OCS Study MMS 2005-068

Final Report

Mapping and Characterization of Recurring Spring Leads and Landfast Ice in the Beaufort and Chukchi Seas

Hajo Eicken*[1]
Lewis H. Shapiro[1]
Allison Graves Gaylord[2]
Andrew Mahoney[1]
Patrick W. Cotter[1]

[1]Geophysical Institute
University of Alaska Fairbanks
Fairbanks, AK 99775-7320

[2]Nuna Technologies
Homer, AK 99603

March 2006

MMS Contract 0103CT71707

U.S. Department of the Interior
Minerals Management Service (MMS)
Alaska Outer Continental Shelf Region
Anchorage, Alaska

Disclaimer:

This report was prepared under contract between the Minerals Management Service (MMS) and the Geophysical Institute at the University of Alaska Fairbanks. This report has been technically reviewed by the MMS and approved for publication. Approval does not signify that the contents necessarily reflect the views and policies of the Service, nor does mention of trade names or commercial products constitute endorsement or recommendation for use. It is, however, exempt from review and compliance with the MMS editorial standards.

Mapping and Characterization of Recurring Spring Leads and Landfast ice in the Beaufort and Chukchi Seas

Hajo Eicken*
Lewis H. Shapiro
Andrew Mahoney
Patrick W. Cotter

Geophysical Institute
University of Alaska Fairbanks
903 Koyukuk Drive
PO Box 757320
Fairbanks, AK 99775-7320

Allison Graves Gaylord

Nuna Technologies
PO Box 1483
Homer, AK 99603

This study was funded by the U.S. Department of the Interior, Minerals Management Service (MMS), Alaska Outer Continental Shelf Region, Anchorage Alaska, under Contract Number 0103CT71707, as part of the MMS Alaska Environmental Studies Program.

March, 2006

*Corresponding author
Email: hajo.eicken@gi.alaska.edu

Project Organization

Report authors

Hajo Eicken – *Principal Investigator*
• Oversaw project progress and completion
• Responsible for delivery of final products and reports (incl. interaction between project team and funding agency)
• Primary responsibility for tasks 1, 2, and 5 (with significant contributions by Dr. Shapiro and Mrs. Graves Gaylord)
• Shared responsibility for completion of tasks 3 and 4 (with Mrs. Graves Gaylord)
• Supervised student research assistants and image analyst; principal thesis advisor for Mr. Andrew Mahoney
• Analysis of lead and fast-ice patterns, derivation of statistical measures of landfast ice and lead variability
• Analysis of observed spatio-temporal variability in the context of atmospheric and oceanic variability and change

Lewis H. Shapiro – *Co-Principal Investigator*
• Primary responsibility for documentation of landfast ice edge position and development of coastal lead systems between 1975 and 1985 based on archived (historical) data
• Provided insight and guidance on developing criteria for the classification of coastal lead systems
• Contributed to completion of Task 5 in offering an explanation for the observed patterns in lead system and landfast ice development on different spatial and temporal scales
• Co-advised students involved in the research project, in particular with respect to identification and classification of relevant features
• Analysis of observed spatio-temporal variability in the context of atmospheric and oceanic variability and change

Allison Graves Gaylord - *Consultant*
• Supported data acquisition efforts including the search and retrieval of Radarsat SAR imagery from the Alaska Satellite Facility archive, plus the integration of ancillary GIS data (bathymetry, Alaska Sea Ice Atlas grids) and the automation of selected historical paper maps as needed.
• Processed imagery to a standard map projection and datum chosen for the project to help synthesize data of varying scales.
• Assisted with image interpretation and classification to delineate sea ice characterizations of landfast ice.
• Created ArcGIS shapefiles, grids and geodatabases depicting the landfast ice edge across the Alaska Beaufort Sea to the Canadian Mackenzie Delta. Created ArcGIS geodatabases of annual lead patterns.
• Developed FGDC metadata templates for the data sets
• Assisted in the compilation of spreadsheets to catalog the images and image quality used for the analysis.
• Assisted in maintaining the project website.

Andrew Mahoney – *Doctoral degree student*
• Supported data analysis through development of programs dedicated to automation of landfast ice edge detection and lead patterns
• Processed Radarsat SAR imagery and developed automated routines for image (pre)processing and geolocation
• Comparison of landfast ice patterns with changes in the oceanic, atmospheric and sea-ice environment in the Chukchi and Beaufort Sea (incl. the integration of field measurements carried out as part of the thesis research)

Patrick Cotter – *Research Technician*
• Miscellaneous project support (help with compilation of bibliography, scanning of archives for suitable imagery, preprocessing, etc.)
• Assisted in the compilation of an image catalog and an image-quality catalog used for the lead analysis.
• Processed AVHRR imagery, including georeferencing, cloud masking and binarization
• Maintenance of project web site
• Created ArcGIS grids and shapefiles from AVHRR data depicting the distribution of recurring lead patterns

Table of Contents

List of Figures

List of Tables

Glossary of Abbreviations

ASF	Alaska Satellite Facility
AVHRR	Advanced Very High Resolution Radiometer
CP	Characteristic Pattern; a daily sea level pressure field that is statistically similar to a minimum number of other daily fields (section 3.4.2)
ENC	Electronic Nautical Chart
ENVI	commercial IDL-based image processing software package, by RSI
FDD	Freezing Degree Days; cumulative daily mean air temperature (°C) since onset of freezing (section 3.4.3)
FGDC	Federal Geographic Data Committee
GEODAS	GEOphysical DAta System
GINA	Geographic Information Network of Alaska
GIS	Geographic Information System
HRPT	High Resolution Picture Transmission
IBCAO	International Bathymetric Chart of the Arctic Ocean
IDL	commercial high-level programming language, by RSI
MMS	Minerals Management Service
MODIS	MODerate resolution Imaging Spectroradiometer
NDI	Nautical Data International (for the Canadian Hydrographic Service)
NGDC	National Geophysical Data Center
NIC	National Ice Center
NOAA	National Oceanic and Atmospheric Administration
SAR	Synthetic Aperture Radar
SLIE	Seaward Landfast Ice Edge
SwathView	Proprietary interface for viewing satellite swaths
TDD	Thawing Degree Days; cumulative daily mean air temperature (°C) since onset of thawing (section 3.4.3)
TeraScan	software for processing raw remote sensing data
WMO	World Meteorological Organization

Abstract

The aim of this project was to map and document the spatial and temporal distribution of recurring lead systems and coastal polynyas and landfast ice off the coast of northern Alaska in the Chukchi and Beaufort Seas between Wainwright bordering the Chukchi Sea and the Mackenzie River Delta in the Canadian Beaufort Sea. The extent and duration of the landfast ice along this stretch of coast was analyzed with Radarsat Synthetic Aperture Radar (SAR) between 1996 and 2004 and supplemented with Advanced Very High Resolution Radiometer (AVHRR) data, for the time period between 1993 and 1996. Lead distributions were quantified from AVHRR data for the period between 1993 and 2004. These data were compared to older AVHRR imagery and older published data from the 1970's and 1980's. Monthly mean landfast ice edge positions and spatial statistics of lead distributions were derived from these data for the time period of stable, closed sea-ice cover. Longer-term spatio-temporal variations in landfast ice extent and lead patterns were assessed in the context of large-scale atmospheric and oceanic change. Project products and deliverables include ArcGIS grids and shapefiles of monthly landfast ice extents and lead distributions with accompanying metadata. Published articles and reports of relevance to the project were also compiled in a Procite bibliography database.

Executive Summary

The Arctic sea-ice cover has undergone significant changes in the past two decades. These changes include a reduction in summer ice extent (with four consecutive record minima attained between 2001 and 2005) as well as substantial thinning of the ice pack. The western Arctic, i.e., the Chukchi and Beaufort Seas, has seen the largest anomalies in summer ice extent, as well as a substantial reduction in the amount of multiyear ice over the Beaufort and Chukchi shelves. The present project was aimed at mapping and documenting changes in the spatial and temporal distribution of spring lead systems and landfast ice extent off the coast of northern Alaska. In addition to providing baseline data against which to evaluate further changes, the work also examined present-day conditions in relation to earlier studies conducted in the 1970s as part of the Outer Continental Shelf Environmental Assessment Project and discussed the role of different forcing mechanisms in controlling spatial and temporal patterns of variability in lead distribution and landfast ice extent.

The study area extended from the eastern Chukchi Sea, southwest of Barrow to Wainwright, Alaska across the Beaufort Sea to the Canadian Mackenzie River Delta System, with the northern boundary at roughly 74°N (qualitative analysis of lead patterns included areas extending into the Canada Basin and the High Canadian Arctic as well). Lead distributions and patterns were examined with the aid of Advanced Very High Resolution Radiometer (AVHRR) data archived at the Geographic Information Network of Alaska (GINA) at the University of Alaska Fairbanks (UAF). At least one AVHRR scene was examined (in the visible and thermal infra-red (IR) channels 1 and 4) for each day from early December to late June of the ice years from 1993-94 through 2003-04, noting cloud-free sectors and general lead characteristics for further processing of a subset of these roughly 2000 scenes. Based on the qualitative analysis of these scenes, a number of characteristic, recurring sequences or patterns of lead evolution were described and interpreted in the context of the large-scale rheology of the ice pack.

Based on the visual inspection of scenes suitable for further processing, a subset of 385 scenes was geolocated through individual navigation of scenes (geolocation error <3 km) and reprojected into an Albers Conical Equal Area (AK) projection at 1.2 km grid cell size. The study area was divided into 12 subregions and only those that were cloud free were considered in further analysis. The fraction of leads within each pixel was determined based on brightness temperature or reflectance using an algorithm developed by Lindsay and Rothrock (1995) that has been extended to take into account regional variations in ice temperature and to correct for thin cloud cover. Binary images denoting leads (for pixels containing 25% or more thin ice or open water) and ice were obtained for further processing. Further analysis of these images included calculation of total lead fraction, the geographic location, area, perimeter, and major/minor dimensions of individual leads, and derived statistics including lead number densities and size distributions. Products from this analysis include processed imagery (GeoTIFF format), lead grid and shape files in ArcGIS format and lead statistics, available through the project web site (mms.gina.alaska.edu) and to be submitted to national sea-ice data distribution centers (including National Snow and Ice Data Center).

Landfast ice extent has been studied by determining the location of the seaward landfast ice edge (SLIE) in Radarsat Synthetic Aperture (SAR) imagery. The SLIE is simple to define conceptually but more difficult to determine in practice, partly since both the location and a lack of motion must be determined over time, implying that a single observation is insufficient. We have examined different definitions of landfast ice used by others and then propose our own, consisting of two criteria: 1) the ice is contiguous with the land, and 2) the ice lacks detectable motion for approximately 20 days. Based on this definition, we then processed SAR data for the time period 1996 to 2004. One mosaic composed of geolocated Radarsat ScanSAR Wide scenes (geolocation error <0.5 km) was compiled every 10 days (with a total of roughly 1000 scenes) and the SLIE determined using a combination of automated and manual delineation. From these SLIE delineations, further parameters describing the seasonal evolution and width of the landfast ice were derived. Products from this analysis include SAR mosaics (GeoTIFF format), SLIE grid and shapefiles in ArcGIS format and derived SLIE statistics.

Ancillary data processing includes the compilation of a bathymetric data set mostly from National Oceanographic and Atmospheric Administration (NOAA) data sources, computation of freezing and thawing degree days from National Center for Environmental Prediction (NCEP) reanalysis models, and an objective synoptic classification of sea level atmospheric pressure patterns from NCEP reanalysis.

The analysis of lead distributions shows a distinct seasonal cycle in the lead fraction (ranging between <2 % in winter to >10 % in late spring), as well as lead size and number density. While there is substantial interannual variability in lead characteristics, with no statistically significant trends or correlations to key atmospheric variables, spatial patterns of lead occurrence and size are consistent from year to year. Highest lead fractions and largest sizes are observed in the eastern Chukchi Sea and off the Mackenzie Delta, with fewer and smaller leads present in the central Beaufort Sea. This is a result of the prevailing easterly wind directions, forcing ice offshore and creating recurring flaw leads and polynyas along the landfast ice edge. The Mackenzie shelf exhibits the highest lead fractions in the study area in late spring due to the impact of river break-up. Lead size (area) distributions conform to a power law, as does the relation between lead size and lead number density, confirming the scale-invariant nature of lead morphology and distribution. A key event in the seasonal cycle is the transition between the regime of distinct linear leads in winter and the ubiquitous appearance of patches of open water surrounding floes in spring ("spring ice"), typically occurring in late April or early May (with a trend towards earlier dates in recent years). An increase in lead number density from values below 0.001 km^{-2} to more than 0.003 km^{-2} marks this transition.

Monthly maps of lead occurrence probability reflect the key processes controlling lead patterns, including flaw leads and polynyas, advection of floes past grounded ice on Hanna Shoal, the appearance of arced leads that radiate from Point Barrow and propagate into areas of more stagnant ice in the central and eastern Beaufort Sea as well as arches that form along the margin of ice that is confined in the "dead space" of the eastern Beaufort Sea. These patterns have been examined and classified into about a dozen characteristic patterns and evolution sequences that occur throughout the years. Furthermore, examination of AVHRR imagery from the 1970s revealed that these patterns occurred in a similar fashion during the heavier ice years of the mid-1970s.

Based on the SLIE data set, the spatial and temporal variability in the extent of landfast ice, the water depth it occupies and the timing of key events in its annual cycle have been examined. We identified four zones of coherent seasonal variability and the key elements of coastal and bathymetric configuration that define these zones. In all four zones the SLIE was observed to advance incrementally into deeper water with some sections advancing first, followed by neighboring sections. By the end of the season, prior to break-up, the distribution of water depths at the SLIE in all zones exhibited strong modes ranging between 16 m and 22 m.

This is in good agreement with past observations that noted the similarity between the 20 m isobath and the landfast ice edge. The retreat of the SLIE takes place far more quickly than the advance and is therefore not as well captured in the Radarsat imagery. However, the similarity in water depth distributions at the start and end of the annual landfast ice cycle suggests that as the SLIE retreats, it occupies the same locations that it did while advancing.

We also examined interannual variability and identified the components of atmospheric circulation and air temperature that are most important for the formation and break-up of the landfast ice. A comparison with earlier work from the 1970's suggests that the annual cycle of landfast ice has been significantly shorter in recent years, caused by later formation and earlier break-up. We also note that any comparisons must take into account relevant definitions and methods. This is particularly so with operational datasets that lack the benefit of hindsight such as the National Ice Center Ice Charts, which can differ significantly from our own for the same time period. Examination of air temperatures over the region showed multi-decadal trends towards an earlier onset of thawing in spring, and later onset of freezing in fall. A strong interannual correlation suggests that the former is responsible for the early landfast ice break-up in recent years. However, the timing of landfast ice formation appears to correlate best with the timing of pack ice incursion into coastal waters, suggesting that the observed latening of landfast ice formation could be related to the more northward retreat of the perennial ice edge in recent years.

Major conclusions from this work include the following: (1) Lead distribution and landfast ice extent patterns are consistent throughout the study period between 1993 and 2004 and compare well with observations from earlier studies completed in the 1970s. (2) Landfast ice extent is controlled by the combination of coastal bathymetry, heat exchange with the atmosphere (and to a lesser extent atmospheric circulation) and ice-pack interaction. (3) With a general warming trend in the region during the study period, the landfast ice season is significantly shorter, with a less stable ice cover. Lead patterns and fractions or sizes, on the other hand do not show any significant trend over the study period. (4) The large-scale pattern of high lead activity and landfast ice variability in the eastern Chukchi Sea and the Mackenzie shelf area and much more quiescent conditions in the central Beaufort Sea are explained by a combination of coastal morphology in relation to prevailing wind direction, the rheology of the ice pack and its confinement in the "dead space" of the Beaufort Sea and Canadian Basin, and the impact of river influx on break-up in the Mackenzie Delta.

1. Introduction

Over the past two decades the Arctic sea-ice cover has undergone significant change. A record minimum summer ice extent has been recorded for four out of the past five summers in the Arctic (Stroeve et al., 2005). The retreat of the summer Arctic ice cover has been most pronounced in the Western Arctic, specifically the East Siberian, Chukchi and Beaufort Seas (Comiso, 2002). With the perennial ice retreating to the North and changes in surface circulation (Drobot and Maslanik, 2003; Tucker et al., 2001), the western Arctic shelf seas have also experienced a loss of multiyear ice in the winter (Belchansky et al., 2004). While there are few if any systematic direct observations of the extent and impacts of these changes in the Alaska coastal zone and inner-shelf waters, native communities have reported for some time about substantial changes in the sea-ice regime, including later onset of ice formation and a less stable and less predictable ice cover (George et al., 2004; Huntington, 2000; Krupnik and Jolly, 2002). Along with the changes in ice extent and seasonality, a significant reduction in ice thickness throughout the Arctic has been observed in deep-water, off-shelf areas accessible by submarine (Rothrock and Zhang, 2005; Tucker et al., 2001).

Given the importance of Alaska coastal and inner-shelf waters from an ecological, economic and sociological perspective, in particular in the light of recent sales of offshore oil and gas leases, there is a clear need for information on the current status of the coastal sea ice regime. Since little research has been completed on ice conditions in this region since the Outer Continental Shelf Environmental Assessment Program (OCSEAP) in the 1970s and 1980s, such work is timely both from the perspective of changing ice conditions as well as advances in satellite remote sensing and digital image processing. Thus, we note that the most recent, thorough analyses of landfast ice conditions and lead distributions in the Alaska coastal regions have been determined by hand, working with transparencies of low-resolution AVHRR data (Barry et al., 1979a; Miles and Barry, 1998; Stringer, 1978; Stringer et al., 1980).

The aim of the present study is to provide quantitative information on the seasonal and interannual variability in ice conditions, specifically landfast sea-ice extent and stability and distribution and morphology of spring lead systems (for definitions of these terms and in-depth discussions of previous work on these topics please see Sections 3.3 and 4.1 of this report), for the time period 1996 to 2004 and 1993 to 2004, respectively. In order to extract quantitative information from remote-sensing data, a number of techniques and approaches were developed or adapted. The resulting imagery and data sets (and ancillary data) were compiled into geodatabases and are provided as part of this report. Upon formal release by the Minerals Management Service they will also be made available online through established geodata distribution centers. As part of this project and in collaboration with the Geographic Information Network of Alaska (GINA) at the University of Alaska Fairbanks, we have also established a dedicated web site that serves as a clearinghouse and point-of-reference for project collaborators, program managers and others, with a separate, limited-access section that provides access to all resulting datasets (mms.gina.alaska.edu).

1.1. Lead distribution patterns

This study is based largely on the hypothesis that the deformation patterns of the pack ice in the Beaufort Sea generally (but not always) reflect the interaction of the moving ice with the fixed coastlines to the East (Canadian Arctic islands) and South (north coast of Alaska; a map of the study region is shown in Figure 1.1.1). The mean sense of displacement of the ice pack is clockwise around the Beaufort Gyre so it is generally southerly and westerly along the Alaska coast, with occasional excursions to the East. However, the latter are severely limited by the shapes of the coastlines. Northerly and southerly displacements also occur, but they too are limited in both time and distance. The only bathymetric features hypothesized to have a measurable and relevant impact on lead distributions are shoals that are shallow enough to allow for grounding of pressure ridges (mostly limited to Hanna Shoal).

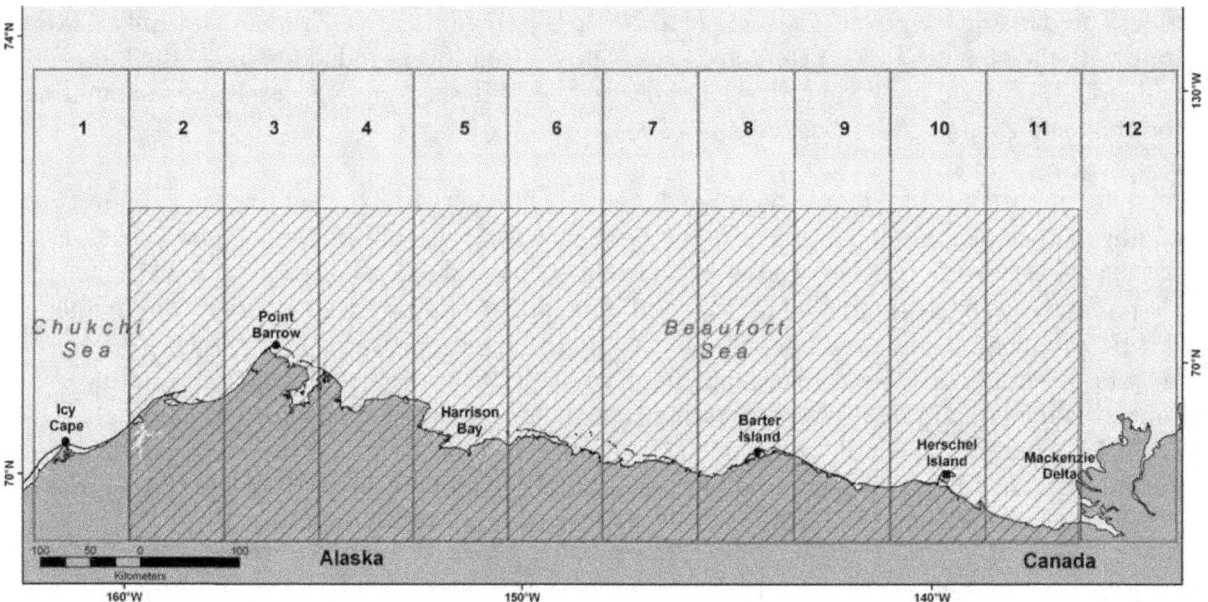

Figure 1.1.1. Study area and sub-regions for quantitative analysis of lead distribution and morphology in AVHRR scenes (outlined in red) and study area for analysis of landfast ice extent (hatched area)

Pack ice deforms by generating leads, along or across which differential motion occurs. On some scales, the process can be modeled as if the ice is a continuum following some constitutive law. However, on the spatial and time scales of the satellite imagery used to study lead distributions, the deformation clearly depends on lead formation. The driving conditions repeat with the passage of weather systems and the consistency of ocean currents, and given that the boundaries are rigid it is expected that many lead patterns would occur repeatedly in the same or different years. Some variations should occur because of differences in the configuration of the landfast ice and the composition of the pack ice. However, similar lead patterns should be recognizable. Descriptions and examples of repeated lead patterns and other deformation features constitute an important part of this report.

The quantitative analysis of lead distributions and morphology for the time period 1993 to 2004 complements the general analysis of deformation and lead patterns and provides for planning tools with respect to lead recurrence probabilities, lead morphology and size and linkages of lead distributions to large-scale atmospheric and ice-dynamics parameters.

1.2. Landfast ice extent and stability

Along the coast of Arctic Alaska, landfast sea ice serves as a platform for marine mammals, (e.g., polar bears and ringed seals) provides access from the land to hunting grounds and is utilized as a platform and for transportation in offshore oil development. The annual landfast ice cycle can be broadly characterized by a gradual seaward advance from the coast beginning in late fall or early winter (October - November) followed by a rapid retreat coinciding with the onset of spring (May-June). The range of dates comes from spatial differences in the arrival of the seasons as well as interannual variability in the behavior of the landfast ice.

Although stationary by definition, landfast ice is formed and deformed by a combination of dynamic and thermodynamic processes, which follow their own annual cycles and vary geographically in their presence and importance. Consequently, the extent and appearance of landfast ice differ significantly between regions of the Arctic. In much of the Russian Arctic, the landfast ice extends hundreds of kilometers from the coast (Barnett, 1991; Eicken et al., 2005; Zubov, 1945), which is one or two orders of magnitude greater than the typical width of landfast ice in Arctic Alaska (Barry et al., 1979b; Stringer et al., 1980). Such basin-scale differences in spatial extent can be largely related to differences in nearshore bathymetry, but there is no Arctic-wide relationship between the water depth and the location of the landfast ice edge. Among the different water depths that have been cited as the limits of landfast ice extent are 25m along the Siberian coast (Zubov, 1945), 10m in the Kara Sea (Divine et al., 2004); between 18m and 30m in the Beaufort Sea (Kovacs, 1976; Kovacs and Mellor, 1974; Reimnitz and Barnes, 1974; Service, 1968; Shapiro, 1975; Stringer, 1974; Stringer et al., 1980; Weeks et al., 1977), 100m near Severnaya Zemlya (Divine et al., 2004) and 180m off the eastern coast of Baffin Island (Jacobs et al., 1975).

The lack of a universal water depth that limits landfast ice extent does not mean that landfast ice does not interact with the seabed, but instead that landfast ice extent in different areas of the Arctic is controlled by different mechanisms. For example, Zubov (Zubov, 1945) states that the combination of barrier islands and involuted coastlines, a lack of strong currents and tides, and shallow water is conducive to the presence of landfast ice. However, offshore of northern Alaska and northwest Canada, deep-keeled ridges are formed by the convergence and shear of westward drifting ice in the Beaufort Gyre against the landfast ice dominated coast. These play an important role in anchoring the advance of landfast ice (Reimnitz et al., 1977; Shapiro, 1975).

Having established that there are broad differences in landfast ice appearance and behavior throughout the Arctic, this study will focus on northern Alaska and Northwestern Canada (Jacobs et al., 1975). In particular, we will examine the relationship between water depth and landfast sea ice extent and the underlying processes responsible in different locations. However, we will also address the development of the landfast ice and the processes that drive its annual cycle. The formation of landfast ice is a complex process involving *in-situ* freezing of open water in sheltered regions of the coast as well as the assimilation of pack ice from offshore. As a result, the landfast ice grows seaward but may break up and reform a number of times before it achieves stability. As well as being of great importance to native subsistence activities (George et al., 2004), both the date at which the landfast ice becomes stable and the length of time that it remains so are of considerable economic importance for offshore development.

The details of the smaller scale processes behind the response of landfast ice to the annual cycle of forces are the subject of other ongoing research by the authors. Here, our aims are to identify the key linkages between landfast ice and coastal bathymetry and atmospheric forcing at the regional scale. To achieve this goal, we will characterize the behavior of landfast ice according to its extent, the water depth it occupies and the timing of key events in its annual cycle. We will also identify components of coastal morphology and nearshore bathymetry that characterize sections of coastline. Finally we will derive annual mean measures of air temperature and sea level pressure patterns. Examining spatial and interannual variability in all these variables in a fashion consistent with earlier studies completed in the 1970's (Barry et al., 1979b; Stringer et al., 1980) will also allow us to address the causes underlying multi-decadal changes in Alaska landfast ice.

2. Objectives

The objectives fall broadly into four different categories.

1. Document and map the spatial and temporal distribution of recurring spring leads system and polynyas from the eastern Chukchi Sea, southwest of Barrow to Wainwright, Alaska across the Beaufort Sea to the Canadian Mackenzie River Delta System for the time period 1993 to 2004 based on Advanced Very High Resolution Radiometer (AVHRR) data. Draw on older archived AVHRR data from the 1970s and 1980s as well as publications from that time period to document potential changes in the lead regime.
2. Document and map the yearly spatial and temporal changes by month of the stable landfast ice distribution across the Eastern Chukchi Sea and the Alaska Beaufort Sea to the Canadian Mackenzie Delta based on analysis of high-resolution Radarsat Synthetic Aperture Radar (SAR) imagery.
3. Document trends in lead and stable landfast characteristics over the time period covered and in relation to earlier studies from the 1970s and 1980s, especially as related to large-scale ice thinning and shrinking of summer minimum ice extent in the region. Offer up preliminary explanations of these changes in the context of atmosphere-ice-ocean interaction.
4. Document and discuss the dominant mode(s) of spring lead/ice pack interaction as well as any potential significance these might have on the landfast ice regime.

In meeting these objectives, a number of data sets and other research products (lead and landfast ice bibliography, summary statistics, publications) have been produced. The project goals include dissemination of these research products of the research to the general public, through a combination of a dedicated project web site (mms.gina.alaska.edu), collaboration with the Geographic Information Network of Alaska (GINA) at UAF and, eventually, through submission of data sets to data distribution and archival centers and manuscript to peer-reviewed scientific journals for publication.

3. Methods and Data Sets

3.1. Characterization of large-scale lead patterns

The hypothesis is based upon long term observations by one of the authors using AVHRR imagery of the Bering, Beaufort and Chukchi Seas' sea ice cover in connection with various research and operational projects. These observations were done over a span of years, and none involved systematic recorded observation and recording of the ice features or lead patterns. However, it was apparent that some features and patterns of leads were seen often enough to suggest that they were repeatable. Combining that with the ideas about interactions with the coast and the normal circulation of the Beaufort Sea ice cover directly leads to the hypothesis.

The present study was completed primarily using software called 'SWATHVIEW' and the images came from the data archive of the Geographic Information Network of Alaska (GINA). GINA acquires virtually every available image from the AVHRR and Moderate Resolution Imaging Spectrometer (MODIS) satellites and SWATHVIEW provides a convenient method of accessing the images; it can also display them at scales ranging from 1 to 20 km per pixel on the screen. For this project, the images were usually examined at 2km/pixel (corresponding to a scale of 1:5,900,000), because that allowed all of the study area to be displayed on the monitor. However, enlargements of particular features were used occasionally.

Unfortunately, until almost the very end of this study, SWATHVIEW had no provision for storing all or part of an image for later use, but it did allow the image on the screen to be printed. Printing led to significant degradation of the image quality, but it was the only way to retain an image for reference. It became apparent early in the study, that it was important to have prints available, so almost every image in which the study area was not completely covered by clouds was printed.

At least one AVHRR image was examined for each day from early December to late June of the ice years from 1993-94 through 2003-04 (except for a few days when the AVHRR ground station was not functioning; the MODIS system was used for such days when possible). Thus, about 2000 images were examined for the study. Descriptive notes were made for each image. Cloud free sectors of the study area that could be used for analysis of lead length, orientation and area were noted and that information was used to select images to be processed by GINA for that analysis. In addition, if an open or newly refrozen lead could be identified at the landfast ice edge, that information was also recorded for use as possible ground truth for the SAR imagery used in the study.

There is no existing classification or systematic nomenclature for the pack ice features and lead patterns discussed here. In their absence, in order to recognize that a feature or pattern was repeated or recurring, it was necessary to recall having seen it at least a few times during the process of examining the images. A search could then be made to find the earlier occurrences of the feature or patterns and verify the similarity. This proved to be a tedious process which was made more difficult because the first pass through the images took place over about a year, while

GINA prepared the imagery for use in the SWATHVIEW application. However, recurring patterns and features were recognized and named. That simplified the process of taking notes and also provided a series of key words that could be used to rapidly scan the notes to locate days when particular features were identified.

An attempt was made to organize the results of the study into a spread sheet, so statistics of the frequencies of occurrence of lead patterns and other features could be tabulated. However, it was soon clear that this was too time-consuming to be practical because of the need to account for the distribution of cloud cover over the study area for every day in order to make the statistics valid. In addition, we found that, although a pattern might be recognizable on an image for a period of days, it was not necessarily active over that time. New leads freeze over rapidly and their appearance on SWATHVIEW may not change significantly until they are snow covered. In that case, they are of no significance to ice deformation processes because new leads are required for the ice to deform. As a result, the only way to determine if a pattern was active over time would be to look for evidence of differential ice motion between AVHRR scenes. Given the resolution limits of SWATHVIEW it was not practical to attempt to do that and the lack of that information would have made the value of the statistics of the occurrence of patterns even more uncertain. Finally, as noted, a pattern had to be observed at least a few times before its characteristics and repeatability were recognized. Thus, occurrences before the name was applied may not have been recorded and could only be found by scanning back the imagery. This is a time-consuming task and was not generally attempted.

More important than the statistics, with experience we recognized that many of the lead patterns were simply steps in sequences of patterns. Thus, the persistence of any pattern, and the one that followed it, depended on the rate at which weather systems with sufficient energy to drive the pack ice affected the area. However, the progression of patterns through a sequence is an interesting aspect of the question of repeatability. It is discussed in later sections of the report.

It would clearly be useful to be able to quantitatively interpret the progress of patterns through a sequence in terms of the environmental forces which drive them. However, we know of no models that account for the observed fracturing which, in the southern Beaufort Sea depends on the unknown conditions at the pack ice/landfast ice boundary. However, the general sense of pack ice motion can often be determined from SWATHVIEW by comparison of successive AVHRR images, and that can be interpreted to give information on the displacement boundary conditions on the deformation. Thus, while the forces driving the movements are not known, their effect can be seen in the motion of the pack ice which, in turn, provides a basis for some interpretation of the genesis of the lead patterns.

It is important to emphasize that, regardless of whether the driving forces are known, the lead patterns are real indicators of the deformation of the pack ice. Thus, they represent a ground truth that numerical models of the geometry of the deformation pattern should be consistent with. In fact, it should be possible to suggest lead orientations from calculated displacement patterns. Studies of that type should provide insight into the nature of the boundary conditions. This is mentioned in other sections of the report and summarized in the Discussion (Section 5.2) at the end.

3.2. Mapping of lead distribution and morphology

3.2.1. Acquisition and processing of satellite imagery

For the quantitative analysis of lead distribution and morphology, the study area was expanded from that specified in the MMS Request for Proposals (Figure 1.1.1). This was done to provide a better perspective on regional lead characteristics and capture key geographic areas associated with specific lead patterns, such as leads over Hanna Shoal and in Mackenzie Bay. The region encompassed by the AVHRR study area covers approximately 540,000 km^2, bounded by the Mackenzie Delta in the East, Icy Cape in the West and extending 470 kilometers north-south . The study area is divided into 12 subregions, covering approximately 45,000 km^2 each.

A total of 385 unique AVHRR scenes were ordered and downloaded from the GINA server and processed. AVHRR data had been down-linked through the International Observatory of the North and its predecessors at the Geophysical Institute, UAF. Of these images, 11 were analyzed in both the thermal and visible ranges, for a total of 396 analyzed scenes. In addition to the image processing to extract lead fraction described below, each image was manually inspected to identify areas of cloud cover. Whole subregions of data were selectively eliminated if a significant fraction of their surface was obscured by clouds or if clouds were being misidentified as leads by the algorithm described below. Figure 3.2.1 shows the total number of scenes per subregion that were analyzed in this study. Figure 3.2.2 shows that the winter and spring months were sampled equally, with fewer sufficiently cloud-free scenes available from the transition months, December and June.

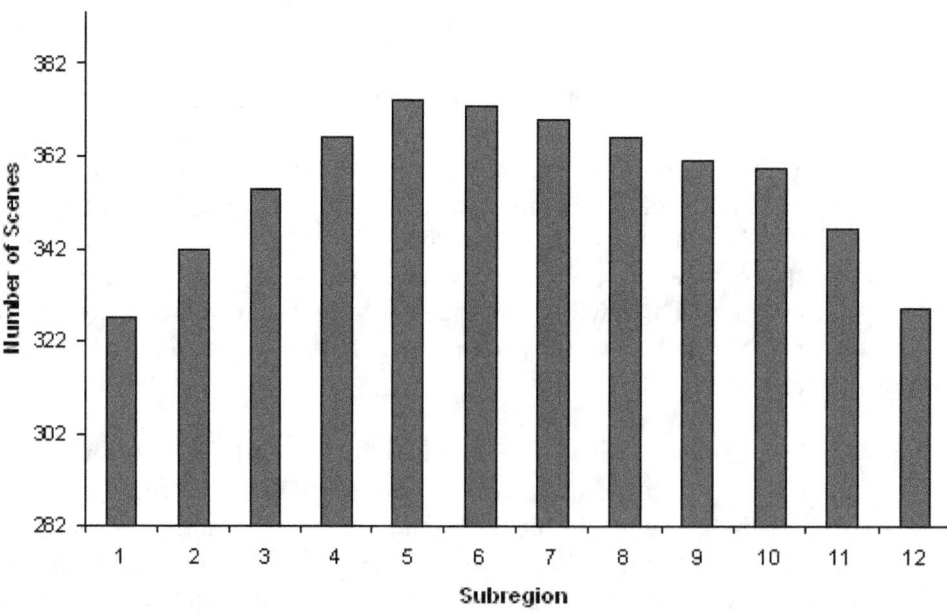

Figure 3.2.1. Number of AVHRR scenes analyzed per subregion during the study period (1993-2004).

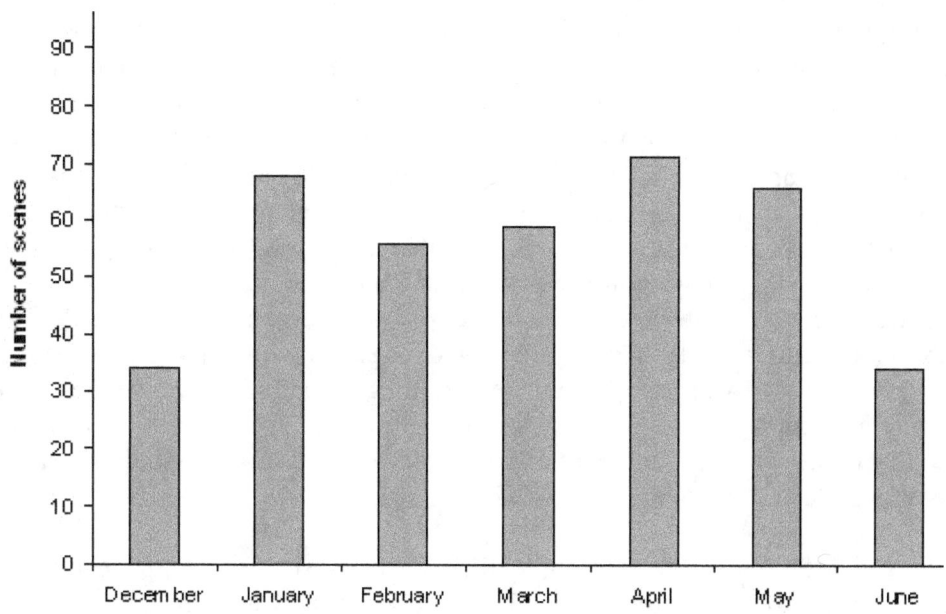

Figure 3.2.2. Number of AVHRR scenes analyzed for each month during the study period (1993-2004).

Raw, High Resolution Picture Transmission (HRPT) data were ingested for each AVHRR scene and processed in TeraScan (SeaSpace, 2003). Calibration and conversion of visible and thermal channel data to surface reflectance and brightness temperature, respectively, was carried out as specified in the NOAA Polar Orbiter Data User's Guide (2003, www2.ncdc.noaa.gov/docs/podug/html/c3/sec3-3.htm).

Geo-location was accomplished by adjusting the pitch, tilt, roll, and yaw parameters within the XVU function of TeraScan until the image aligned with an overlain, georeferenced coast. Error was less than 3 kilometers, and generally within 1.2 kilometers. Georeferenced images in a polar stereographic projection were exported from TeraScan as HDF files.

These HDF files were subsequently imported into ENVI (Research Systems, Inc., 2003) where they were reprojected into an Albers Conical Equal Area (AK) projection using the NAD (1983) datum (see Section 3.5). Also using ENVI, the land area was masked, and the image was cropped to the study region. These files were exported as 16-bit integer files, with pixel values representing albedo in hundredths of percent and brightness temperature in hundredths of °C for channel 1 and channel 4 images respectively. Landmask values were set to 10001(corresponding to 100.01%) and –5000 (corresponding to –50 °C) for channel 1 and channel 4 images respectively.

The fraction of leads within each pixel was determined based on the brightness temperatures or reflectances of open water and the surrounding thick ice, as described by Lindsay and Rothrock

(1995). Here, we have corrected for regional differences in surface temperature and reflectance, as well as thin cloud cover, by determining the fraction of leads within a moving 50 by 50 pixel (55 x 55 km) square window, with the fraction of thick ice based on the upper and lower quartile reflectance and brightness temperature, respectively. For a few cases of more expansive stretches of open water, manual adjustments of open water extent have been made. The resulting image indicating the fraction of open water was then binarized about a threshold corresponding to an open water fraction of 25% in each pixel, (equivalent to a value of $\delta = 0.25$ deemed optimal based on work by Lindsay and Rothrock, 1995) with pixels containing less open water designated as ice and those at or above 25% designated as leads. The resulting binary images are then imported into the NIH Image software package (rsb.info.nih.gov/nih-image/index.html) for derivation of lead location, shape and size statistics, open water fractions and other information for each subregion. Prior to analysis, single, isolated pixels which were found to be the result of noise in the data were removed from the segmented image. Lead statistics were exported from NIH Image into Microsoft Excel format. Data were eliminated from statistical analysis if the ice was obscured by clouds in a particular subregion as determined from manual inspection of images in both visible and thermal channels.

The binarized GeoTIFF images delineating leads, were converted to ArcGIS format using a batch utility in ArcToolbox. Another batch file was used in ArcCatalog (ESRI, 2002) to define the map projection and datum. Each Grid file was then exported to an ESRI interchange format (*.e00) using batch utilities within ArcToolbox to ensure clean data transfer. Low resolution browse images (*.jpg format) were generated for display on the project web site. Final processing included a batch import of the appropriate FGDC compliant metadata. Final data sets were bundled with WinZip (WinZip Computing, Inc., 2004) for posting to the web to ensure clean data transfer of the components of the grid, plus the associated metadata record and browse image.

Monthly lead probabilities were calculated from the binarized lead images by summing all the images for each month. In the resulting images, the pixel value represented the number of images in which a lead was observed at the location during a particular month. These were converted to probabilities by dividing by the total number of images stacked for each month. This was done individually for each of the subregions 1-12 to take account of those that were excluded from certain images due to cloud cover.

3.2.2. Defining leads and validating the lead detection approach

Lead definitions

The World Meteorological Organization's Sea Ice Nomenclature defines a lead as "any fracture or passage-way through sea ice which is navigable by surface vessels" (1985). Expanding the definition from its original operational scope in the context of ice navigation, leads are commonly taken to be linear features of open water or thin ice present within the ice pack (Lindsay and Rothrock, 1994; Lindsay and Rothrock, 1995). Their importance derives from the high rates of energy exchange that are sustained in areas of thin ice (Maykut, 1986), either as a result of heat conduction through an open-water or thin-ice surface (Alam and Curry, 1998) or as a result of absorption of shortwave radiation fostered by the low albedo of thin ice or open water

(Pegau and Paulson, 2001; Perovich, 1990). At the same time, leads are of great ecological importance both as potential access points to open water for marine birds and mammals (Bump and Lovvorn, 2004; Stirling, 1997) and as a habitat (Melnikov, 1997). In the present study we are following common practice by applying a lead definition and corresponding lead detection criterion that does not distinguish between open leads and those covered by thin ice up to roughly 0.15 to 0.2 m thick (i.e., nilas and grey ice according to WMO nomenclature). This is motivated by the fact that thermally as well as optically, thin ice with albedos typically less than 0.2 and high surface temperatures is often indistinguishable from open water (Perovich, 1998). Furthermore, under freezing conditions, ice grows to several centimeter thickness within a few hours and even in cases of wind clearing leads of newly forming frazil ice, open water typically cannot be sustained for more than 24 hours (Alam and Curry, 1998; Bauer and Martin, 1983). Even after onset of surface melt, it is not uncommon to observe nighttime freezing of leads well into June.

Identification of leads in remote sensing imagery is complicated by a number of factors, including ambiguous signatures of open water and thin ice in SAR data (Kwok and Cunningham, 1994), atmospheric and resolution effects in visible-range and thermal IR AVHRR data (Key et al., 1993) and lack of resolution in passive microwave data (Fett et al., 1997). Several studies indicate that for analysis of lead patterns and distributions, AVHRR imagery provides for a dataset that represents the best compromise between resolution, coverage and discriminatory power (Key et al., 1993; Lindsay and Rothrock, 1995; Miles and Barry, 1998; Tschudi et al., 2002). In recent years, derivation of ice deformation fields from sequences of Radarsat SAR imagery has been used successfully to map pack ice openings at the scale of 5 km and upwards indirectly (Kwok, 1998; Kwok and Cunningham, 2002). However, this approach is only of limited value for a study in seasonal ice (where ice deformation fields are not easily obtained due to ambiguities in backscatter characteristics) and computationally intensive (so far only a limited number of years have been processed) and was hence not applicable in the current study. Here, we have followed the approach developed by (Lindsay and Rothrock, 1994; Lindsay and Rothrock, 1995) for extracting lead distributions from AVHRR radiance data for the visible-range (channel 1) and thermal-IR (channel 4), converted to reflectances and brightness temperatures, respectively. Specifically, we can calculate the fraction of leads δ_T within each pixel based on the surface brightness temperature of the entire pixel T, that of open water ($T_w = -1.8\ °C$) and that of surrounding thick ice (T_i):

$$\delta_T = \frac{T_i - T}{T_i - T_w} \ .$$

The surface brightness temperature of the surrounding thick ice is derived from the lower quartile brightness temperature determined for a 50x50 pixel window centered on each pixel. The corresponding approach is taken in the analysis of visible range data, with ρ_i, and ρ_w denoting the reflectances of open water (0.1) and the surrounding thick ice (upper quartile within the 50x50 pixel mask):

$$\delta_R = \frac{\rho_i - \rho}{\rho_i - \rho_w} \ .$$

The fraction of open water is then indicated by the magnitude of δ_T or δ_R. In following Lindsay and Rothrock's approach, we have chosen a value of 0.25 as the cutoff value, with cells (pixels) exhibiting a $\delta > 0.25$ designated as lead and those smaller designated as ice. Selecting a value

11

smaller than 0.5 (i.e., a cell composed out of equal fractions of ice and lead) is driven by the fact that two processes tend to result in an underestimation of the fraction of lead present. First, thin ice in a lead will result in lowered surface temperatures and raised reflectances, thereby lowering δ. Second, atmospheric effects such as formation of vapor plumes further reduce detectability of leads (Key et al., 1993).

Validation of lead detection and mapping approach with field observations

In order to evaluate the accuracy and reliability of the lead detection and mapping approach we have compared the results of our AVHRR data analysis with ground observations. The Shelf-Basin Interactions Study's spring process cruise with USCGC *HEALY* in May-June 2002 presented one of the first opportunities to access the study area with a surface vessel during the ice-growth season. One of us (H.E.) carried out a detailed ice observations program during this expedition that is utilized here. Due to prevailing cloud cover, coincident ship-based observations and cloud-free AVHRR scenes were only available for May 23 and June 8, 2002. Figure 3.2.3 shows the geolocated AVHRR scene for May 23 and the corresponding binary image after automated lead detection (Figure 3.2.4). The box corresponds to the area covered by the ship's track and for which ship-based ice observations are available for a 36 hour period bracketing the satellite scene. The ship-based observation program is described in detail in (Eicken et al., 2006).

The photographs in Figure 3.2.5 show typical ice conditions with systems of leads containing a range of floe size distributions developing in between larger ice floes. Up until the first week of June new ice up to 10 cm thick kept forming in leads (Figure 3.2.5, right). As is evident from the photographs and confirmed by the ship-based ice observations, with the exception of the coastal flaw lead and polynya system lining the landfast ice edge and a few major openings in the pack, individual leads were mostly a few tens to a few hundred meters wide (Figure 3.2.5, left). With smaller floes present within lead systems, occurrences of open water or new ice extending over the entire area of a complete AVHRR grid cell (pixel) 1.2 x 1.2 km^2 in size were quite rare, supporting a lead detection criterion δ of 0.25. Furthermore, the ground observations also confirm that measures of lead size (in particular width) based on low-resolution remote sensing data sets such as AVHRR are not necessarily directly related to the size of openings detected at the scale of an observer on the ice. This may have important operational implications from the perspective of marine ecology and oil spill mitigation. This finding is also in line with an earlier study, examining measures of lead sizes for Landsat imagery of leads north of Alaska artificially degraded to pixel sizes ranging between 80 and 1280 m (Key et al., 1993) and comparisons between airborne imagery and AVHRR (Tschudi et al., 2002). In fact, the ice observations during the *HEALY* cruise suggest that even Landsat imagery at 30 m pixel size may still be overestimating lead widths as the prevailing deformation regime in the study area typically results in complex lead geometries with interspersed floe fragments and stacked arrays of smaller leads (Schulson, 2004), as also discussed in Section 4.3.

While such resolution dependence needs to be taken into account when interpreting measures of lead size (see Section 4.1), the comparison between ground observations and AVHRR imagery indicates reasonable agreement between these two data sets. Thus, observations on May 23 for

12

the area shown in Figure 3.2.5 yield a mean lead fraction of 0.14, while the AVHRR scene indicates a lead fraction of 0.12 for the same area. Comparison of ground observations and AVHRR imagery for June 8 in an area of very high ice concentration yields values of 0.01 and 0.02 respectively. Considering the errors involved in ground-based observations this finding is encouraging and indicates that the data derived from this analysis are reflective of conditions relevant in an operational context.

Figure 3.2.3. AVHRR scene (Channel 1, visible range) for study area on May 23, 2002 (landmask is shown in white).

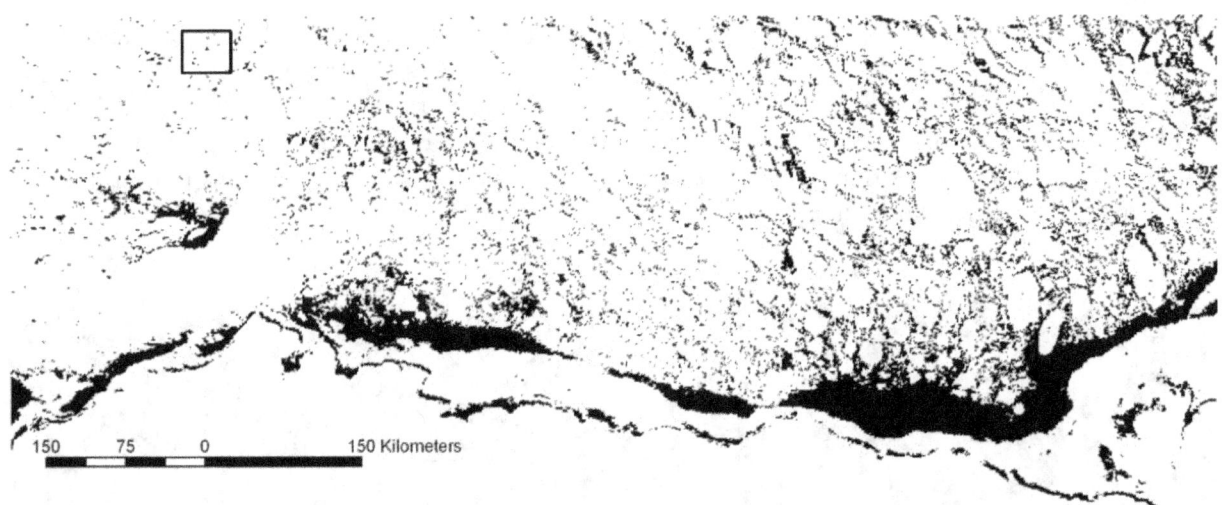

Figure 3.2.4. Binarized image derived from scene shown in Figure 3.2.3. showing the result of the lead detection algorithm (leads are shown in black, ice and the land mask in white). The box marks the location of the area in which ground observations were obtained, with an areal lead fraction of 0.12.

Figure 3.2.5. Aerial photographs of leads as seen during the 2002 field expedition (May 15; leads shown in photographs are several tens of meters to several hundreds of meters wide). Photo at left shows system of leads and adjacent deformed ice. Image at right shows floes and brash ice in a newly formed lead. Note the rims of newly formed thin ice lining most floes.

3.3. Mapping of landfast ice extent and stability

3.3.1. Definition of landfast ice

In order to quantify landfast ice extent and examine spatio-temporal variability, a rigorous definition of landfast ice is required that can be applied to the available data. Numerous definitions of landfast ice are found in the literature, which differ according to the processes considered relevant to a particular study. According to Weaver (1951), "fast ice or landfast ice is the young coastal ice which, in stationary sheets, builds seaward from the shore of landmasses … by being more or less attached to the shore, or by being otherwise confined". The World Meteorological Organization (WMO) (1985) defines fast ice as "Sea ice which remains fast along the coast, where it is attached to the shore, to an ice wall, to an ice front, or over shoals, or between grounded icebergs". Stringer (1978) describes the fast ice zone as 'the area generally shoreward of the 20m isobath with quite stable ice much of the year' and only includes ice contiguous with the shore. Barry et al. (1979b) list three criteria that can distinguish landfast ice from other forms of sea ice: '(i) the ice remains relatively immobile near the shore for a specified time interval; (ii) the ice extends from the coast as a continuous sheet; (iii) the ice is grounded or forms a continuous sheet which is bounded at the seaward edge by an intermittent or nearly continuous zone of grounded ridges'. Stringer et al. (1980) use the term "contiguous ice" synonymously with "fast ice" as described by the WMO. Zubov (1945) does not give a definition of what he calls fast ice, but instead describes the conditions that favor its growth from coastlines and islands. Grounded ridges are not mentioned, although thickening through rafting is, which probably reflects the different physical regime under which landfast ice in the Russian Arctic forms.

These definitions and descriptions all agree that landfast ice (or fast ice) is adjacent to the coast and characterized by a relative lack of motion, although none explicitly specify a time interval over which this must occur. Furthermore, as will be discussed in detail below, it is generally not possible to identify sea ice that is grounded or otherwise anchored from remotely sensed data. However, it is possible to identify sea ice that is both stationary and contiguous with the coast. In the context of this report we limit the definition of landfast sea ice to these criteria:

> the sea ice is contiguous with the shoreline

> the sea ice lacks motion detectable in satellite imagery for approximately 20 days

Stringer (1978), Stringer et al. (1980), Barry et al. (1979b) and Barry (1979) used similar criteria where overlap was available between consecutive Landfast scenes allowing them determine a lack of motion over a time period of between 1 and 4 days. Where no overlap occurred however, the flaw lead or edge of the contiguous ice was used instead. The National Ice Center (NIC) adopts a similar definition when comparing a variety of remote sensing products to produce weekly ice charts. However, their primary criterion is uniformity of color (in visible range imagery) or texture (in microwave or infra-red imagery) shoreward of a clearly defined edge (J. Pena, personal communication, 2005). We must also stress that our definition is one that can only be applied retrospectively and so our results will be inherently different to operational datasets such as the NIC ice charts.

Our definition uses no flaw lead or textural information and employs a longer time period that was deemed geophysically meaningful and appropriate for nearshore operations in ice-covered waters. It is short enough to capture both the annual cycle of advance and retreat as well as the higher frequency variability due to stable extensions and breakouts. It also spans more than a single synoptic period and so precludes sea ice that merely comes to rest temporarily and lacks a mechanism to hold it fast against offshore or alongshore forcing. It is also important to note that we exclude islands from our definition of the coastline, with the exceptions of Herschel and Barter Islands, which are larger than most others and separated from the mainland by only a very narrow stretch of water. This decision was made to avoid complex topological problems that would result when trying to calculate distances from the coast. The effect of this is to exclude ice that is attached to barrier islands but is not contiguous with the mainland. This usually only occurs late in the spring however, when offshore ice operations have typically ceased.

3.3.2. Remote sensing of landfast ice

Owing to the broad extent of landfast ice along coastlines where access is difficult, remote sensing offers an ideal way to observe its annual cycle. Landsat I and II channel 7 (0.8 – 1.1 μm) data were used in an extensive series of studies of Alaska's landfast ice during the 1970's prior to leasing parts of the continental shelf for oil exploration (Barry et al., 1979b; Stringer, 1978; Stringer et al., 1980). The high resolution (80m) near-infrared images allowed identification of sea ice that was contiguous with the coast with sufficient detail to be able to detect small-scale motion. However, due to the darkness of the polar winter, the studies were focused on the landfast ice extent from February to early spring and the subsequent decay process. The repeat interval between orbits was 18 days, but at the latitude of the northern Alaska coast, overlap between orbits allowed regions of the coast to be covered on up to 4 consecutive days. Radarsat synthetic aperture radar (SAR) data from the Alaska Satellite Facility provides imagery of Earth's surface independent of clouds and darkness. The moderate resolution ScanSAR data has a repeat interval of approximately 3 days and a pixel size of 150 m and pixel spacing of 100 m and so is capable of detecting features and motion of a similar scale to those identified in Landsat images. However, there are a number of processes not associated with detectable motion that can lead to a change in the backscatter over time, which make the identification of stationary ice more difficult. Different incidence angles between orbits can cause this, but the sea ice itself also evolves and this, in turn, alters the radar interaction with the ice thereby resulting in a different backscatter coefficient.

Frost flowers on newly formed sea ice can generate the strongest backscatter (Onstott, 1992), though wind or snow on the surface soon dampen their effect. Once formed, sea ice desalinates over time (Weeks and Ackley, 1986). As a result, the radar energy penetrates more deeply, which leads to an increase in backscatter. Deformation of level ice increases the surface roughness and also the backscatter coefficient (Hallikainen and Winebrenner, 1992). It should be noted that the term roughness is used in relation to the radar wavelength. Hence small-scale height variations on the sea ice can yield a similar backscatter coefficient to large ridge fields, which contain both large- and small-scale roughness. Fetterer et al. (1994) found that new ice and open water can exhibit a wide range of backscatter coefficients since the surfaces of both can be very smooth or roughened by small-scale ice deformation or wind-induced waves.

The strongest changes in backscatter of landfast ice occur at the end of the sea ice season and are associated with warming and melting of the ice and snow. Holt and Digby(1985) combined field observations of the evolution of the ice and snow cover with space borne and airborne SAR measurements and describe processes that lead to rapid fluctuations in backscatter over landfast ice during the melt period. The production of superimposed ice nodules in the snow early in the spring, followed by flooding and then draining of the ice surface can lead to an increase in the backscatter, followed by a sudden decrease and then another increase (Barber et al., 1995).

By its coastal nature, landfast ice can be influenced by rivers where they meet the sea. The freshwater reduces the salinity of the seawater near the mouth of the river and therefore the bulk salinity of ice that forms from it. This increases the penetration depth and allows scattering from the ice-water interface leading to a high backscatter coefficient. Where the water is shallow enough however, the ice can freeze to the bed, whereupon there is no ice-water interface and the dielectric contrast at the bottom of the bed is greatly reduced. This leads to a sudden reduction in the backscatter, which allows identification of the bottom fast ice zone (Eicken et al., 2005; Solomon et al., 2004). In the spring, the river water floods the landfast ice, reducing the backscatter coefficient to that of calm open water. Early in this process it can be seen that the ice beyond the flooded area remains stable and is still contiguous with the coast. However, later in process, near larger rivers, such as the Kuparuk and Colville Deltas in Alaska and the Mackenzie Delta in Canada, the flooded area can be so extensive that it becomes difficult to determine whether the ice beyond can still be classified as landfast. The effect is an underestimate of landfast ice extent and overestimate of the stage of decay in these areas.

3.3.3. Study area and subregions

The study area is shown in Figure 1.1.1. It measures 955 km by 330 km in an Albers equal area projection (see Section 3.5) such that at its center point its axes are aligned east-west and north-south. Mosaicked SAR imagery is cropped to fit this rectangle. Within the study area are 10 subregions, (Figure 3.3.1), each measuring 95.5 km by 132 km and chosen such that it can be almost wholly taken from a single parent image leaving it free of mosaicking artifacts. These subregions were only used in the image processing stage to derive the location of the seaward landfast ice edge (SLIE) and do not appear on the subsequent data analysis. Their use is explained below.

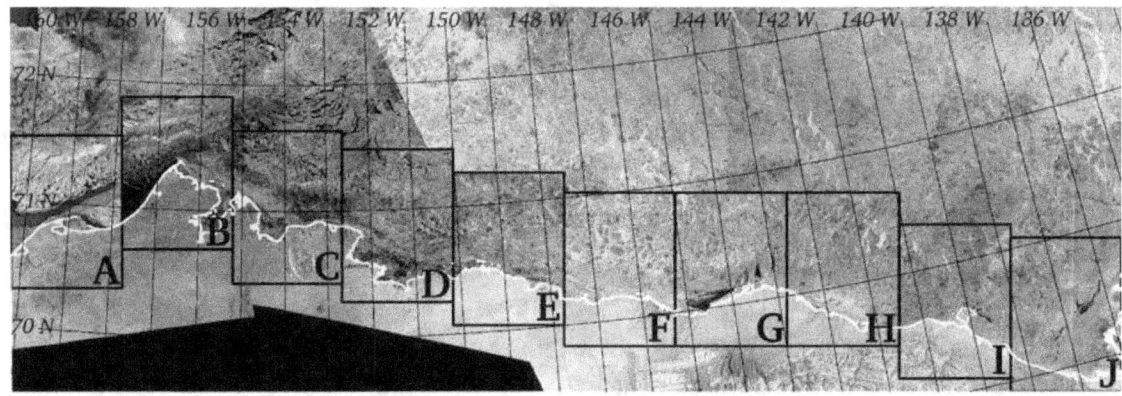

Figure 3.3.1. The full extent (955 × 330 km) of the study area shown by a mosaic of four (4) parent Radarsat scenes. Also shown are the (95.5 × 132 km) subregion boundaries. Note that the subregions are cropped from the parent scenes so that they do not contain any mosaicking edges. SAR imagery © Canadian Space Agency (2002)

3.3.4. Data assimilation

Moderate resolution Radarsat ScanSAR wide beam data were ordered via the Alaska Satellite Facility (ASF) electronic data gateway and were chosen to provide complete coverage of the study area approximately every 10 days between October and July for each of the 8 annual cycles between 1996 and 2004. The data were made available in GeoTIFF format by the ASF Advanced Product Design group with a geolocation accuracy stated to be 5 pixels or 500m. Each image covers an area 550 km by 550 km and is one of a group of parent scenes for a mosaic cropped to the study area. Each mosaic is made up of between 3 and 5 parent scenes separated in time by between 2 and 4 days. Approximately 1000 parent scenes were used to create 238 mosaics during the 8-year study period

Prior to any landfast ice analysis in the images, the data were checked to ensure adequate coverage of the study area and each subregion. In addition, scenes with a large geolocation error were identified and either corrected with a simple horizontal translation or removed from the dataset. The stated geolocation accuracy could give rise to co-location errors of up to 10 pixels or 1 km between parts of two mosaics, though where possible this was reduced to less than 500 m.

3.3.5. Image processing to identify landfast ice

If the backscatter from a sea ice surface changed over time only through ice motion, then landfast ice ought to exhibit a constant backscatter, since it is stationary according to our definition (Section 3.3.1). However, due to the processes described in Section 3.3.2, the backscatter of landfast ice can still change over time while the ice remains stationary. This means that simple subtraction of collocated images is not capable of discerning motion. However, the processes that change the backscatter from the ice surface act least strongly on ridges and areas of deformed ice and consequently the features of the SAR imagery that exhibit most consistency over time are stationary linear regions of high backscatter. These are typically a few hundred meters wide and parallel or sub-parallel with the coast. A technique for distinguishing landfast ice must therefore be able to recognize these features and their orientation.

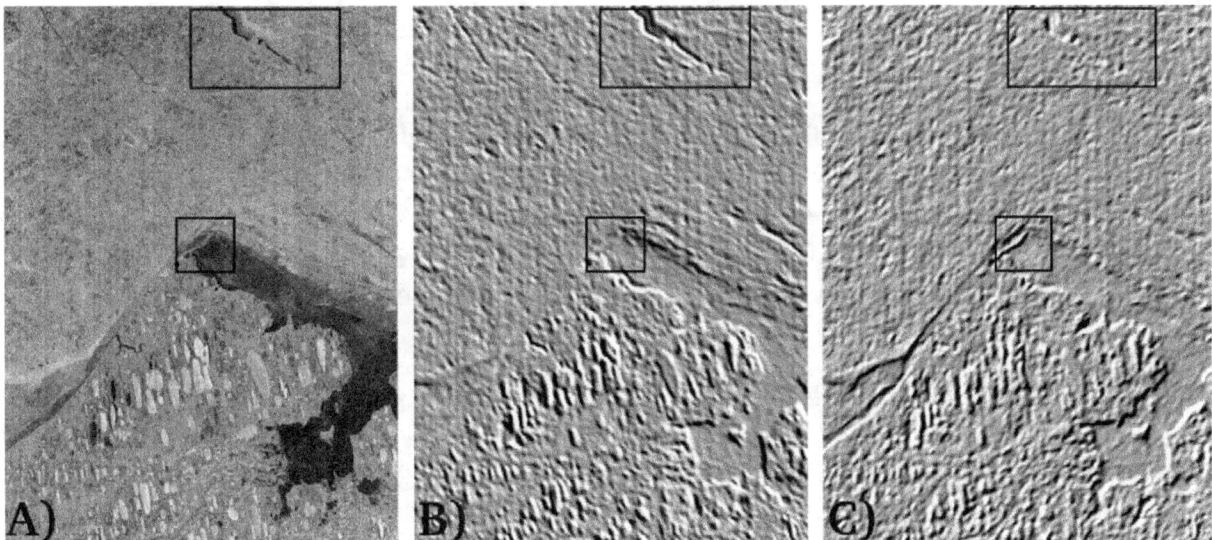

Figure 3.3.2. a) Calibrated Radarsat ScanSAR image over Barrow, Alaska, January 6 2002, corresponding to region B in Figure 3.3.1. The image has been smoothed by 5x5 pixel (500m) filter, b) Horizontal component of grayscale gradient field, c) Vertical component of grayscale gradient field. Bright areas are positive gradients and dark areas are negative gradients, with axes positive to the right and downwards. Note how features have different orientations in the horizontal and vertical component images, such as those indicated by the boxed regions.

The technique we used calculates the horizontal and vertical grey value gradient fields in 3 consecutive images and then calculates the magnitude of the difference in gradient fields. We call the result a gradient difference image. Calculation of the gradient fields is similar to the application of a LaPlacian filter, which is commonly used to detect edges in images, except we only calculate first derivatives and treat the horizontal and vertical components separately in order to preserve the information regarding the orientation of the edge features

The 2-dimensional vector gradient of a scalar field, Φ, is given by equation 3.1:

$$\nabla\Phi = \frac{\partial\Phi}{\partial x}\underline{i} + \frac{\partial\Phi}{\partial y}\underline{j}$$

equation 3.1

where $\underline{i}$ and $\underline{j}$ are horizontal and vertical unit vectors respectively in the image plane. We can apply this to a digital SAR image, if Φ is the backscatter grey values and we approximate equation 3.1 with finite differences:

$$\nabla\Phi_{x,y} \approx \left(\frac{\Phi_{x-d,y} - \Phi_{x+d,y}}{d}\right)\underline{i} + \left(\frac{\Phi_{x,y-d} - \Phi_{x,y+d}}{d}\right)\underline{j}$$

equation 3.2

where x and y are the image co-ordinates and d is the number of pixels between which the gradient is calculated.

By calculating the vector spatial grayscale gradient field of a single SAR image we generate two images that represent the horizontal and vertical components of the gradient field (Figure 3.3.2 B and C respectively). The combination of both components describes the magnitude and orientation of edges in the original image.

To identify regions of the image that remained constant and therefore may represent landfast ice, we calculated the vector gradient fields of three (3) consecutive SAR images and derived the magnitude of net difference between them. In order to preserve the directional information during this calculation, the net difference of each component of the gradient fields is treated separately. Calculation of the net difference between horizontal components is described by:

$$\Delta_{net}\nabla_H = \left|\nabla_H\Phi_1 - \nabla_H\Phi_2\right| + \left|\nabla_H\Phi_1 - \nabla_H\Phi_3\right| + \left|\nabla_H\Phi_2 - \nabla_H\Phi_3\right| \qquad \text{equation 3.3}$$

Where Φ_1, Φ_2 and Φ_3 are the 3 consecutive SAR images and ∇_H is the horizontal gradient component. The same equation is applied for the vertical gradient component.

The final gradient difference image is the Pythagorean sum of the horizontal and vertical components. Figure 3.3.3 shows the gradient difference image that was derived from 3 consecutive SAR images. These images off Barrow, Alaska represent the coverage of one of ten subregions into which the whole study area was divided. In doing so, we were able to calculate the gradient fields of images that were free from mosaicking edges that contribute artificial gradients.

Landfast ice occupies the dark region of low gradient difference values adjacent to the coast. The seaward boundary of this zone, which corresponds to the seaward landfast ice edge (SLIE), is often marked by bright linear regions of high gradient difference, which are the result of a flaw lead existing at that location in one of the 3 parent images. However, no single threshold value of backscatter gradient difference was found to uniquely identify landfast ice and so the SLIE is discontinuous. An algorithm to locate and connect the SLIE was developed but this proved successful only during the middle of winter when the backscatter signatures of landfast ice are most constant. At other times, regions of high gradient difference could be found within the landfast ice particularly during the spring when surface flooding from rivers occurs. Different incidence angles between ascending and descendig orbits also introduced backscatter gradients.

As a result of these difficulties, the gradient difference technique failed to provide the automated and objective method of delineating the SLIE that we were looking for. However, the mosaics of the gradient difference images were still used in conjunction with manual examination of the parent images when image quality was poor and also to reduce some of the subjectivity in such a manual approach. This technique is described in section 3.3.6.

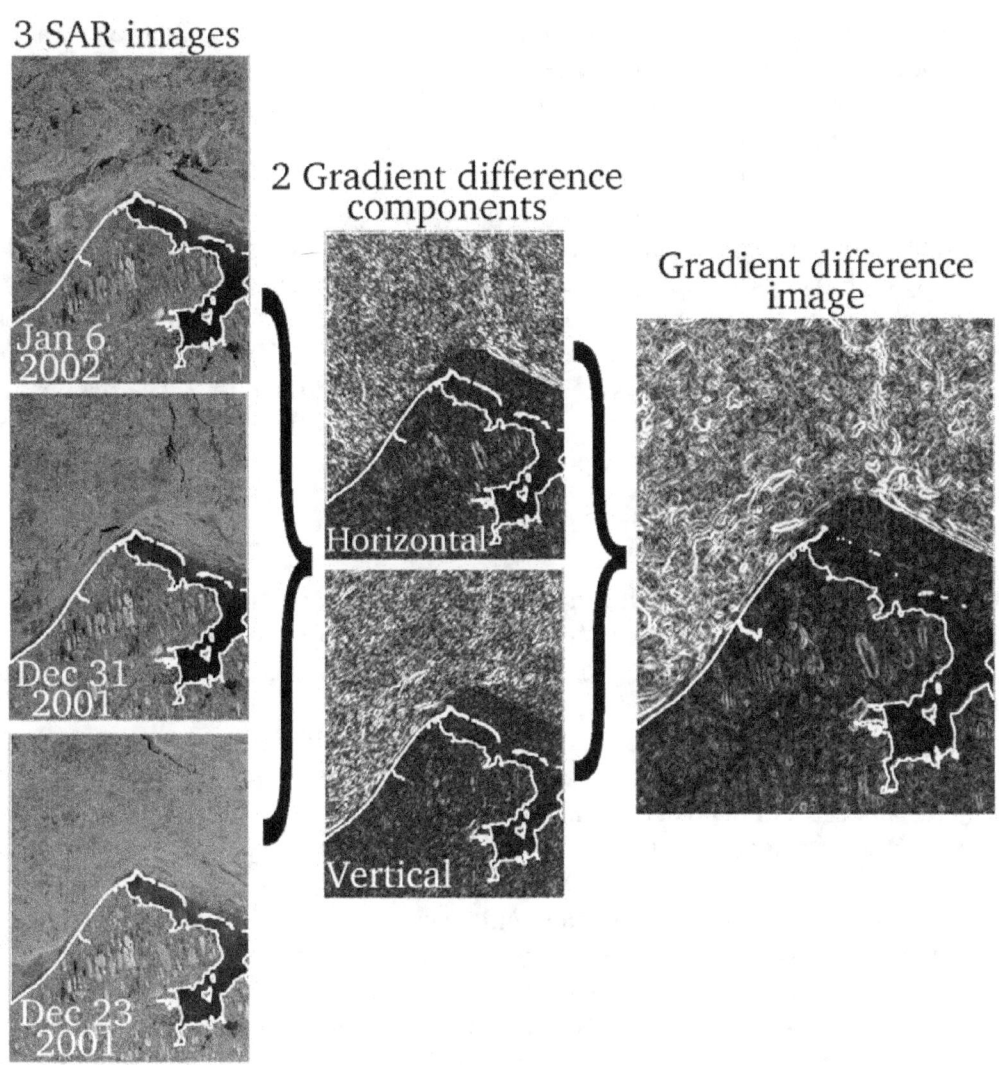

Figure 3.3.3. A gradient difference image and the 3 SAR images from which it was derived. Landfast ice appears dark since the ridges within it retain a more constant backscatter over time. The horizontal and vertical differences are calculated separately from the corresponding components of the vector gradient fields, which are not shown.

3.3.6. Delineation of landfast ice from consecutive SAR mosaics

Although a fully automated method for delineating the SLIE proved elusive (Section 3.3.5), a rigorous technique of manual examination of 3 consecutive SAR mosaics and a gradient difference image was used for the purposes of this study. Sets of 3 consecutive mosaics were examined together to identify regions of ice exhibiting a lack of motion determined by a constant backscatter signature. The georeferencing accuracy of the data allowed us to confidently identify motion greater than 500m. This involved a detailed manual examination of each set of 3 mosaics by process of flickering on a computer screen. The gradient difference image was used to better discriminate changes in backscatter in low-contrast images.

The SLIE delineated in this fashion is a line representing the minimum offshore extent of contiguous stationary ice during the period represented by the 3 mosaics. We distinguish between a seaward and an inshore landfast ice edge. The latter develops during break-up when river flooding and the development of an inshore lead, mostly in areas of bottomfast ice (Reimnitz, 2000), can result in open water inside of the SLIE, as identified in SAR and AVHRR imagery (see also Section 4.1). A more specific date can be assigned to the SLIE at a given location by referring to the mean date of the first mosaic during time periods when the landfast ice is advancing and to that of the last mosaic during periods of landfast ice retreat. Since different parts of the landfast ice may be advancing and retreating at the same time, it is not meaningful to attribute a single date to the entire delineated SLIE. This delineation technique yields the shape of the SLIE and allows us to examine changes in landfast ice area over time. However, to analyze variability in extent over space and time, we need to determine the width of landfast sea ice relative to the coast throughout the study area.

3.3.7. Measuring landfast ice width

The measurement of landfast ice width is not as simple a task as it initially appears, since the value yielded depends upon the direction from the coast in which the measurement is taken. A direction normal to the coast line at the point of interest is preferable, but at convex regions of the coast with high curvature a single direction can be both difficult to define and misrepresentative. To overcome this, a set of transects were defined based on a fixed set of rules. First a line of offshore points was defined such that every point on the line was 150 km from the nearest point of land. It should be noted again that islands are excluded from this coastline, with the exception of Barter and Herschel Island (see Section 3.3.1) Every 1 km along this line, a point was connected by a transect to the nearest point on the coast, so that some coast points were connected by more than one transect and others by none. Finally, unconnected points on the coast were connected to the nearest point on the offshore line to fill-in concave regions of the coast. The result of this process is a set of 1935 approximately coast-normal transects which serve as a curvilinear co-ordinate system for defining the location of the SLIE. The measurements of width along these transects are then binned into 200 groups, each representing 9 or 10 measurements, for which average measurements were calculated (Figure 3.3.4).

This approach works well for relatively simple coastlines. However, for more complex coastlines, with deeply concave embayments, the line of offshore points must be closer to land, which limits the width of landfast ice that can be measured. The distance of 150 km that was chosen here strikes a balance between these two constraints. As a result, the waters of Admiralty Bay between Point Barrow and Pitt Point are not represented and there are other small "shadows" behind headlands where the transects do not reach. Also, on rare occasions when the SLIE was more than 150 km from the coast (see Section 1.3.5) the measurement was truncated (deemed of negligible effect on the following analysis). The exclusion of islands from our coastline means that ice attached to barrier islands, but separated from the mainland is not considered landfast ice and so is not included in the width measurement.

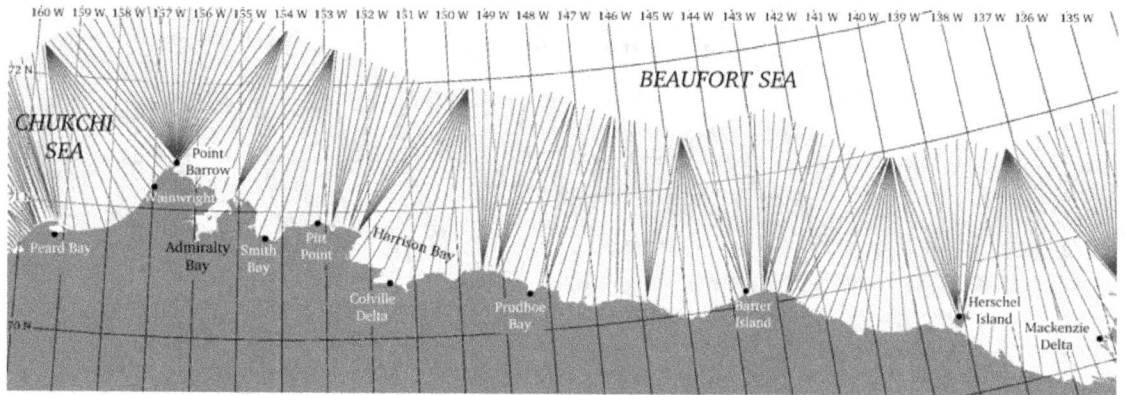

Figure 3.3.4. 200 transects along which landfast ice width is measured. Each transect represents a group of between 9 and 10 measurements that are averaged.

3.3.8. Identifying key events in landfast ice development

By measuring average landfast ice width at 200 coastal locations (Section 3.3.7) during 8 annual cycles, we were able to obtain 1600 time series charting the annual development of landfast ice. Figure 3.3.5 shows the time-series of landfast ice width and water depth at the SLIE for a transect starting at the Colville Delta (see Figure 3.3.4 for coastal locations) for the 2001-02 cycle. Automated algorithms are then applied to these time series to determine the timing of 4 key events at each coastal location during each landfast ice cycle as defined below:

> **First ice on coasts**. The first occurrence of more than 500m of ice at the coast is taken to represent the time at which ice started forming, given the geolocation accuracy of the SAR imagery.

> **Stable landfast ice**. Stability of the landfast ice is more difficult to define. Here, the stable period is defined as the longest period during which the SLIE occupies water 15 m or deeper. The onset of this period is used to define key event 2.

> **Break-up**. This is characterized by a sharp decrease in landfast ice width toward the end of the season and its occurrence is defined by the most negative gradient in the tail of the season once the gradient remains less than or equal to zero. It should be noted that this doesn't necessarily coincide with the end of the stable period.

> **Ice-free coasts**. Once the landfast ice width drops to less than 500m, the coast is deemed ice-free.

The selection of these four criteria is illustrated in Figure 3.3.5 but we should note that not all annual time series fit this pattern and determination of all key events by these criteria was not possible for all locations in all years. This varied across the study region however, and overall the algorithms worked best with time series from the western Beaufort Sea region. Due to restrictions of data availability, the date of the first mosaics acquired for each annual cycle varied. As a result, landfast ice was already present along an average of 67% of the coast in 1996, 1997 and 1998, when the first available mosaics were acquired latest in the year. In the remaining years this only occurred in 6% of time series and so these and the entire first 3 years are excluded from the analysis of the dates of landfast ice formation.

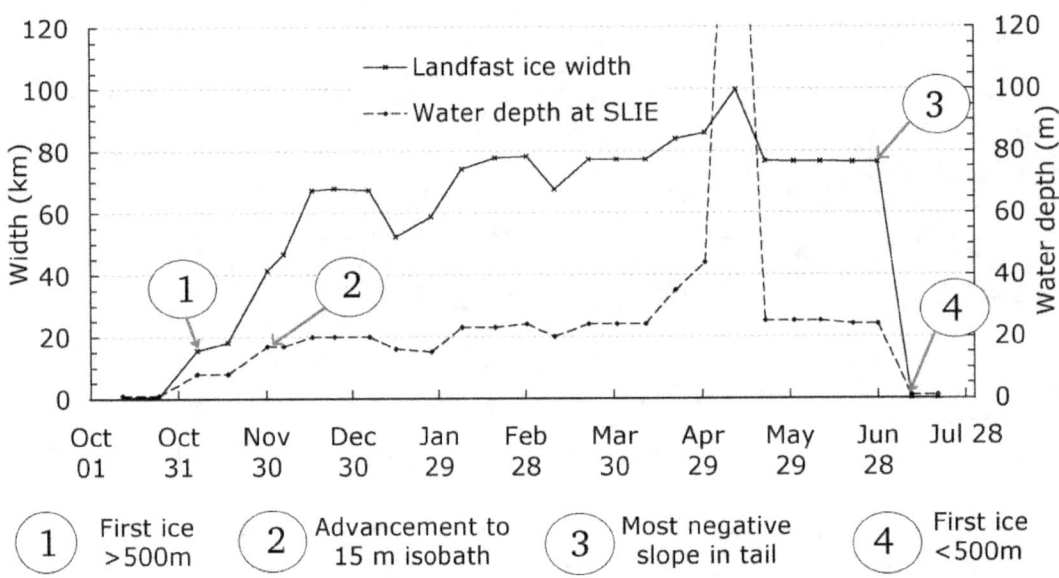

Figure 3.3.5. Development of landfast ice at the Colville Delta between October 2001 and July 2002, showing features of the time series that are used to determine the occurrence dates of four key events in the annual cycle. See text for explanation.

In all of the 1600 time series of landfast ice width, determination of the onsets of stability failed in 8% of instances. Figure 3.3.5 shows that the depth at the SLIE at this location fluctuates around 18 m and hence that the determination of stability can be sensitive to the depth criterion. For this reason a depth of 15 m was chosen instead of 18 m, which is the depth suggested by the analysis discussed in Section 4.2.3. This is also the criterion for stability used by Barry et al. (1979b), with whose results we will compare ours in Section 4.2.4. The onset of break-up was not determined on 28% of occasions, mostly along coasts with a narrow belt of landfast ice. Ice-free coasts remained unobserved in less that 1% of all measurements. In all these cases, the results were excluded from subsequent analysis.

As mentioned in Section 3.3.6, the date corresponding to a particular mosaic can be assigned to a point on the SLIE by considering the change of SLIE position over time. Since a SLIE represents the minimum extent of unmoving contiguous ice in 3 mosaics, we can assign any part of the SLIE that is advancing to the date of the first mosaic. Similarly, if a part of the SLIE is retreating then we can assign it to the last mosaic. This technique is applied to the data in order to determine the most accurate date possible for each event. The methods described above for determining the dates will always give the date of the first mosaics in which the event is observed, meaning that these will inherently err on the side of being up to 10 days after the actual occurrence. Hence, the dates used in the subsequent analysis are all shifted backwards by 5 days, allowing us to estimate an error of ±5 days.

3.3.9. Calculation of mean monthly SLIE statistics

24

Calculation of monthly statistics for the location of the SLIE is complicated by the fact that each SLIE represents a period of time that may span more than one calendar month. This is due to the ~20-day period that is integral to our definition of landfast ice. Two techniques have been used to assign the SLIE data into monthly bins. In both methods, the SLIE must first be defined relative to the coast according the distance along a set of predefined vectors. These are shown in Figure 3.3.4, but it should be noted that for the purposes of creating the monthly SLIEs, all 1935 transects were used without re-binning (see Section 3.3.7). The first method assigns weighted fractions of these distances to different months according to how much of the overall time span of each SLIE falls in those months. This is performed on each year of the study period to yield 8 mean SLIE positions for each calendar month, from which monthly minima, means and maxima are calculated for the entire study period.

The second technique calculates the positions relative to the coast of all the SLIEs in a given year. At each point along the coast, it is then possible to determine whether the SLIE is advancing or retreating at any time. Since a SLIE represents the minimum extent of unmoving contiguous ice in 3 mosaics, we can assign any part of the SLIE that is advancing to the date of the first of mosaic. Similarly, if a part of the SLIE is retreating then we can assign it to the last mosaic. This technique allows us to assign SLIE position data to different months without any averaging.

In both techniques, the monthly SLIEs are drawn by connecting points defined by distances along each of the transects. A comparison between the monthly SLIE positions calculated by each technique for May is shown in Figure 3.3.6, from which it is clear that the greatest differences are in the minima and maxima. There is very little difference in the location of the mean SLIE position. The differences in the minimum positions between the two techniques are due to the additional averaging step when assigning SLIE positions to different months. Consequently, the absolute minimum position will not be captured. Between the maximum positions calculated by each method, the greatest differences are in the eastern portion of the study area, which is where large stable extensions have been observed. Method 2 does still not capture the full extent due to the maximum length of the vectors used to measure landfast ice width (Figure 3.3.4). Method 1 calculates an even lesser extent due to additional averaging.

Figure 3.3.7 shows the mean difference in location for each month, calculated by summing the differences in area and dividing by the length of the coastline, which is on the order 1,000 km. This demonstrates that differences in the mean location remain small for all months. The differences in minimum positions are typically less than 5 km and reflect smoothing of sudden break-outs after which the landfast ice quickly re-advances. The effect of these is somewhat greater in April when early break-outs are more common. The greatest differences between maximum extents occur in February, March and April, which is the time period during which most stable extensions are observed. While the presence of stable extensions warrants further study to understand the possible oceanographic and ecological implications, their effect on offshore development planning is likely to be small.

25

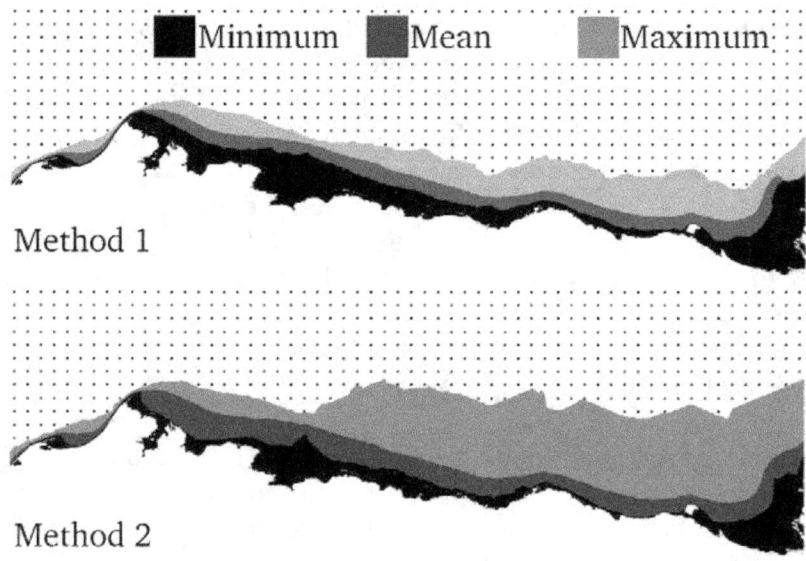

Figure 3.3.6: Comparison between the minimum, mean and maximum SLIE positions for May calculated by two different methods.

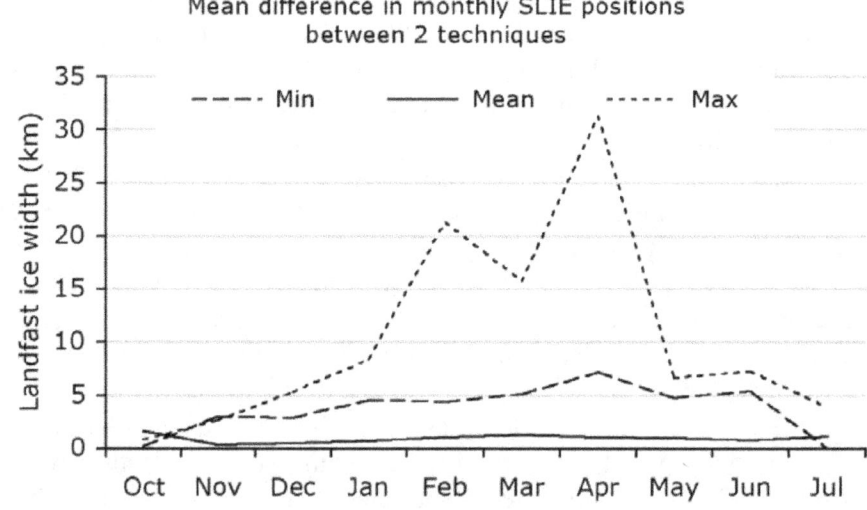

Figure 3.3.7: Mean difference between two methods for calculating monthly minimum, mean and maximum SLIE position.

In consideration of all the above, we feel that the monthly SLIE positions calculated using the first method are entirely adequate for planning purposes. Furthermore, the additional averaging helps remove artifacts from the original data such as those shown in Figure 3.3.8, making the results more suitable for model input. However the advantage to the second method comes with the ability to calculate distributions and modes of the SLIE position for different points along the coast for each month. Therefore we include the results of the first method in ArcGIS format as per Section 3.5 in the data distribution DVD, while the results of the second method are presented in the detailed analysis of landfast ice extent in Section 4.2 below.

Figure 3.3.8: The landfast ice area for the period February 16 – March 8, 2000, overlain semi-transparently on the first of the 3 mosaics of period. This shows how mosaic boundaries, which effectively represent temporal boundaries in the image, lead to artifacts along the SLIE.

3.4. Ancillary data sets

3.4.1. Bathymetry

Bathymetry data were needed for the analysis of the Seaward Landfast Ice Edge (SLIE) and to illustrate the influence of the seafloor on the characterization of common lead patterns. Regional GIS data sets provided online by the US Geological Survey were appropriate as an aid in describing lead characterization (http://www.absc.usgs.gov/research/walrus/bering/bathy/index.htm), but lacked sufficient detail for SLIE analysis. After a survey of existing data sources, it was concluded that most sources only covered a portion of the study area or proved to be too coarse for use in SLIE analysis. As a result, a custom binary data set was developed from several sources.

Table 3.4.1: Summary of bathymetric datasets acquired in the process of developing a gridded bathymetry of the landfast ice study area.

	Dataset	Source	Region
1	GEODAS depth soundings	NGDC	Nearshore Chukchi and Beaufort Seas
2	ENC sounding data	NOAA	Chukchi Sea
3	ENC sounding data	NOAA	Beaufort Sea
4	Nautical chart #16082	NOAA	Point Barrow
5	Outer Continental Shelf Study MMS 2002-017	MMS	
6	Digital Ocean Chart 7662	NDI	Mackenzie Bay
7	Digital Ocean Chart 7661	NDI	Demarcation Bay To Philips Bay
8	IBCAO Sheet 3	IBCAO	Arctic Ocean

The bathymetry developed for SLIE analysis is a 100-meter cell size Digital Elevation Model (DEM) covering the offshore area from Peard Bay, Alaska to Mackenzie Bay, Canada. Sounding point measurements from 8 different datasets were acquired (Table 3.4.1, Figure 3.4.1). Furthermore, detailed comparison of the IBCAO data with neighboring soundings from the NOAA data sets showed significant differences in some locations. These disparities were not consistent, but appear limited to water depths deeper than 100 m. In addition, the IBCAO data points are densely spaced along contours, which bias the overall bathymetry to these depths. Therefore, certain points were excluded from the datasets according to two criteria. First, the IBCAO contours shallower than 100 m were discarded to eliminate the bias in the waters most commonly occupied by landfast ice. Second, the sounding points from datasets 2 and 3 that lay offshore of the IBCAO 100 m isobath were removed.

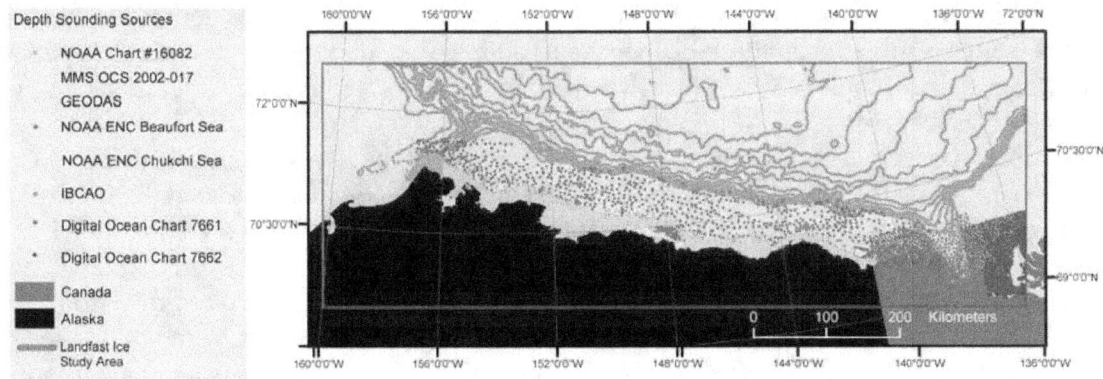

Figure 3.4.1: Bathymetry data sources for landfast ice analysis.

This yielded over 39,000 points distributed unevenly across the study area grid. Thirty thousand (30,000) of these soundings were from dataset 1 (GEODAS) and lay densely spaced in the nearshore zone of the Alaska Chukchi and Beaufort Seas (Figure 3.4.1). The points from dataset 8, (IBCAO sheet 3,) were also densely spaced but only along isobaths (every 100 m between 100m and 500 m, and every 500 m between 1000 m and 3500 m). In order to produce a more even distribution and also to reduce the computation time, these points were then thinned so that no data point lay within 1 km of another data point. This resulted in 24,438 points. To produce the final gridded bathymetry data, an inverse distance weighting algorithm within IDL was applied to these points. The result is shown in Figure 3.4.2. Many different techniques were tested including kriging, co-kriging, topogrid and inverse distance weighted routines within various modules of ESRI's ArcInfo, ArcGIS and ArcView software as well as equivalent algorithms within IDL. Although rigorous statistical comparisons were not performed, there were no apparent significant differences between output from ESRI software and IDL and the adopted IDL algorithm proved the most efficient method to generate an acceptable product.

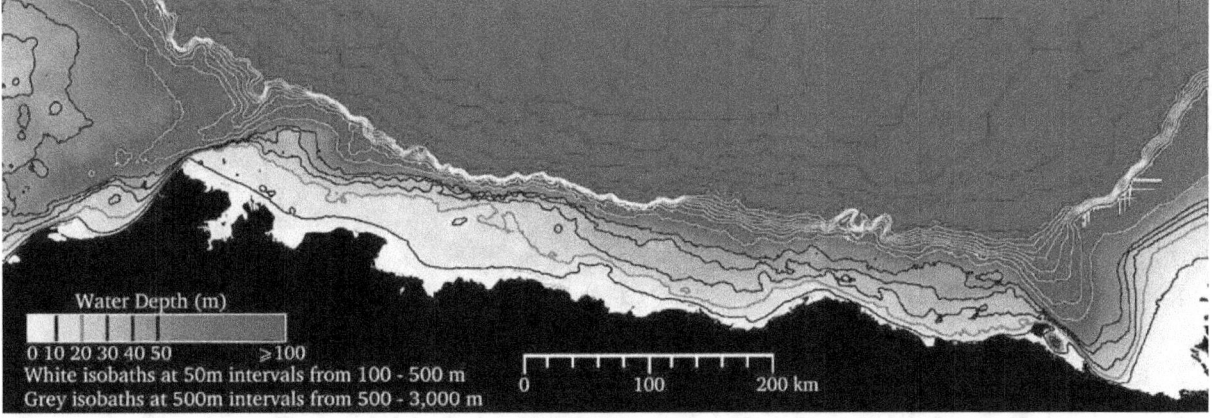

Figure 3.4.2: Radarsat study area bathymetry. The color scale indicates water depth between 0 and 100 m, with black contours at 10, 30, 40 and 50 m depths. The 20 m depth contour is shown in red. Beyond 100 m, black and gray contours are used at 50 m and 500 m intervals respectively.

29

It should be noted that the effective spatial and bathymetric resolutions of the grid vary due to the different datasets used in different areas (Figure 3.4.1). In particular, water depths less than 100 m will be better resolved than those deeper than 100 m. Also, due to lack of data, the spatial resolution deeper than 50 m northwest of the Mackenzie Delta is effectively coarser than elsewhere. These aspects of the DEM only have a small impact on the waters that landfast ice typically occupies, hence we believe the product is adequate for the purposes of analyzing typical relationships between water depth and landfast ice extent. We also note that the 20 m isobath in Figure 3.4.2 lies up to 20 km further offshore when compared with the corresponding IBCAO isobath in the region between the eastern end of Barrow Canyon and western side of Harrison Bay. In this region, the water depths in Figure 3.4.2 were interpolated entirely from NOAA ENC soundings (dataset 3). Therefore, without the original soundings from which the IBCAO data were interpolated, we give more credence to the NOAA soundings and have more confidence in our bathymetric grid in this region.

Therefore, the 100-meter DEM shown in Figure 3.4.2 should be considered a working product. Other regional initiatives are also striving to compile more detailed bathymetry for the Chukchi and Beaufort Seas. These include the Barrow Coastal Observatory, the Arctic Observation System and the Alaska Ocean Observing System. The Hawaii Mapping Research Group based out of the University of Hawaii at Manoa is currently processing multibeam surveys conducted from the 2005 Healy cruise, plus other data sources in an effort to create an improved grid. Such efforts should eventually yield an improved data set.

3.4.2. Objective Synoptic Classification of Sea Level Atmospheric Pressure Patterns

Daily mean sea level pressure fields were acquired from the National Centers for Environmental Prediction (NCEP) over an area extending from 55 °N to 80 °N and 180 °W to 120 °W. All data available up to the end of the study period were acquired, from 1948 to 2004. An objective classification scheme was used to identify key daily pressure patterns (Barry, 1976; Barry, 1979; Kirchhofer, 1974; Serreze and Etringer, 2003). In this scheme, each daily field is normalized by its own mean and standard deviation and then the sum of the square of the differences was calculated between all pairs. The same technique is then also applied to generate difference values for subregions of fields. Pairs of daily pressure fields with difference values below certain thresholds are deemed similar. Individual fields with more than 5 other fields similar to them are identified as characteristic patterns (CPs), which collectively describe the most important patterns in terms of describing to overall variability of sea level pressure. Other fields are then assigned to the CP with which they share the lowest difference value. The CPs are then placed in order so that CP 1 has the most fields assigned to it. The threshold difference values are chosen subjectively and can be adjusted to determine the number of CPs identified. In this study we chose the same values as Barry (1979) and obtained 60 CPs characterizing the 20,820 daily fields between 1948 and 2004.

3.4.3. Freezing and thawing degree days

In addition to the examining the surface pressure patterns, we also examined NCEP surface air temperature data to calculate accumulated freezing and thawing degree days. Freezing degree days (FDDs) are calculated by summing the daily mean air temperatures of days with mean temperature below freezing since the onset of freezing. We define the date of the onset of freezing as being the first day with an average temperature below zero that is also the first day of a 30-day period that has an average temperature below 0 ºC. Thawing degree days (TDDs) and the onset of thawing are defined similarly for days with temperatures above 0 ºC.

3.5. Dissemination and archival of resultant data sets

All project data were processed to the standard Alaska Statewide Albers map projection and federal datum standard to promote data integration. These project data include remotely sensed imagery, specifically AVHRR scenes and RADARSAT mosaics in GeoTIFF format plus ArcGIS grids, shapefiles and vector-based geodatabases. Following are the detailed projection and datum parameters:

Map Projection Name: Albers Conical Equal Area
Standard Parallel: 55.000000
Standard Parallel: 65.000000
Longitude of Central Meridian: -154.000000
Latitude of Projection Origin: 50.000000
False Easting: 0.000000
False Northing: 0.000000

Planar Coordinate Information
Planar Distance Units: meters
Coordinate Encoding Method: coordinate pair

Coordinate Representation
Abscissa Resolution: 0.002048
Ordinate Resolution: 0.002048

Geodetic Model
Horizontal Datum Name: North American Datum of 1983
Ellipsoid Name: Geodetic Reference System 80
Semi-major Axis: 6378137.000000
Denominator of Flattening Ratio: 298.257222

This project required processing a large volume of imagery and derived data. Over 1000 Radarsat data granules were acquired and processed into image mosaics in GeoTIFF format spanning the study area. Radarsat mosaics, derived GIS SLIE delineations and monthly averages total nearly 11 GB worth of data for the ice seasons beginning in the Fall of 1996 through Spring of 2004. 385 AVHRR scenes were acquired and processed into GeoTIFF format as well. A total of nearly 3 GB of AVHRR imagery and derived GIS data were produced for 1993-2004 ice seasons.

Standard naming conventions were adopted as an aid for data management and to address the file naming constraints of ArcGIS grid and coverage data formats. The final deliverables for the project include data in ArcGIS grid format that imposes a 13-character file limitation that was taken into consideration in developing the naming conventions. The file names rely on the use of the directory structure to organize the files in individual folders by year. Individual file names incorporate the number associated with the day of that year for each of the data sets. Detailed information on the file naming conventions is available on the project web site and in the metadata files.

In addition to the ArcGIS grids requested in the original RFP, ArcGIS shapefiles and vector-based geodatabases were prepared. The geodatabases organize the SLIE and lead data by ice season, plus include monthly SLIE minimum, mean, maximum and median data. Ancillary GIS data compiled for this project include depth sounding points (over 412,000 points) and bathymetry data (100 meter and 1 kilometer grids.) FGDC XML metadata templates have been associated with each data set.

These geospatial data sets and associated metadata, plus lead statistic summaries, are available on a password protected web site hosted by the Geographic Information Network of Alaska (GINA) at the University of Alaska Fairbanks. This project web site organizes resultant data sets by ice season and is accessible at: http://mms.gina.alaska.edu. The site proved to be a useful tool for sharing data products and ongoing progress with the MMS contracting officer. Processed imagery, ArcGIS data (prepared in version 8.3) and associated Federal Geographic Data Committee (FGDC) metadata hosted on this site will be ingested into the FGDC clearinghouse at GINA once a final agency review is completed. The archives at the National Oceanographic Data Center (NODC) and National Snow and Ice Data Center (NSIDC) will be notified of these products as well to foster further dissemination through the creation of project catalog pages and harvest of standard FGDC metadata.

4. Results

4.1. Mapping of lead distribution and morphology

4.1.1. Seasonal, interannual and regional variability in lead areal fractions

The total lead fraction averaged by month for the entire study area is shown in Figure 4.1.1. While there is substantial interannual and regional variability, most years nevertheless exhibit a distinct seasonal cycle with lead fractions above 0.02 in December and January and peaking at 0.10 in June. Minimum lead fractions in February coincide roughly with the lowest temperatures, typically found in the last week of February or first week of March based on Barrow surface air temperature climatology (Alaska Climate Research Center, 2005, climate.gi.alaska.edu). Also, there is a marginally significant, inverse correlation between the accumulated number of freezing degree days and areal lead fractions in the Barrow subregion. The distribution of leads shows a distinct regional pattern, with the region west of Point Barrow (Figure 4.1.2) exhibiting the highest lead fractions during winter. The smallest lead fractions were found consistently in subregions 5 (Harrison Bay) through 7 (Prudhoe Bay), with values lower than those for the westernmost subregions by a factor of 2 to 4. The easternmost part of the study region off the Mackenzie Delta exhibits lead fractions that typically range at roughly half of the values in the westernmost subregions during winter and then increase to 0.1 and above in May and June (Figure 4.1.3, see also Table 4.1.1) with the opening of large leads and coastal polynyas off the Mackenzie Delta. As indicated in Figure 4.1.2, interannual variability in the observed wintertime lead areal fraction is substantial and highest in subregions 1-3. In May and June, interannual variability is highest in the easternmost part of the study region. This interannual variability is partly due to differences in cloud cover and availability of imagery suitable for analysis, such as in 1994-95 and 1998-99 when only 21 and 19 images, respectively, were available for analysis, resulting in potential bias for low open water fractions in the winter months. However, the broader regional patterns, such as minimum interannual variability in subregion 4 (Smith Bay) and maximum variability west of Point Barrow for December through April and off the Mackenzie Delta for May and June, hold up to further scrutiny. These regional variability patterns are also manifest in monthly mean lead distributions (Figure 4.1.3), with December and May exhibiting the strongest regional contrast (see also Table 4.1.1).

Table 4.1.1: Mean and standard deviation (σ) of lead areal fractions, number densities, and size parameters for all years (1993-2004).

Parameter	Entire Study Area		West Subregions 1-3		West-Central Subregions 4-6		East-Central Subregions 7-9		East Subregions 10-12	
	Dec-Apr	May-Jun	Dec-Apr	May-Jun	Dec-Apr	May-Jun	Dec-Apr	May-Jun	Dec-Apr	May-Jun
Areal Fraction %	1.9	7.6	3.4	7.2	1.3	3.6	1.3	4.4	1.7	14
σ	1.7	6.2	3.3	4.4	1.5	3.1	2.1	4.3	2.5	16
Number Density (10^{-3} km^{-2})	0.6	2.3	0.9	2.0	0.6	2.1	0.5	2.5	0.4	2.5
σ	0.4	1.4	0.7	1.3	0.5	1.4	0.6	2.0	0.5	2.0
Area (km^2)	36.0	42.0	60.5	79.5	38.7	41.9	47.7	82.6	31.2	115
σ	28.6	40.4	67.7	137	61.2	49.7	144	188	45.7	298
Perimeter (km)	23.4	17.9	30.0	23.1	23.8	19.0	22.6	19.9	18.8	23.7
σ	8.1	3.6	17.8	11.5	18.6	6.4	28.9	17.7	18.4	10.7
Major Axis (km)	7.4	5.6	8.7	6.7	7.3	5.8	6.8	5.9	5.9	6.7
σ	2.0	0.8	4.0	3.5	3.9	1.6	5.5	3.1	5.3	2.0
Minor Axis (km)	2.5	2.4	3.0	2.6	2.3	2.3	2.1	2.4	1.9	2.8
σ	0.40	0.33	1.0	0.79	0.68	0.33	1.0	1.2	1.3	1.0
Number of Scenes	203	68	202	66	203	68	203	67	202	67

Areal fraction: total surface area of leads divided by total surface area of the subregion; Number density: total number of leads divided by total surface area of subregion; Area: surface area of individual leads; Perimeter: perimeter (circumference) of individual leads; Major and minor axis: major and minor axis of an ellipse that provides the best fit to the lead outline; Number of scenes: number of scenes in which subregions were cloud-free and could be analyzed.

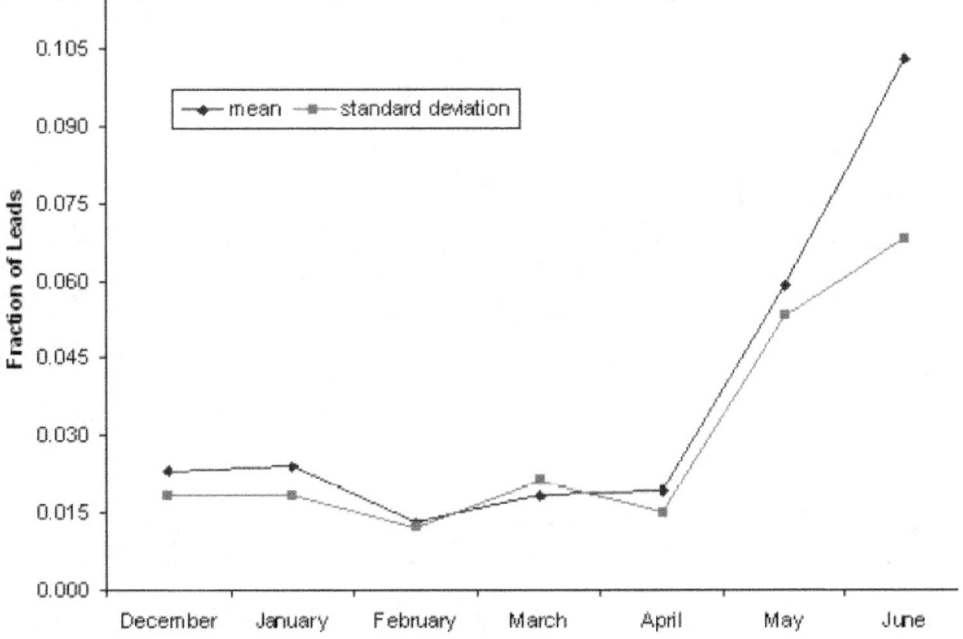

Figure 4.1.1. Monthly mean lead fractions and standard deviations for the entire study area and study period (1993-2004).

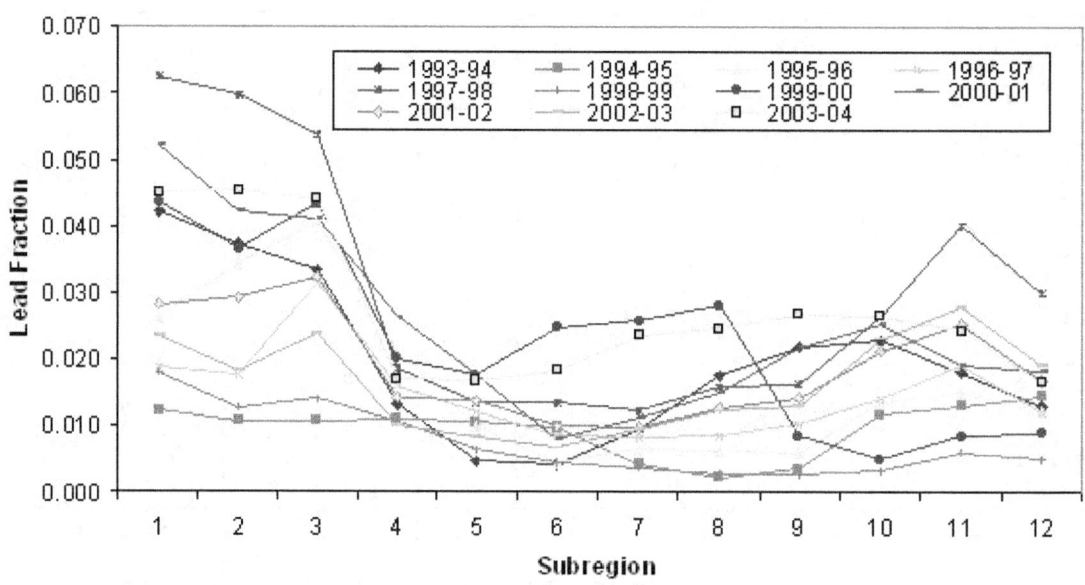

Figure 4.1.2. Mean lead fractions for December through April shown by subregion for all years (1993-2004).

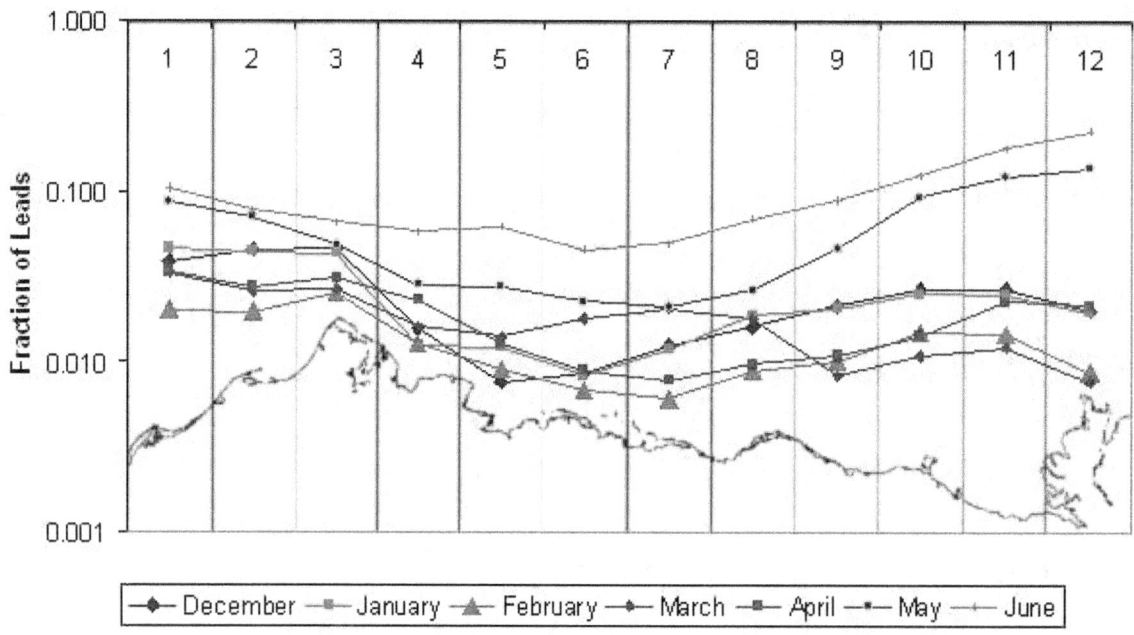

Figure 4.1.3. Mean monthly lead fractions shown by subregion, averaged over all years (1993-2004). Note that the vertical scale is logarithmic.

4.1.2. Regional and seasonal variability in number density and size of leads

The number of leads was determined for each subregion through automated counting of contiguous lead areas (as seen, e.g., in Figure 4.1.2). Each lead was only considered once based on the location of its centerpoint (center of ellipse fit to lead outline). Typical lead numbers for the entire study area ranged between few tens to several hundreds in winter and early spring to more than one thousand in May and June. From these data sets, lead areal densities have been computed (number of leads per km^{-2} of ocean area). The seasonal cycle of lead number density closely follows that of lead areal fraction (Figure 4.1.5) with a linear correlation coefficient of R=0.67 between the two variables. Lead number density increases substantially from mid-April onwards. In winter (December-April), lead number densities are highest in the westernmost part of the study area, with minimum values in the west central and east central sectors, while in May-June maximum values are found in the easternmost sector (Table 4.1.1).

As indicated in Figure 4.1.6, at least part of the data conforms to a power-law type relationship between lead size (major axis of best-fitting ellipse d_{mj}) and lead number density N_l. The entire data is best described by

$$N_l = 0.0675 \, d_{mj}^{-2.30}$$

The magnitude of the power-law exponent b is somewhat higher for our data set than the values of b between 1.5 and 1.7 found by Lindsay and Rothrock (1995) for lead width (measured along a randomly projected line) for 40,000 km^2 cell sizes. Estimates of b obtained from submarine transects at higher spatial resolution range between 2 and 2.29 (Wadhams, 1981; Wadhams et al., 1985). A distinct separation of data points for the winter/early-spring and the late-spring/summer regime is apparent in our data set, reflecting the lead regime discussed in more detail in Section 5.2.

Several variables have been determined to describe the morphology and size of individual leads. These include the lead area, perimeter, and the major and minor axis lengths of a best-fitting ellipse as shown in Table 4.1.1. As is evident from Figure 4.1.2 and Figure 4.1.3, leads extend over a broad range of sizes and hence mean lead area or perimeter, as well as other size parameters, are of lesser value in quantifying and distinguishing between different lead regimes. Overall, mean lead area is linearly correlated with lead perimeter (R = 0.88 for December-April and 0.68 for May-June) as well as width lead major axis (R = 0.71 for December-April and 0.63 for May-June). With leads typically narrow and irregular in shape, lead minor axes exceed the pixel size only by a factor of two to three, with lead (ellipse) aspect ratios averaging at 3.0 in December through April and 2.3 in May and June. The regional contrasts apparent in Table 4.1.1 are marginally significant and mostly reflect the appearance of large coastal leads and polynyas in the western and eastern subregions of the study area.

The size distribution (lead area) derived from all individual measurements for lead sizes <500 km^2 is plotted in Figure 4.1.7. The lead area distribution is well described by a power-law type relationship:

December-April: $\quad f(A) = 9.0721 \, A^{-1.8662}$

May-June: $\quad f(A) = 10.275 \, A^{-2.0048}$

and there is no indication of a change in slope towards smaller bin sizes that would have been indicative of a log-normal distribution. Note that the lower frequency of the smallest bin size (which includes single-pixel leads) is a result of the morphological filtering of scenes to reduce image noise. The power-law distribution is also borne out by field observations (see, e.g., Figure 4.1.3) and studies of high-resolution imagery, suggesting (multi-)fractal size distributions at the scales relevant for this study. The differences between the winter and late spring (May-June) area distributions are significant at the 95%-level and indicate that despite an overall increase in lead areal fractions, the size distribution is dominated by the increase in the number of smaller leads in late spring and early summer.

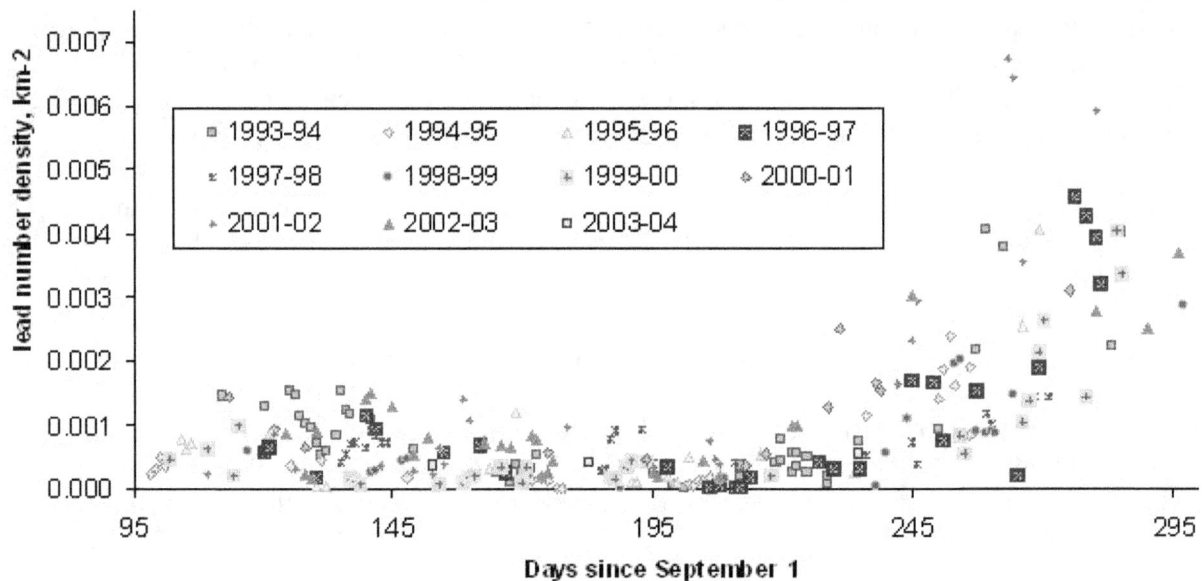

Figure 4.1.4. Seasonal cycle of lead number density shown for the entire study for all years (1993-2004).

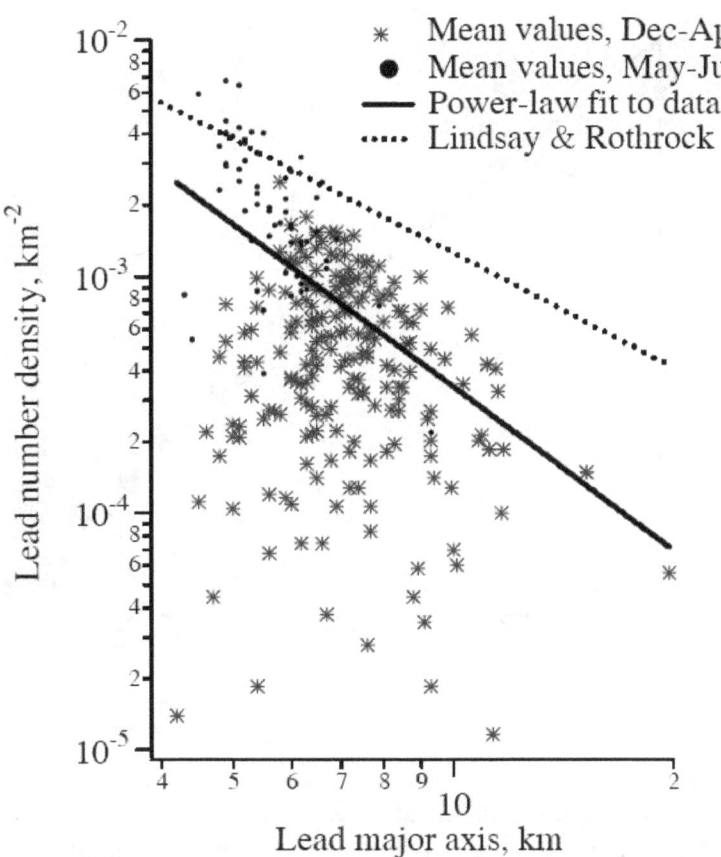

Figure 4.1.5. Mean lead number density plotted as a function of mean lead major axis (best-fitting ellipse) for all years (1993-2004). A best-fit power-law function is also shown, along with the power-law type relationship found by Lindsay and Rothrock (1995) in their data.

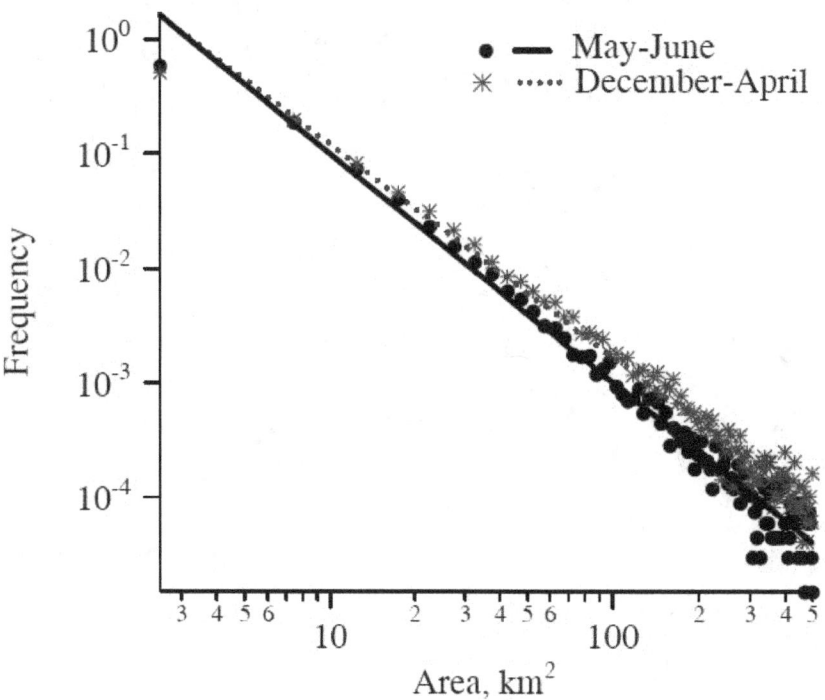

Figure 4.1.6. Lead area frequency distribution for all leads for all years (1993-2004) for December through April and May and June. Note that due to their small number, leads >500 km² have been excluded from the analysis. The frequency of the smallest bin size (0-5 km²) is affected by the morphological filtering of the original data to reduce image noise (see Section 4.1.1). Lines indicate power-law fit to the data set.

4.2. Landfast ice variability and stability

4.2.1. Location of the SLIE

As described in Section 3.3.6, SLIEs were delineated using a combination of 3 consecutive Radarsat mosaics and the corresponding gradient difference mosaics. Consequently, for each season, there were 2 fewer SLIEs identified than there were mosaics available. Figure 4.2.1 shows the position of all 222 SLIEs obtained over all 8 annual cycles. The lines representing the SLIEs were widened to 1 km and then stacked so that the value at a point, indicated by its grey value, represents the relative frequency with which a SLIE occurred at that location and can be viewed as a measure of SLIE stability. When all the SLIEs are combined in this fashion, a zone of preferred locations is readily apparent, within which are nodes of greater stability. The locations of the nodes are indicated by the dotted ellipses in Figure 4.2.1.

In Figure 4.2.2 the landfast ice areas shoreward of each SLIEs are stacked by year such that the grey value indicates the relative frequency with which landfast ice was observed at any point in the study area in each annual cycle. The individual SLIEs for each year are overlain in black and thus have the appearance of frequency contours. The nodes shown in Figure 4.2.1 are indicated by regions at which SLIEs converge and it can seen that there are some nodes that appear each year while others move or are absent in some years. The strong correlation between the 20m isobath and such nodes and the overall concentration of SLIEs suggests that these nodes correspond to locations where the SLIE is pinned by grounded ridges. The role of bathymetry in confining the SLIE will be examined in more detail in Section 4.2.3, though the interannual variability in the position and presence suggests that bathymetry is not the only important control on regional landfast ice extent.

The maximum extent of landfast ice in each year is indicated by the darkest areas, which show obvious interannual differences. During 4 different annual cycles, vast extents of motionless ice were identified, which we refer to as stable extensions following Stringer et al. (1980). Although others have also observed similar features (Barry, 1979; Barry et al., 1979b) they have not typically been considered part of the landfast ice. We include them here in keeping with our definition (Section 3.3.1) and discuss them in more detail in Section 4.2.5. Some SLIEs in Figure 4.2.2 appear to have irregular and jagged edges. These result from boundaries between the parent images within a mosaic that effectively represent temporal discontinuities and are unavoidable in a study area greater in extent than the swath-width of the Radarsat imagery. Figure 3.3.8 shows an example of their origin.

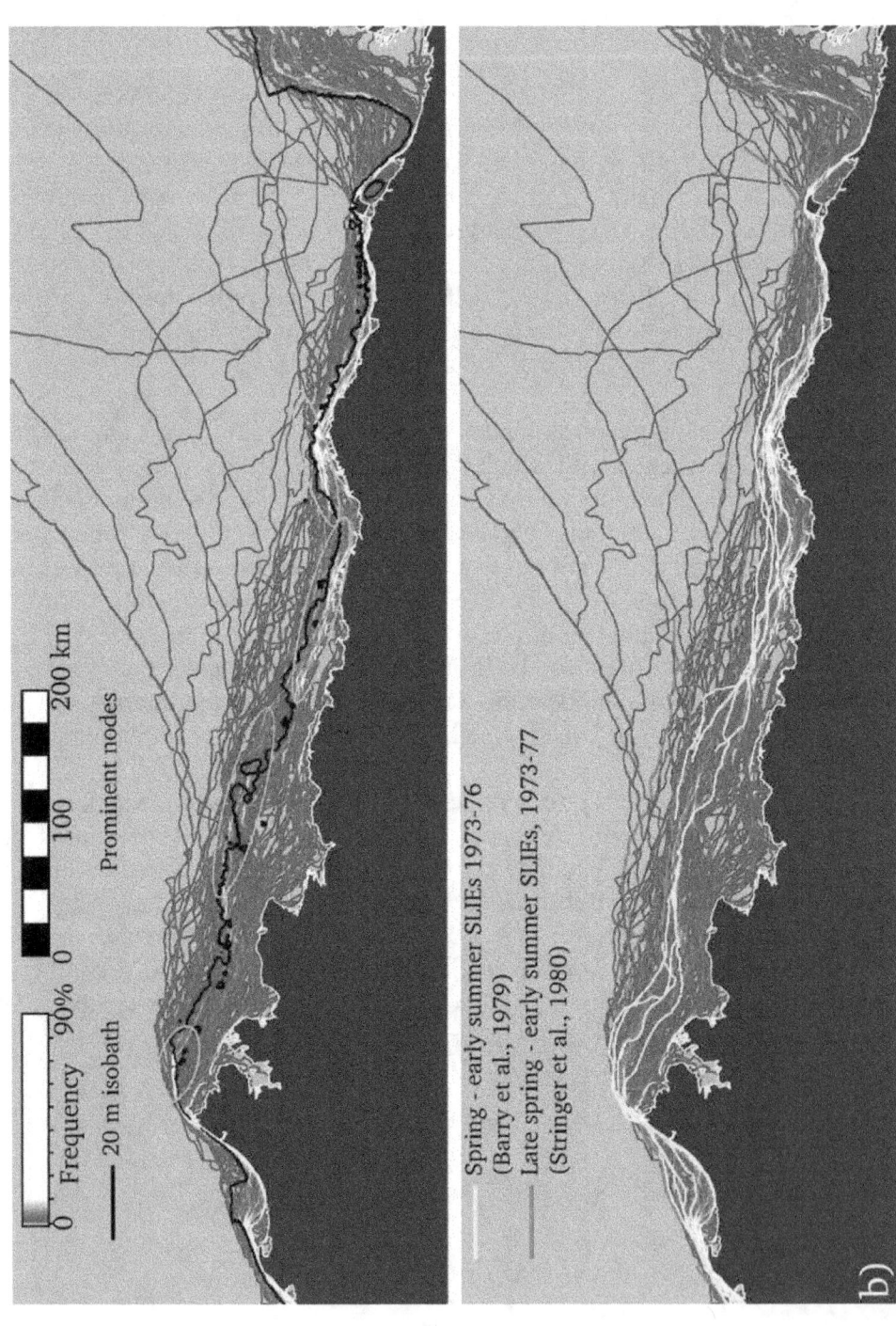

Figure 4.2.1: All 222 SLIEs stacked so that the color value of a line indicates the relative frequency with which the SLIE occurred at that point during the 8-year study period. A white zone of preferred occupation is evident, within which are discrete nodes where the SLIE is more stable. a) The black line shows the 20 m isobath and the orange ellipses indicate the locations of prominent nodes. b) The end-of-season SLIE locations as derived by Barry et al. (1979) and Stringer et al. (1980) shown in yellow and red respectively

42

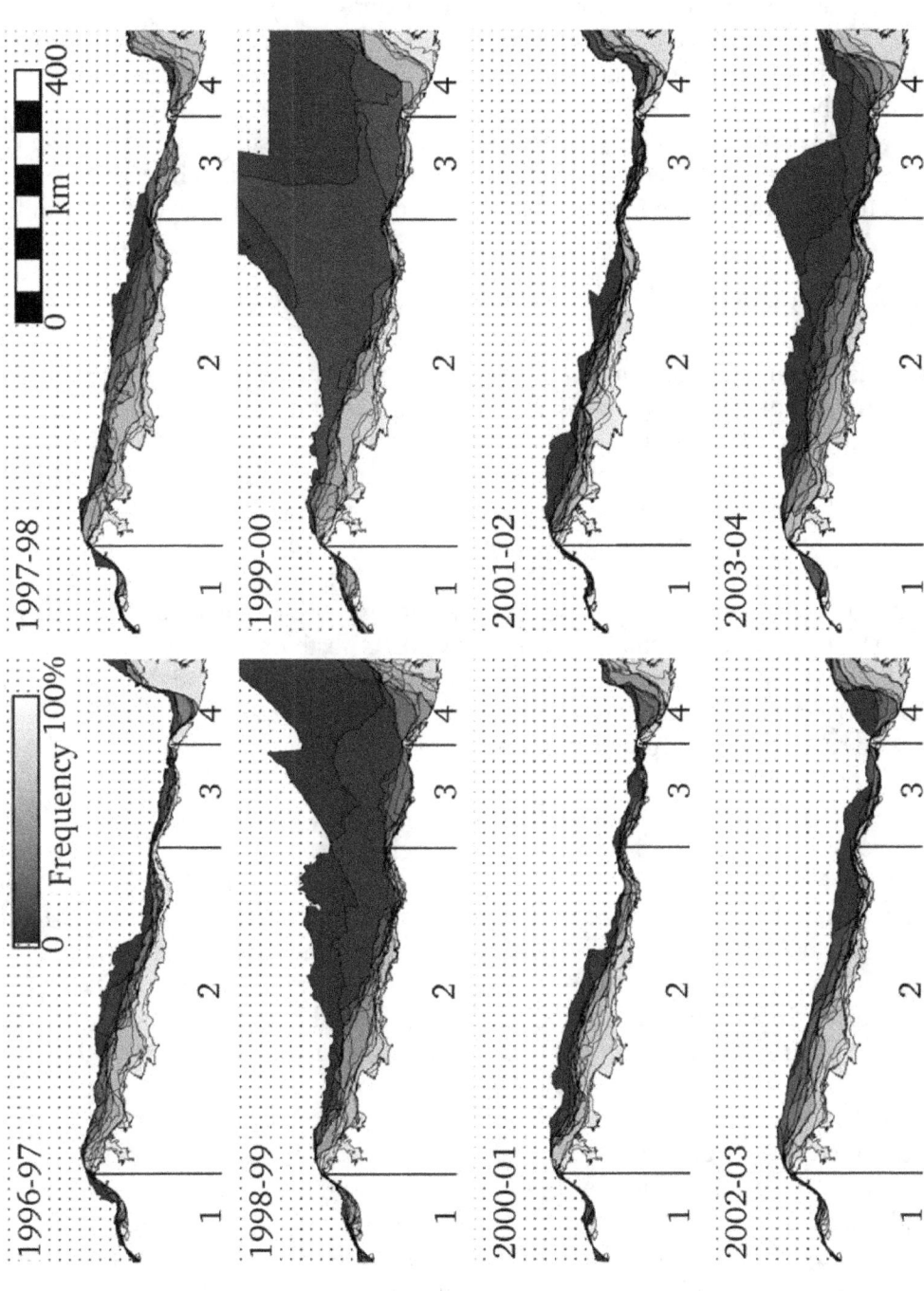

Figure 4.2.2: The position of all SLIEs for each year, with the landfast area of each stacked such that the grey shade of the area represents the fraction of the annual cycle (October-July) for which that area was occupied by landfast sea ice. The numbers 1-4 indicate the locations of the zones described in Section 4.2.1. The darkest shades indicate the maximum extent of landfast sea ice in that year. The dotted area indicates where landfast ice was never observed. The black lines indicate the locations of the individual SLIEs.

43

Across the study area, there are strong contrasts in landfast ice extent and the density of SLIEs, which allow certain zones to be distinguished. These zones are shown in Figure 4.2.2. Perhaps the most apparent boundary between two such zones occurs at Point Barrow (see Figure 3.3.4 or FOLD_OUT MAP for coastal locations). To the west of Point Barrow, in the Chukchi Sea (Zone 1), the landfast sea ice occupies a much narrower strip and the SLIEs appear much more densely spaced than to the east in the western portion of the Beaufort Sea (Zone 2). Zone 3 extends between Barter and Herschel Islands, where the landfast ice extent and variability resemble that of the Chukchi Sea except when large stable extensions of landfast ice occur, which dominate the overall variability. East of Herschel Island is a fourth zone, in which the ice is influenced by the Mackenzie River and the coastline of the Mackenzie Delta, most of which lies beyond our study area.

4.2.2. Monthly landfast ice extents

Although Figure 4.2.2 is useful in delineating interannual variability in the location of the SLIE, it provides no information on the changes that take place during the annual cycle. Such information is partly contained in maps of mean, minimum and maximum monthly landfast extent (Figure 4.2.3). These were calculated by assigning each width measurement of each SLIE (Section 3.3.7) to a calendar month and calculating monthly statistics for each coast point. Monthly SLIEs were then redrawn drawn from the mean width measurements. It should be noted that widths are truncated by the maximum length of the coast vectors, which will affect the maximum extents and, to a lesser degree, the mean extents during those months when vast stable extensions occurred. The jagged extension of the maximum SLIE north of Herschel Island in February results from a mosaicking boundary as described in Section 3.3.9. In the shoulder seasons, those regions not adequately captured by the SLIE width measurement technique (Section 3.3.7) show up as anomalous regions of permanent landfast ice.

Figure 4.2.3 illustrates the mean annual cycle and its variability across the study area. It can be seen that the landfast ice grows gradually from October through to February and the monthly mean extent is greatest in March and April for most of the study area except for the central portion of zone 2 (see Figure 4.2.2 for zone locations), where it is greatest in May. During March and April, there is the greatest difference between the monthly mean and maximum extents, which reflects the occurrence of stable extensions (Section 4.2.5) during these months. The real extents of these stable extensions do not appear in Figure 4.2.3 for the reasons discussed above, but they can be seen in Figure 4.2.2, although this does not indicate at what time of year they occur.

The advance of landfast ice is not a continuous process and can involve many stages of formation, break-up and reformation. Hence, except in October when the landfast may not have had time to form and break-up, the monthly minimum SLIE corresponds to most severe break-out that was observed in any month. Figure 4.2.3 shows that up until March, the minimum SLIE position advances behind the mean indicating that break-outs become less severe. However, beginning in April, parts of coast have the opportunity to experience severe break-outs again. This is most obvious in the western Beaufort Sea between the Colville Delta and Point Barrow, which suggests this region is more susceptible to these kinds of events. By contrast, the area north of the Harrison Bay remains stable until June and in fact represents the seaward-most monthly minimum position of the SLIE. The tip of this area corresponds to one of the nodes that can be seen in Figure 4.2.1 and lies above a shoal of shallow water. Water depth at the SLIE is discussed next.

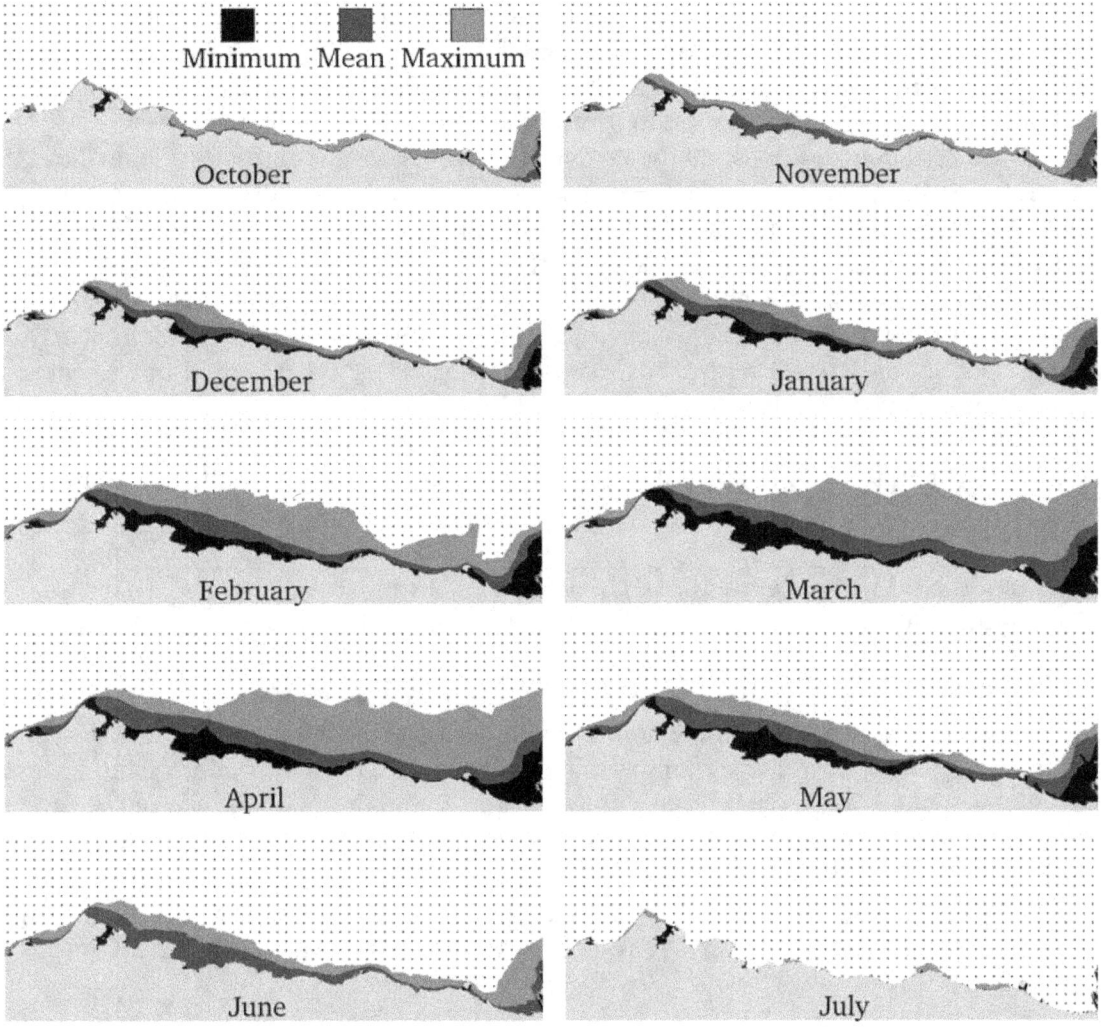

Figure 4.2.3: Minimum, mean and maximum monthly mean landfast sea ice extents showing the change in landfast ice distribution in the study area through the annual cycle. The dotted area indicates where landfast ice was never observed. See text for details on calculating these SLIE positions.

4.2.3. Water depth at the SLIE

Compilation and interpolation of the bathymetric sounding data used in this study is discussed in Section 3.4 and resulting bathymetric DEM is shown in Figure 3.4.2. Of particular interest is the 20m isobath, which is shown in red and has often been noted to coincide with consistent SLIE locations in this region (Stringer, 1980; Kovacs, 1976; Shapiro, 1975, 1976; Reimnitz, 1974). Its overall position and shape resemble those of many of the 222 SLIEs delineated in this study, although this resemblance varies throughout the year and across the study area. Using this bathymetric grid, the variability of water depth at the SLIE has been measured using the same transects used to measure the width of the landfast ice (Section 3.3.7). Hence, we can also examine the spatial variability and annual cycle of landfast ice in terms of water depth at the SLIE.

In Figure 4.2.1 and Figure 4.2.2, the relative stability of the SLIE position can be inferred from the relative frequency and spatial density of SLIEs. Similarly, we assume that water depths in which the SLIE is most frequently observed correspond to depths in which the SLIE is most stable. Figure 4.2.4 shows the distribution of water depths that the SLIE occupies in each of the zones identified in Section 4.2.1 and how this varies through each month of the annual cycle. In each zone, the SLIE advances into deeper water and the histograms evolve toward a uni-modal distribution by the end of winter. However each zone differs according to depth of this mode and the time of year in which it is achieved. These differences are summarized in Table 4.2.1. These depths are useful indicators of stability of the landfast ice, since the histograms do not change significantly once the mode has reached such a depth. However, in keeping with the work of Barry et al. (1979b) and to reduce the sensitivity of the criterion, a depth of 15 m was chosen to the indicate the onset of stabilization (Section 3.3.8)

Table 4.2.1: The modal water depth at the SLIE at the end of winter for each zone and the month in which this distribution is achieved

	Zone 1	Zone 2	Zone 3	Zone 4
Final modal water depth at SLIE	19 m	18 m	22 m	16 m
Month achieved	April	January	February	March

As with the development of landfast ice area, the advance of the SLIE into deeper water is more gradual than its retreat at the end of the annual cycle. Also, advancement to these water depths is not a continuous process. At the beginning of the annual cycle, the distributions in all zones are multi-modal with the strongest modes in shallow water. Through the first few months, however, deeper modes develop at the expense of the shallow modes. Hence, the SLIE appears to advance from one stable water depth to the next in order to reach it final modal depth. Furthermore, the October and July distributions are strikingly similar for all zones. This suggests that although the retreat is more rapid, the SLIE appears to re-occupy the same water depths as during its advance.

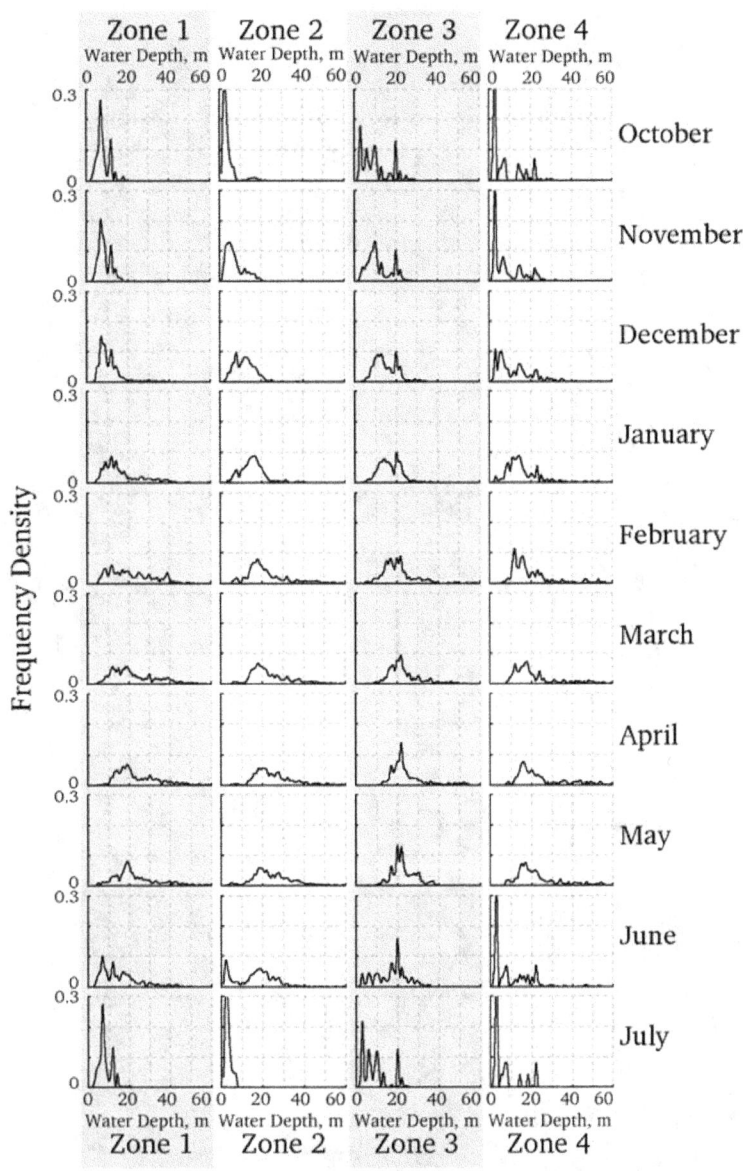

Figure 4.2.4: Monthly histograms of water depth at the SLIE for each of the 4 zones identified in Section 4.2.1 and shown in Figure 4.2.2. Depth bins are 1 m.

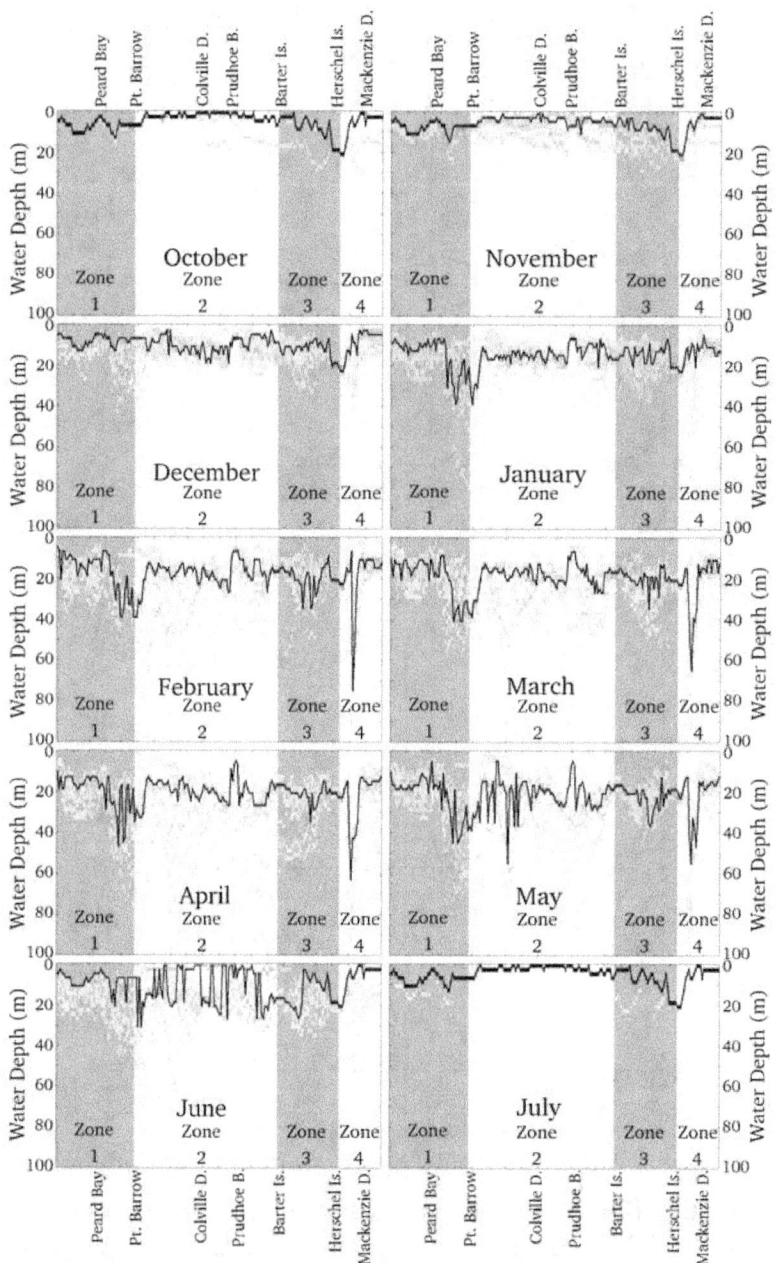

Figure 4.2.5: The modal water depth at the SLIE indicating the depth at which the landfast ice is stable for each coast location and each month. The x-axis represents the 200 coast locations from west to east. Note that this is not a linear axis (see Figure 3.3.4). The grayscale indicates the relative frequency with which the SLIE is located in a given water depth for each location and month, but note that the very deepest waters beneath stable extensions (Section 4.2.5) extend beyond the axes. Teal shaded areas are used to indicate the extents of the 4 previously identified zones (Figure 4.2.2).

More detailed spatial variability of water depths at the SLIE is shown in Figure 4.2.5, which shows the monthly mode and range of water depths occupied by the SLIE as measured along each transect (Figure 3.3.4). The deepest water frequently occupied by the SLIE occurs near Point Barrow (in the upper portion of Barrow Canyon) and in the Mackenzie Channel between Herschel Island and the Mackenzie Delta. In both these locations, the sea bed slopes steeply near the coast (Figure 3.4.2), which together with spatial alignment errors in the data may explain the increased scatter in these parts of the coastline in Figure 4.2.5. The maximum water depths indicated in Figure 4.2.5 clearly show that the SLIE occupies deeper water at other locations, but these depths correspond to the occurrences of stable extensions (Section 4.2.5) and cannot be considered typical. Although the modal water depth curves in Figure 4.2.5 appear noisy, the envelope of each curve is relatively smooth, suggesting that isolated small sections of the SLIE are stabilized in deeper water at the same depth. Furthermore throughout the first few months, more points advance to water depths indicated by the envelope of the previous month. This suggests the intervening sections of the SLIE advance alongside those that stabilized first at that water depth. This therefore seems to be the mechanism by which the SLIE advances from one modal water depth to the next.

The significance of the modal water depths indicated in Figure 4.2.4 and Table 4.2.1 is made clearer in Figure 4.2.5, particularly in zone 2. Before the majority of the SLIE in each zone advances to these depths, very little of the SLIE extends into deeper waters. However, there is a clear transition once a significant fraction of the SLIE occupies the modal water depth. It is only after this that landfast is commonly found in water deeper than the modal depth and is rarely found in shallower water. This is a further indication that stability is strongly linked to bathymetry.

4.2.4. Key events within the annual cycle

The mean annual cycle can be described by the monthly averages as in Figure 4.2.3, but it is also informative to examine the variation in width at individual points along the coast. In doing so, we can examine the annual cycle in finer detail and also consider interannual variability. As described in Section 3.3.7 we calculated landfast ice width at 200 locations along the coast. Time series over all 8 years at 5 of these locations are shown in Figure 4.2.6. Eight annual cycles are clearly seen, each with an asymmetric shape showing a gradual advance and rapid retreat. Short-term variability observed in many of the profiles is discussed in Section 4.2.5.

For each of the 5 time series shown in Figure 4.2.6 and the 195 others throughout the study area, we have derived mean occurrence dates of the 4 key events as described in Section 3.3.8. These are presented in Figure 4.2.7, in which we see can that there is both regional and local variability. Broadly, the date-curve for the first occurrence of ice is u-shaped, with landfast ice typically forming first in zone 2 and later in the zones to the east and west. We see the inverse pattern (n-shaped curve) in the timing of break-up and ice-free conditions across the study area, which shows that the effects of spring begin earliest in those areas where the effects of winter are felt latest and vice-versa. Figure 4.2.7 also shows the variation in the onsets of freezing and thawing (Section 3.4.3). The freezing date curve has a similar u-shape to that of the first occurrence of ice, though less pronounced. The thawing date curve also bears a similar likeness to the date curves for break-up and ice-free coasts. The similarities in shape between the dates curves for the onset of freezing and first appearance of ice and between those for the onset of thawing, break-up and ice-free coasts suggests that air temperature is at least partly responsible for determining the length of the landfast ice season. However, the curvature of the date curves for the onsets of freezing and thawing is insufficient to completely explain the u- and n-shaped date curves of key events 1, 3 and 4. It is therefore likely that other regional differences are also important such as the influence of the Bering Sea in zone 1, the barrier islands and broad shelf of zone 2 and the effect of the Mackenzie River in zone 4. These and other causes of spatial variability across the study area are discussed in Sections 5.2.1 and 5.2.2.

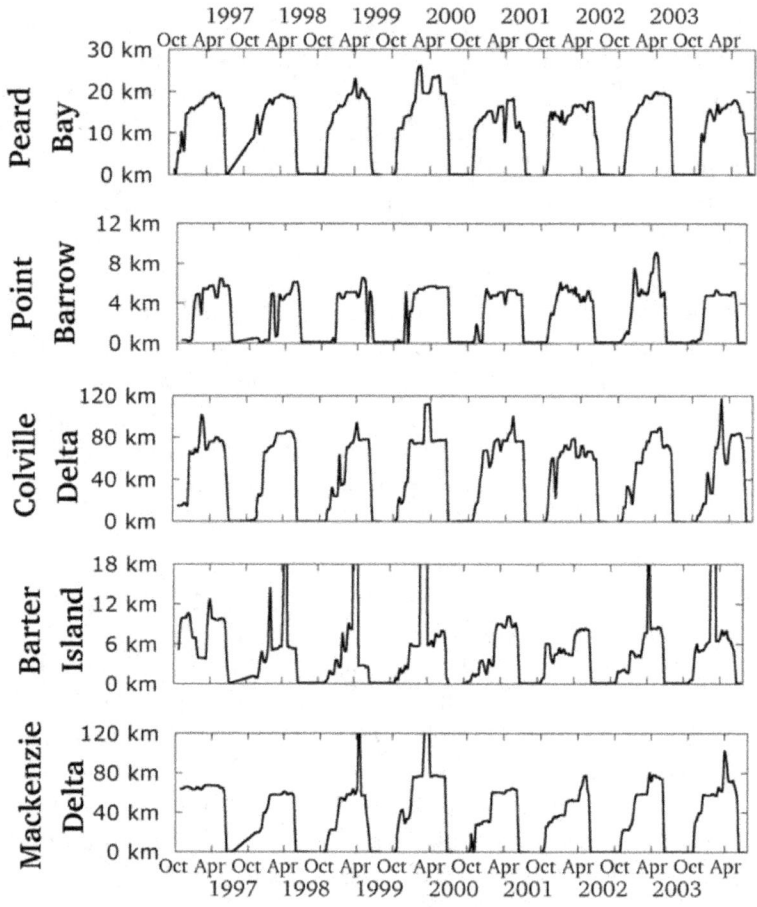

Figure 4.2.6: Time series of landfast ice width at 5 locations along the coast, showing 8 annual cycles as well as short-term variability. Note the different scales on the width axes. Locations of the profiles are shown in Figure 3.3.4.

The date-curve for stabilization of the landfast ice is not shaped like the others and has far greater standard deviations, though it bears the greatest resemblance to the date curve for event 1. There are clearly some regions of the coast that stabilize significantly before others and overall, most of zone 2 appears to stabilize first beginning with Prudhoe Bay. There is also some evidence of a saw-tooth pattern with stabilization progressing westward from those locations that stabilize earliest.

In addition to broad regional trends, we also see higher frequency spatial variability related to coastal morphology and bathymetry. For example, in the shelter of Peard Bay, landfast ice forms significantly earlier than on the coasts nearby, though the effect of the inflow of the Kugrua River here is not known. In addition, the earliest points to stabilize correspond to the locations of shoals (Figure 3.4.2). Such signals can be distinguished from scatter in the data by examining the standard deviations. Furthermore, differences in the magnitude and character of the high-frequency spatial variability in the date-curves appear to correspond to the 4 coastal zones identified in Section 4.2.1. This is most obvious in the case of zone 2, where the standard deviations and range of dates are smallest and the mean date-curves are smoothest (with the exception of the date curve for stabilization). This indicates that the landfast ice of the western Beaufort Sea has the most regular and uniform annual landfast ice cycle. In zones 1, 3 and 4 by comparison, the standard deviations are higher as a result of greater interannual variability and the impact of coastal morphology and bathymetry on the signal is stronger.

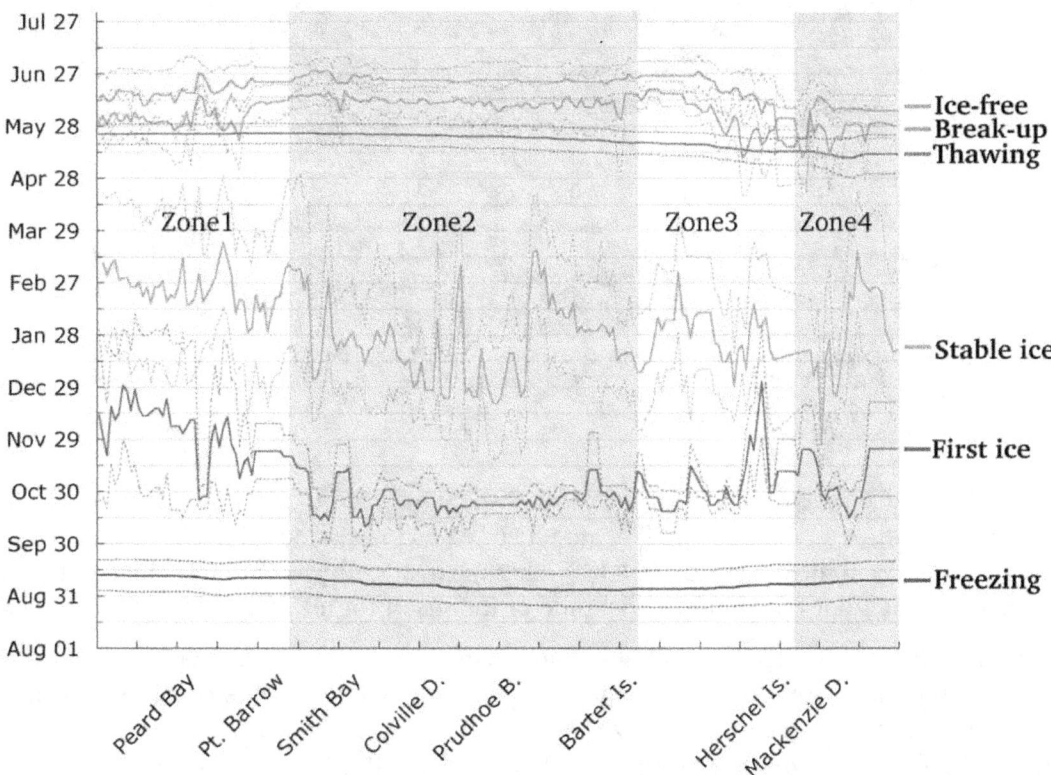

Figure 4.2.7: Spatial variability in the dates of occurrence of 4 key events in the annual cycle and the onsets of freezing and thawing derived from surface observations. The bold lines indicate the mean of the 8-year study period and the dashed lines indicate ±1 standard deviation from the mean. The x-axis represents the 200 coast locations from west to east (see Figure 3.3.4) and the shading indicates the extents of the 4 zones identified in Section 4.2.1

The degree of spatial variability in the key event dates relative to the dates of inset of freezing and thawing indicates that there is no single relationship between the accumulation of FDDs and TDDs and the occurrence of the 4 key events. Figure 4.2.9 shows the mean for each zone of the degree days accrued at the time of each key event and the standard deviations. It is clear that zone 1 requires more FDDs to acquire its first ice than the other zones and less TDDs to incur break-up and ice-free conditions. Also shown are the means of those points within each zone located on headlands or open coasts and those in embayments or lagoons. These suggest that at least part of the variability can be explained by coastal morphology. In zones 1, 3 and 4 landfast ice generally forms before and breaks-up after ice on headlands, as one would expect. The effect of coastal morphology in zone 2 is less pronounced and in fact reversed, which perhaps suggests that offshore bathymetry is more important in this zone.

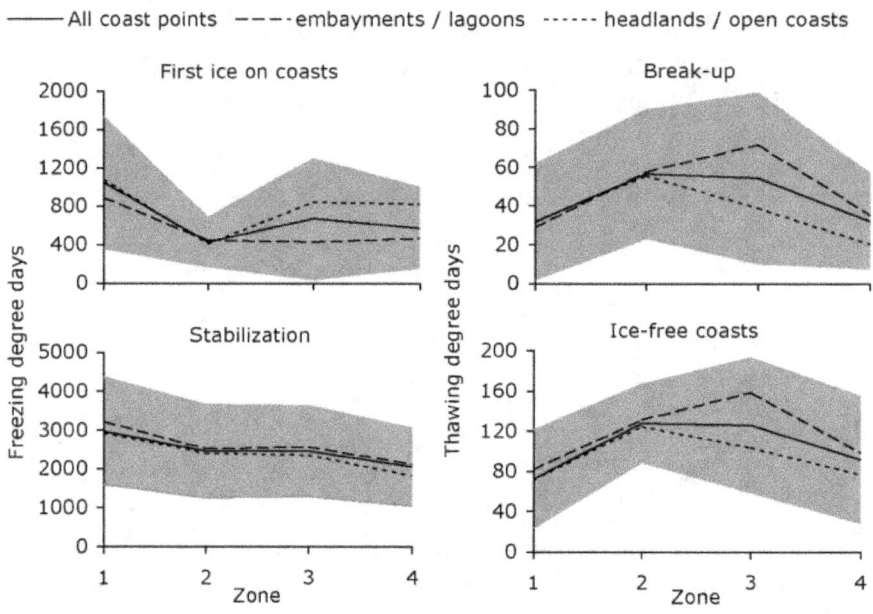

Figure 4.2.8: The mean number of freezing or thawing degree days in each zone accrued at the time of each event. The results are also broken down according to whether a point on the coast lies on a headland or in an embayment. The shaded area indicates one standard deviation either side of the mean for all points.

Examination of the occurrence dates at all locations throughout the study period reveals no strong temporal trends. However, to examine longer term changes, Table 4.2.2 lists the mean occurrence dates for each event for each zone along with the results of (Barry et al., 1979b) for the period 1973-77. However, this comparison is complicated by the use of different methodologies and conventions. Of the 8 events (Barry et al., 1979b) identified, we have chosen the 4 that most closely match ours. We also assume that their Central Chukchi and Central Beaufort regions correspond to our zones 1 and 2 respectively. From this, it seems that the formation of landfast ice is taking place along the Chukchi Coast approximately one month later than between 1973-77, with little change along the central Beaufort Sea Coast. However, each date calculated in this study has an error of approximately ±5 days, while Barry et al. (1979b) give an estimate error of ±10 – 15 days to their means. Table 4.2.2 also gives the mean of the standard deviations at each point with in a zone as a measure of the mean interannual variability, which is particularly large for formation of landfast ice along the Chukchi Coast in this study.

Taking this into account, the apparent latening of the formation of landfast ice along both coasts is within the range of uncertainty.

Table 4.2.2. Mean occurrence dates (1996-2004) for the first appearance of landfast ice, stabilization, break-up and ice-free conditions calculated for each zone. Also given is σ', the mean standard deviation due to interannual variability at each coast point for each zone. For comparison, the results for events most closely matching ours are shown from work by Barry et al. (1979b) for 1973-77.

		This study					Barry et al. (1979b)		
		Zone 1	Zone 2	Zone 3	Zone 4	All zones	Central Chukchi	Central Beaufort	
First Ice*	Mean	Dec 01	Oct 25	Nov 04	Nov 9	Nov 7	Early November	Mid October	First continuous fast ice
	σ'	31.8	9.6	11.4	17.5	16.4			
Stable Ice	Mean	Feb 23	Jan 22	Jan 28	Jan 27	Feb 01	Feb	Jan/Feb	Stable ice inside of 15 m isobath
	σ'	41.9	30.1	32.6	34.9	34.1			
Break up	Mean	Jun 04	Jun 11	Jun 04	May 26	Jun 06	Jun 10	Jun 30	First openings and movement
	σ'	13.9	14.2	13.7	12.6	14.6			
Ice Free	Mean	Jun 18	Jun 24	Jun 24	Jun 06	Jun 18	Jul 05	Aug 01	Nearshore largely free of fast ice
	σ'	12.7	8.4	12.6	10.2	10.4			

*1996-1998 omitted from analysis (see Section 3.3.8)

The indication from Table 4.2.2 is that the timing of stabilization has not changed greatly, though the dates given by (Barry et al.) for this event are not specific. Break-up appears to be occurring earlier along both coastlines, but along that of the Chukchi Sea the difference is only 6 days, which is less than the estimated errors. Along the Beaufort Sea coast though, the difference is 21 days. However, although the description given for "first openings and movement" qualitatively matches the first sudden decrease in landfast ice area, which defines break-up in this study, the dates given for this study are an average of the dates calculated for all coastal points within each zone. Instead, it may be a more appropriate comparison to calculate the mean date on which the landfast ice first breaks up in each zone. This gives a break-up date approximately 3 weeks earlier than the dates in Table 4.2.2, which would represent a significant shortening of the stable landfast ice period.

Ice-free coastlines appear to be occurring over a month earlier along the Beaufort Sea coast and approximately 2 weeks earlier along that of the Chukchi Sea. In the case of the Chukchi Sea, this is toward the outside of the uncertainty range, but maybe significant when taken with the observation of an earlier break-up. Along the coast of the Beaufort Sea however, the magnitude of the change is clearly significant.

4.2.5. Episodic Events

We use the term episodic events to refer to the brief events that occur at irregular intervals and result in a deviation of the SLIE position from the mean annual cycle. The Radarsat imagery used in this study allows us to identify breakouts and stable extensions, where the SLIE lies briefly either significantly landward or seaward, respectively, of its normal position. In the time series of landfast ice width (Figure 4.2.6) these appear as sharp troughs or peaks. On some occasions they correspond to a extension remaining temporarily attached to the landfast ice when a flaw lead opens (such as occurred twice near Barrow in 2003) or when a small area of the drifting pack ice becomes locked-up adjacent to the landfast ice (such as happened at Barter Island in 1998). However, more significant stable extensions occurred on 5 occasions in 4 different years. Their extents are seen in Figure 4.2.2 and the dates for which they were observed are listed in Table 4.2.3. It is clear from these data that stable extensions occur most frequently in March and April in the eastern half of the study area, which is when and where sea ice concentration will be greatest. On these occasions, the SLIE lies over water up to 3,500 m deep, but Mahoney et al.(2005) speculated that the sea ice may be anchored somewhere outside of the study area in the vicinity of Banks Island. Stringer et al. (1980) noted that landfast ice could extend up to 100 km offshore in the absence of disturbance, though Thorndike and Colony (1982) observed such events despite strong winds. It is beyond the scope of this study to consider all the stresses on the ice sheet during these stable extensions, but their correlation with other aspects of landfast ice behavior and occurrence of offshore leads is discussed in Sections 5.2.1 and 5.1.1 respectively.

Table 4.2.3. Dates of occurrence of stable extensions observed in this study. Note that the mosaic dates (Section 3.3.4) give the earliest and latest dates we observed the extension, which may therefore underestimate the duration by up to approximately 20 days.

	First date of first mosaic	Last date of last mosaic	Duration	Location
1	1999/04/04	1999/04/26	22 days	Prudhoe Bay – Mackenzie Delta
2	2000/02/23	2000/04/08	44 days	Pitt Point – Mackenzie Delta
3	2001/04/29	2001/05/22	24 days	Smith Bay – Prudhoe Bay
4	2004/02/15	2004/03/08	22 days	Colville Delta – Prudhoe Bay
5	2004/02/25	2004/03/18	22 days	Barter Island – Mackenzie Delta

Using the same set of Radarsat imagery Blazey et al. (2005) identified 267 breakout events and categorized them according to severity based upon the fraction of the landfast ice width involved and the depth to which the new SLIE retreated. Most severe breakouts occur in June and coincide with the annual break-up of the landfast ice. However, a number were observed at other times of the year, though without any clear pattern. A spatial pattern was observed, however, suggesting that the eastern region of zone 2 is least susceptible to such events, while several breakout events affected the landfast ice immediately between Point Barrow and Smith Bay during winter and early spring. The effects of these are seen in the more shoreward location of the monthly minimum SLIE positions in this area (Figure 4.2.3). The mechanisms of winter breakouts are likely to be different from those occurring at the end of the season when the landfast ice is weaker. A more detailed analysis of breakout events in landfast ice will be the subject of subsequent work.

4.2.6. Characteristic Synoptic Climatology

Since we adopted our methodology from a similar analysis of Beaufort Sea climatology from 1966-1974 by Barry (1976; 1979), a comparison between the results was an obvious course to take. Using the same similarity threshold criteria (Section 3.4.2), we derived almost 3 times as many characteristic patterns (CPs) as Barry over a time period roughly 7 times as long. Overall, we observe the same range of variability in sea level atmospheric pressure patterns and the 3 most prevalent CPs from our study resemble the most prevalent CP of Barry's analysis. There are no patterns identified by Barry that are clearly absent from our results, though the exact orders of prevalence do not agree. This is not surprising, however, since every CP is clearly more frequent in some years than others.

Figure 4.2.10 shows the 31-day running mean of the occurrences of each CP after having been binned by day of year. It is striking that every CP appears modal or bi-modal in its annual distribution. This allows the majority to be categorized as either a winter or summer pattern, with just 6 CPs that show strong peaks only in the transitions between summer and winter. Barry (1979) noted that a high pressure in the north and lows in the south characterize winter pressure patterns in this part of the world. In summer, by contrast, he notes that the central, western and northern regions experience frequent low pressure features while the Pacific High often extends as a ridge over the Gulf of Alaska. Examination of each CP shows that most fit the description for the season in which they most frequently occur. This strong seasonal feature of the data gives us confidence in our characterization of the synoptic climatology, though we note a few exceptions where a pattern that occurs mostly in one season fits the description of the other.

Annual frequencies for each CP were also calculated, each of which showed significant interannual variability. However, linear regressions on each time-series showed no significant trends and a sequential algorithm for detecting climate regime shifts (Rodionov, 2004) detected none. Fourier analyses revealed peaks in occurrence at between 6-and 10-year periods for many CPs and running 10-year means of the yearly frequencies indicated longer-timescale variability.

55

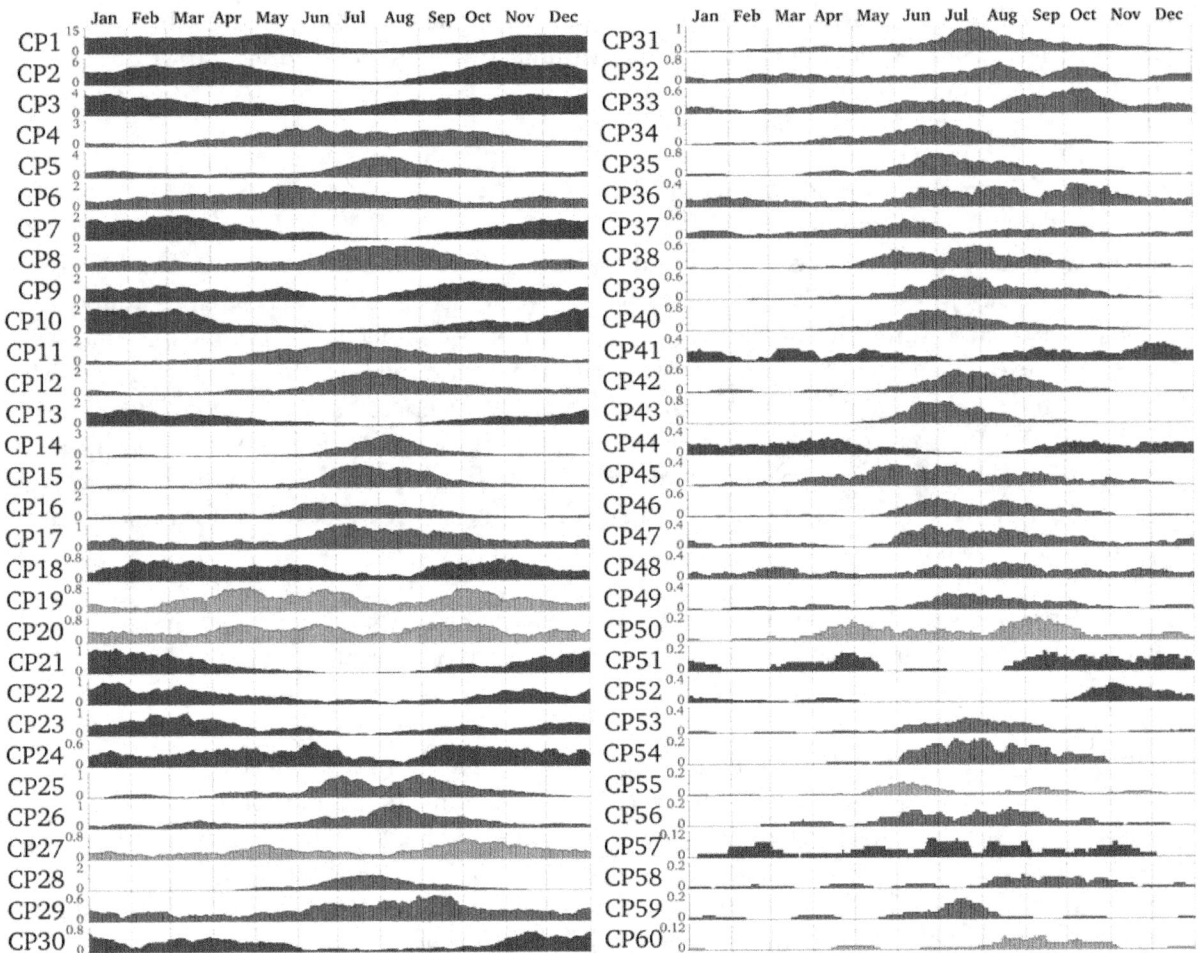

Figure 4.2.9: Running 31-day means of the occurrences of each characteristic pattern (CP) after binning according to day of year. This quantity is taken to represent the monthly occurrence frequency for each CP. Each curve is colored according to whether it occurs mostly in the winter (blue), summer (red) or the shoulder seasons (green). Note different scales on each y-axis.

The calculations of mean monthly and annual occurrences of CPs are two ways to address the temporal variability in the sea level pressure patterns. However, neither method will capture changes in seasonal weather patterns. To reduce the volume of data for such an analysis, CPs were grouped into winter, summer and shoulder season categories according to their season of most frequent occurrence (Figure 4.2.9). The relative contribution of seasons' patterns to each month is shown in Figure 4.2.10 for the period 1948-2004. Although there is a large amount of interannual variability, the 10-year running means of the relative contribution of winter patterns (blue lines) show that each month is characterized by different proportions of each type of pattern. The winter and summer months appear relatively constant in this regard, but September and October show significant trends towards becoming more summer-like such that recent Septembers and Octobers resemble Augusts and Septembers respectively from earlier in the period. June, however, shows a trend towards more winter-like conditions.

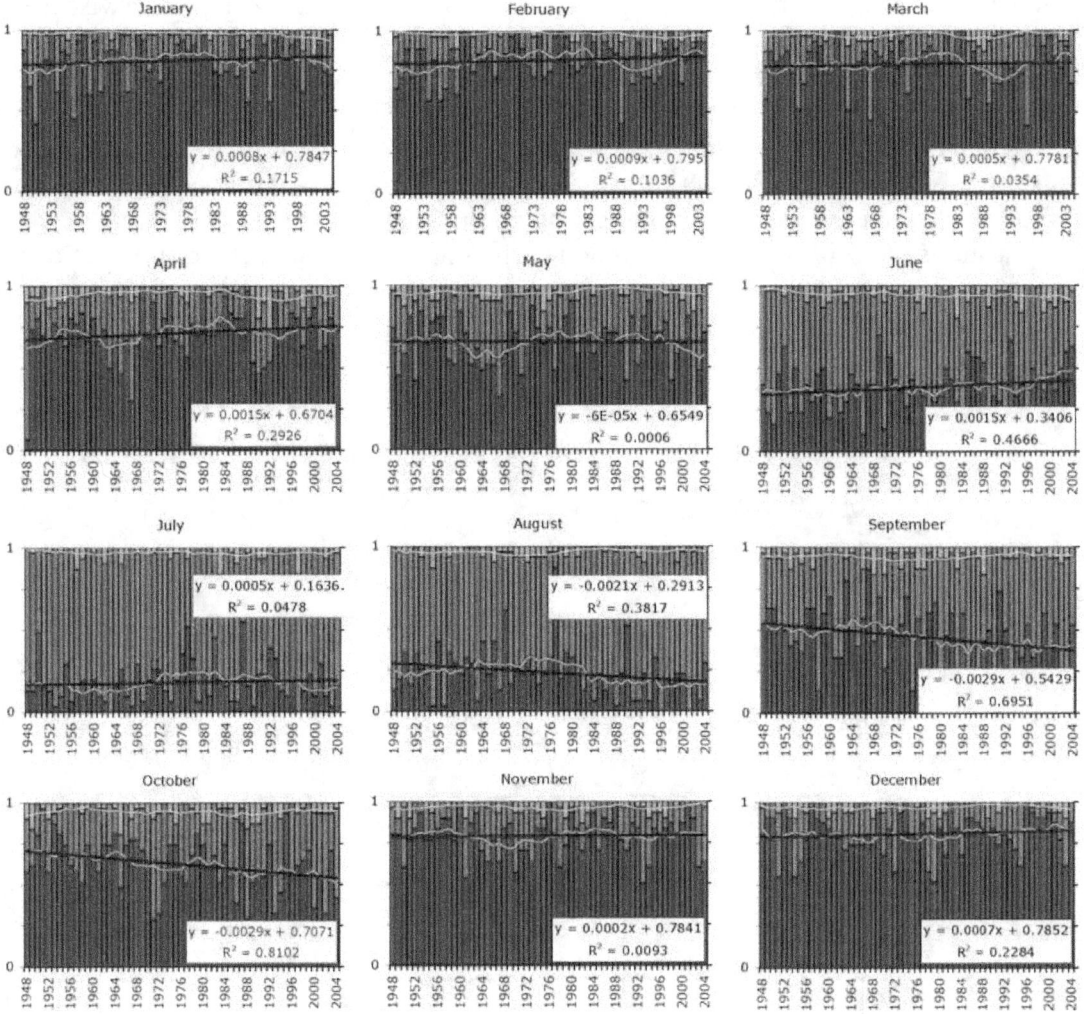

Figure 4.2.10: The relative contribution to each month's pressure patterns from winter (blue), summer (red) and shoulder season (green) patterns (as determined in Figure 4.2.9). The light blue and pink lines show the running 10-year means. The black line shows the trend of the 10-year mean winter contribution to each month.

4.2.7. Freezing and thawing degree day trends

So far, we have examined the onsets of freezing and thawing and the accumulation of their respective degree days in the context of their variability across the study area and their relationship to key events within the annual landfast ice cycle (Section 3.4.3). However, the data also show significant temporal trends that warrant further discussion. Figure 4.2.11 shows the variation over time for each of these quantities. The solid curves show values derived from NCEP data interpolated for Point Barrow (Section 3.4.3), while the dashed curves shows values calculated using the same method with data from Barrow Wiley-Post Airport weather station for the period 1984-2004 (the period available on-line from the National Climatic Data Center). The results from the two datasets differ in the magnitudes of largest peak values, but otherwise are well correlated and in fact converge in recent years.

It is clear that there is significant interannual variability in the data, which will be discussed later along with interannual variability in the landfast ice between 1996 and 2004. In addition, both datasets show trends toward a later onset of freezing and earlier and onset of thawing. There are also trends towards warmer winters and summer. While these trends may have far greater-reaching implications, we will limit our discussion to the impacts on landfast ice and relationship to the observed differences in the mean annual cycle between this study and that of Barry (1979b) and Barry et al. (1979b)

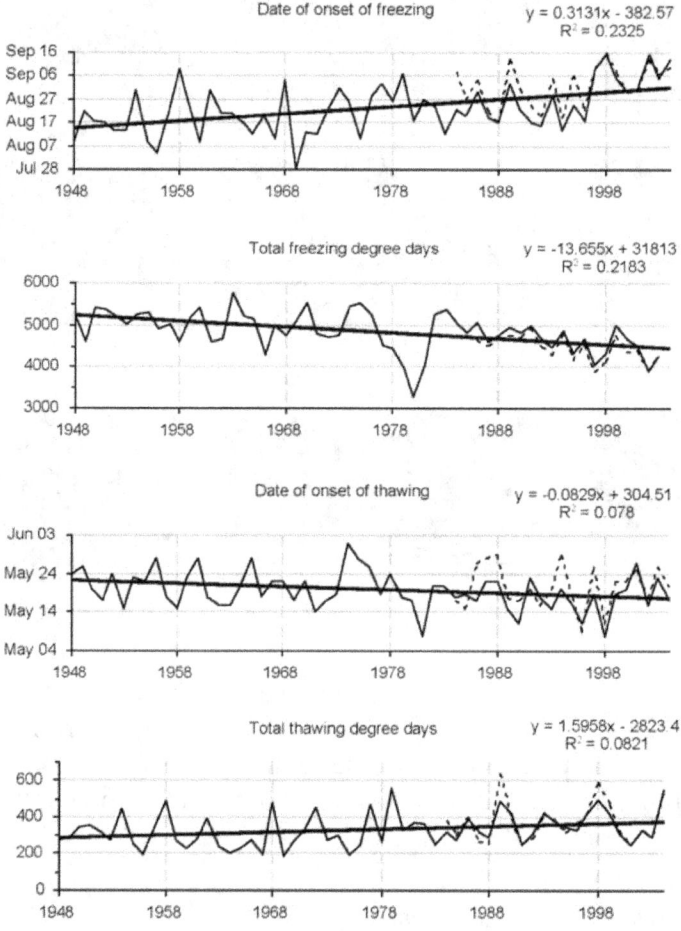

Figure 4.2.11: Dates of onset of freezing and thawing and their respective degree day totals for each year (Section 3.4.3). The solid curve denotes values derived from NCEP data, while the dashed line denotes those calculated from Barrow Wiley Post Airport weather station data for the period 1984-2004. Also shown are linear regression lines.

4.3. Identification and description of pack ice lead patterns

4.3.1 Definitions

The term "lead pattern" is used here in a general sense such that both (1) a lead along the landfast ice edge, or (2) a lead or series of leads that occur in a repeatable configuration or relationship at different times, are considered to satisfy the definition. As noted in Section 3.1, before attaching any significance to a lead pattern, it was necessary to verify that the pattern recurred often enough to be considered repeatable. With that restriction, leads and lead patterns have been recognized that have particular geometric relations to the coast or to the grounded ice mass that forms annually on Hanna Shoal. In some cases, patterns have been found to occur as steps in sequences of patterns that reflect a continuous process.

Two patterns stand out as of particular importance. The first is a lead pattern which we have called the Barrow Arch, and the second is an arcuate structure that trends northeastward from Point Barrow and serves as the boundary between moving pack ice to the north and generally stationary ice between itself and the coast (the stable extension of the landfast ice). The descriptions of these patterns and discussion of their significance to the overall deformation pattern of the Beaufort Sea pack ice are given in Sections 4.3.3 and 4.3.5 respectively.

4.3.2 Lead patterns at the landfast ice/pack ice boundary.

It is important to understand the nature of the interactions between pack ice and the landfast ice edge along the Beaufort Sea coast of Alaska, because leads generated there can involve the entrapment and movement of oil following a spill. Mechanisms of generating leads along that boundary, and the resulting distribution of floes and open water/thin ice are considered in this section. In particular, the features described in this section are found offshore from the edge of the stable landfast ice which coincides with the zone of grounded ridges along the (approximately) 20 m isobath. There are several types of openings that form as a result of interactions along this boundary as described in the following paragraphs. The existence of stable extensions to the landfast ice was noted in Sections 3.3.1 and 4.2.1 and these are covered in Section 4.3.5 below.

Before proceeding farther, it should be noted that in general, compression of the pack ice at a high-angle to the landfast ice edge does not produce leads that propagate along the boundary. It does, however generate leads that can extend far into the pack ice, as described in Section 4.3.4 below.

The simplest mechanism for creating leads along the landfast ice edge is for the pack ice to shift slightly to the north. The result can be a lead that opens along most or all of the boundary between the pack ice and the landfast ice edge from Point Barrow eastward. However, when the Beaufort Sea is ice-covered, northward displacement is limited because of the lack of space to accommodate the movement. As a result, leads formed by northerly shifts of the ice pack tend to be narrow and short-lived.

An important element in the line of ridges that anchors the stable landfast ice is a shoal off Harrison Bay at approximately 71°45'N, 152°W, where the sea floor is shallower than 20 m. The shoal is one of many shown on the maps in Reimnitz and Kempema (1974) and Grantz and Mullen (1992). Ice usually begins to ground there in early winter, but since it is not generally exposed to drifting pack ice, the grounded ice mass is seldom involved in lead patterns that penetrate far into the pack ice. However, it is often the site of a significant stable point in the pattern of landfast ice edges (see Section 4.2.1) and its presence can sometimes be detected by its influence on the shape of the landfast ice edge. Other than that, it is difficult to differentiate the grounded ice on the shoal from the rest of the landfast ice on the AVHRR imagery.

The most common source of leads along the pack ice-landfast ice boundary is a westerly shift of the pack ice when it is in contact with the landfast ice edge. Easterly shifts also occur, but they are less common. Movements in either direction are easily recognized because they tend to leave openings on the lee sides of promontories, including particularly the ice grounded on the shoal off Harrison Bay. Figures 4.3.1 and 4.3.2 provide illustrations of the results of such movements.

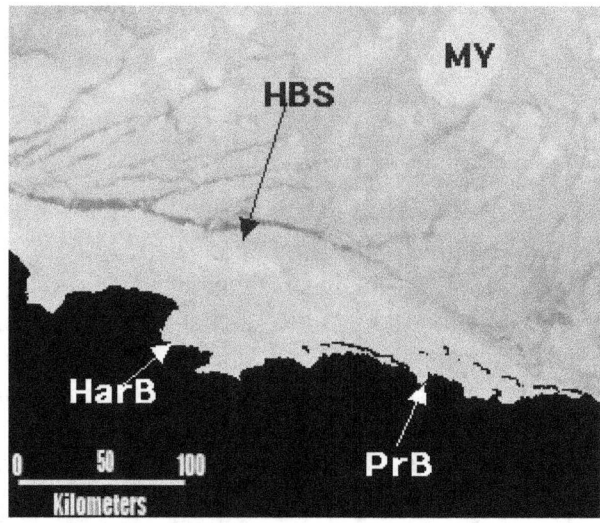

Figure 4.3.1. AVHRR acquired on February 20, 1994 showing an open lead along the landfast ice edge (dark band) resulting from westward shift of the pack ice. Symbols are [HarB] Harrison Bay, [PrB], Prudhoe Bay and [HBS] marks the approximate location of the shoal in outer Harrison Bay (Harrison Bay Shoal). [MY] is a large multiyear ice floe.

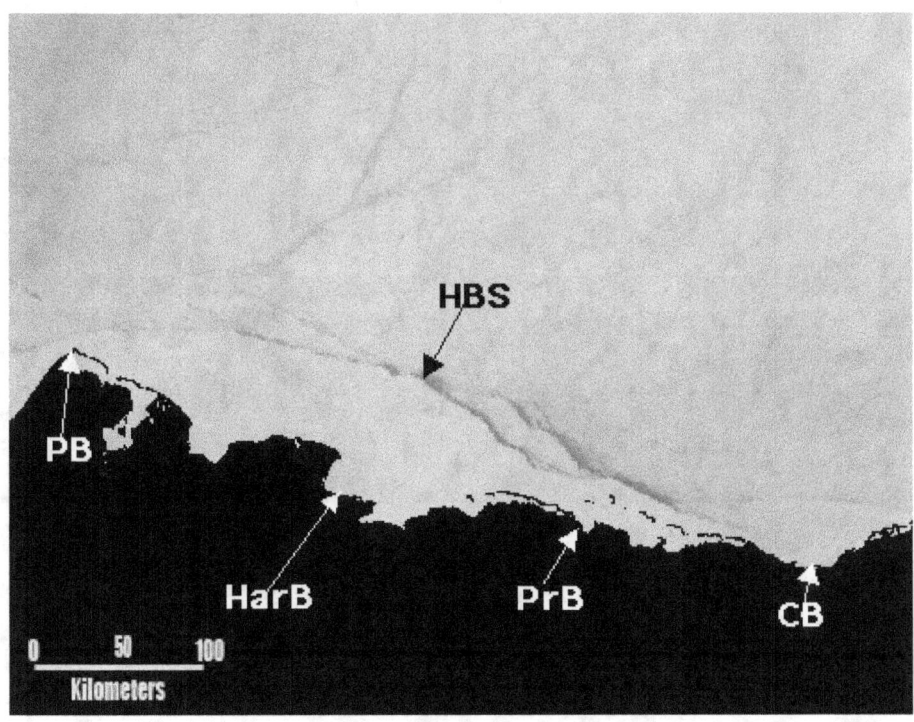

Figure 4.3.2. AVHRR image acquired on March 21, 1995 showing open leads (dark bands) around a breakout from the landfast ice resulting from eastward shift of the pack ice. Symbols are [PB] Point Barrow, [HarB] Harrison Bay, [PrB] Prudhoe Bay, and [CB] Camden Bay. [HBS] is the approximate location of Harrison Bay Shoal.

In Figures 4.3.1 and 4.3.2, lead formation was limited to the immediate boundary between the pack ice and the landfast ice. However, in some cases, movement of the pack ice parallel to the landfast ice edge results in the propagation of leads for several tens of kilometers into the pack ice. When these leads intersect, they produce floes that are caught between the moving pack ice and the stationary landfast ice. Zones of floes in that configuration have been referred to by different authors as "shear zones," (Hibler, et al., 1974) or flaw zones [Section 5.2.1.*(i)* this report]; unfortunately, the nomenclature is not consistent. Examples to which these terms might be applied are shown in Figures 4.3.3 and 4.4.4. Both figures show that space is created between floes, which, as noted above, can affect the transport of spilled oil.

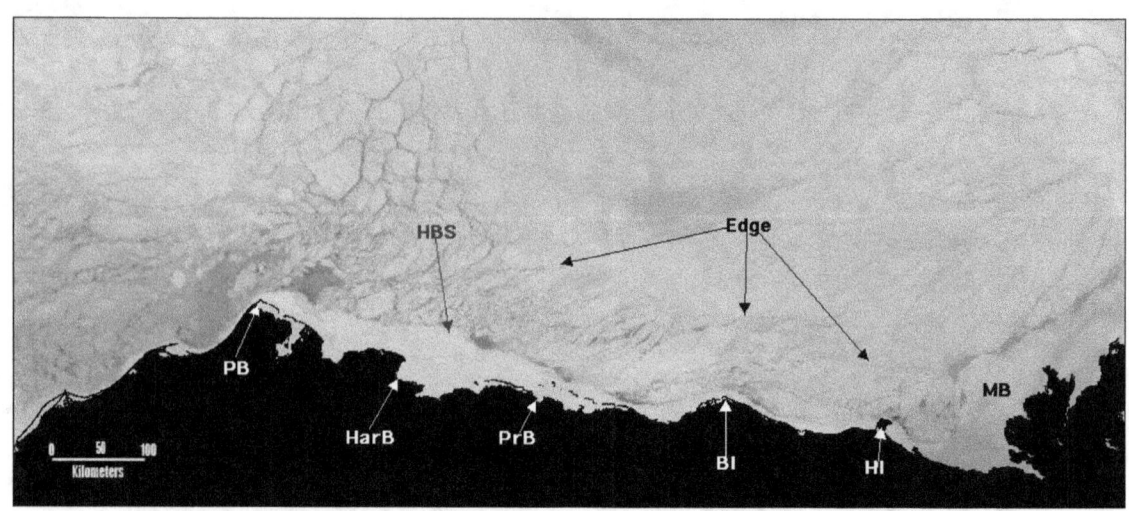

Figure 4.3.3. AVHRR image acquired on February 15, 1996 illustrating the penetration of leads into the pack ice creating individual floes with space between them. "Edge" is the approximate limit of lead penetration. [HBS] is the approximate position of the shoal off Harrison Bay near the landfast ice edge. Dark areas to the east of the shoal indicate that the last pack ice motion was to the east. Other symbols [PB] Point Barrow, [HarB] Harrison Bay, [PrB] Prudhoe Bay, [BI] Barter Island, and [HI] Herschel Island.

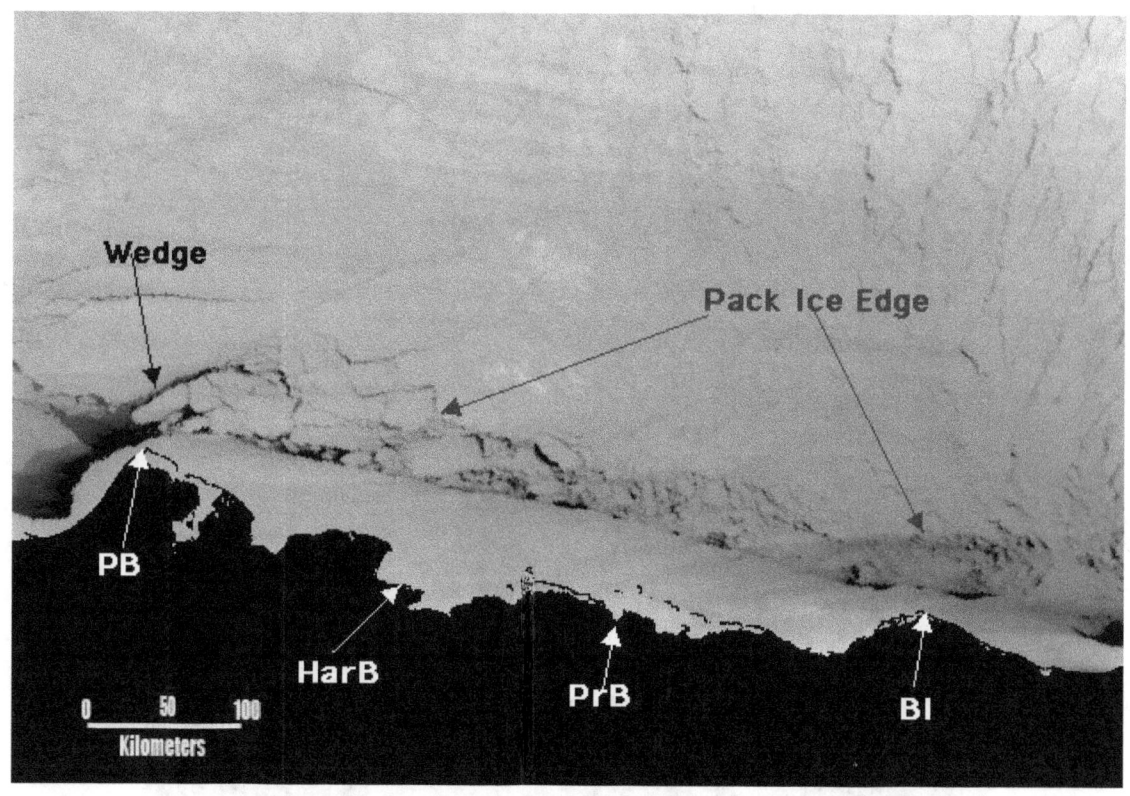

Figure 4.3.4. AVHRR image acquired on March 6, 1998 with a clearly defined zone of floes between the continuous pack ice and the landfast ice edge which probably resulted from westward shift of the pack ice. The feature labeled "wedge" formed from that movement as described in the text. Note that this image was acquired the day after the image shown in Figure 4.3.16 below. Comparison of those figures demonstrates the speed with which zone of floes developed. Symbols are [PB] Point Barrow, [HarB] Harrison Bay, [PrB} Prudhoe Bay and [BI] Barter Island.

Another interesting feature shown in Figure 4.3.4 is termed here a "Point Barrow Wedge." It is the 'wedge' of pack ice that juts westward from just north of Point Barrow into the Chukchi Sea. When present, a wedge indicates that the Beaufort Sea pack ice has shifted to the west. Another example is shown in Figure 4.3.5.

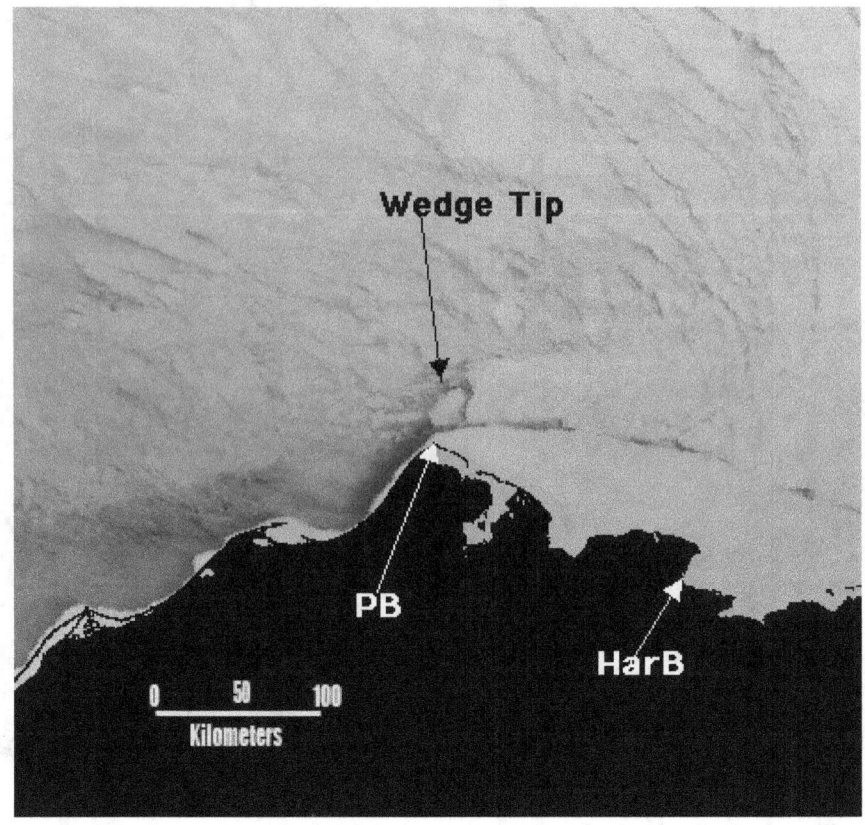

Figure 4.3.5. AVHRR image from December 31, 1995 showing a wedge projecting toward the Chukchi Sea as the result of westward displacement of part of the Beaufort Sea pack ice. Symbols are [PB] Point Barrow, [HarB] Harrison Bay.

An additional point regarding the features described here is that the leads created by the processes, along with other lead patterns described in the following sections, are important habitat for ringed seals and polar bears that reside there through the year (Burns, Shapiro and Fay, 1980). In addition, they are part of the spring migration route followed by bowhead whales (Braham, et al., 1980; Fraker and Cubbage, 1980) heading for the eastern Beaufort Sea.

4 3.3. Arch Structures

(i) Arch Forms and Origins

The terms "Barrow Arch" and "North Slope Arch" are used here to describe the arch-like structural forms that appear in the pack ice near Point Barrow and along the Beaufort Sea coast under some conditions (note that the former is unrelated to the subsurface geologic structure of the same name). Pack ice arch structures are not single leads. Instead, they are assemblages of leads in a particular pattern. An example of a Barrow Arch is shown in Figure 4.3.6 and, since the mechanism by which both types of arch structures form is similar, it will serve as an example to describe the process.

In Figure 4.3.6, a lead extending to the northeast from the landfast ice edge near Point Barrow serves as the east boundary of an arch structure. The crest of the arch is the

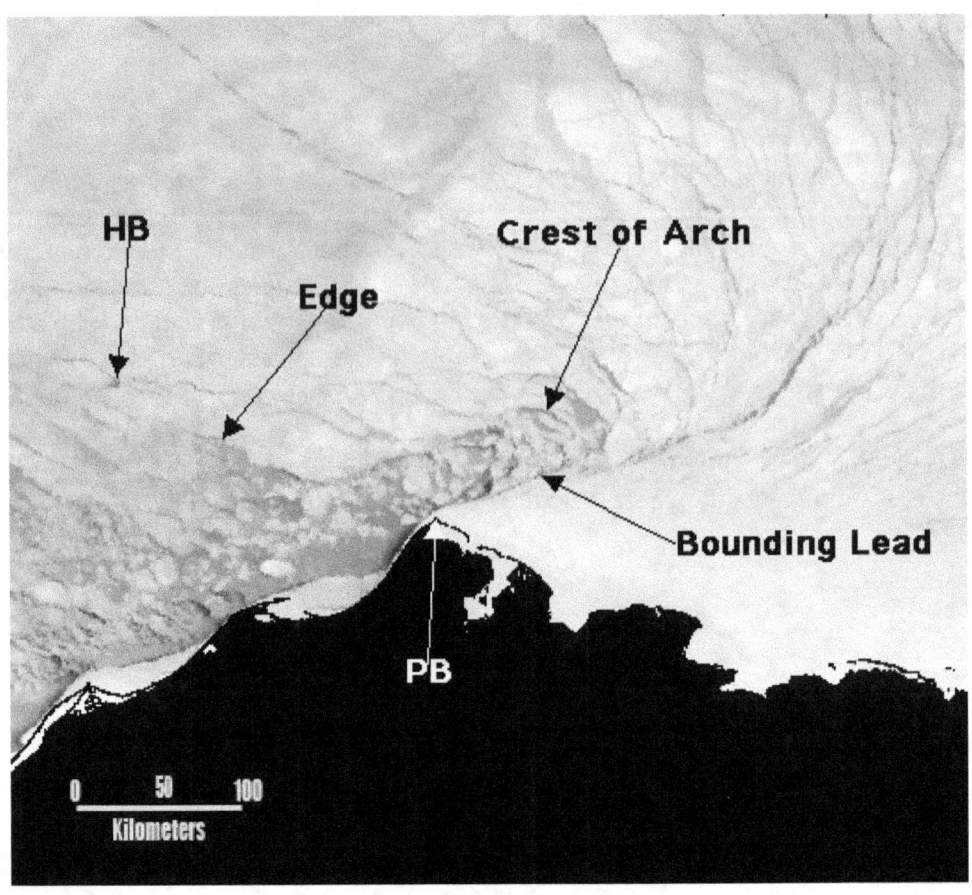

Figure 4.3.6. AVHRR image acquired on December 18, 1999, showing a Barrow Arch structure in early winter with a lead to the grounded ice on Hanna Shoal. The boundary labeled 'edge' marks the southern limit of relatively continuous pack ice. South of the edge the pack is broken into floes which are diverging and drifting southward. Symbols are [HB] Hanna Shoal, and [PB] Point Barrow.

complex of curving leads inside of which the pack ice is breaking into smaller floes. To the northeast along the bounding lead, the pack ice ahead of the crest is relatively continuous, while to the southwest of the crest, the pack ice has been reduced to floes. In this scene, the space between floes is filled with thin ice showing that the structure has been stable for some time. However, the small dark lines offshore from the Chukchi Sea coast are leads of either open water or very thin ice. Some of the leads are arcs concave to the southwest indicating that the near shore pack ice is starting to shift in that direction.

The arch in Figure 4.3.6 probably began as a smaller, but wider structure with the crest closer to Point Barrow. To reach the stage shown in the figure the structure grew by repeated fracturing of the pack ice at the crest of the arch creating the floes. That process has the effect of shifting the crest further along the bounding lead to the northeast. That is the basic mechanism by which such arches evolve.

A similar process operates when pack ice breaks out to the south through Bering Strait (Shapiro and Burns, 1974). However, at Bering Strait, the arch is bounded by leads that extend from fixed points at the coasts on opposite sides of the Strait. The constraints on a Barrow Arch are different; the southeast side of those structures is fixed by the bounding lead from Point Barrow that separates the arch from the more stable pack ice to the east. However, the west side is either unconfined or bounded by a lead that extends to Hanna Shoal. The mechanism of arch formation off Point Barrow is therefore different from that in Bering Strait, and has not been analyzed.

The process of forming a North Slope Arch is similar. However, there are some variations as are described in Section *(iii)*.

(ii) Barrow Arch

The most common feature of the deformation pattern of pack ice in the study area is probably the presence of an arch structure in the vicinity of Point Barrow called here a "Barrow Arch." In fact, such structures are probably the most common lead patterns of the pack ice in the Beaufort Sea, but their occurrence has not previously been reported. Barrow Arches occur in different configurations that probably reflect differences in the driving forces that create them, and the time of year (as that influences the properties of the pack ice). They appear to form as a result of south or southwest displacement of the Beaufort Sea pack ice, which is probably preceded by displacement in the same sense of the pack ice in the eastern Chukchi Sea.

Some variations of Barrow Arch structures are described in the following paragraphs. They are illustrated in Figures 5.2.4 and 5.2.6, in Section 5.2.1*(iii)*, in Figure 4.3.6 above, and in the figures that follow.

Barrow Arches are commonly bounded on the east by a northeast trending lead. Figure 4.3.6, which was described in detail above, is a good example of a Barrow Arch with a lead extending to the northeast. In addition, Figure 5.4.6 in Section 5.2.1*(iii)* shows an arcing lead system from near Point Barrow directly to Hanna Shoal. That structure is a type of Barrow Arch with a bounding lead on its east side but is wider than those in Figures 4.3.7 and 4.3.8 below which, for clarity, are described in extended captions.

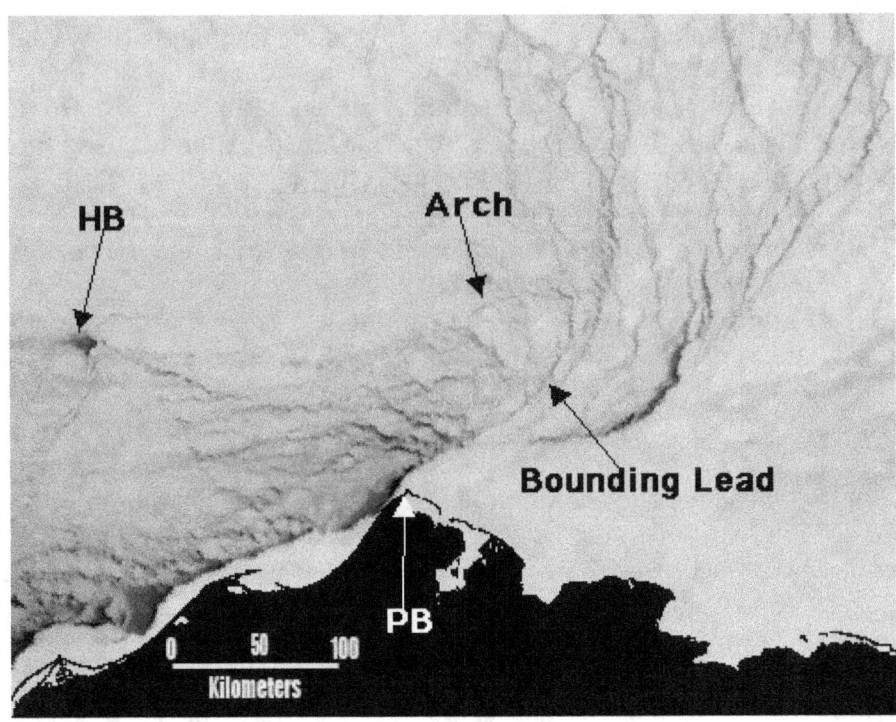

Figure 4.3.7. AVHRR image of a Barrow Arch on April 5, 2000 that is bounded on the east by a lead. The lead is part of a 'Lead Fan' whose members originate at the edge of the landfast ice north of Point Barrow (lead fans are described in Section 4.3.4. below). Note that the bounding lead ends in an arc that encloses the crest of the arch structure suggesting that the crest will not progress further to the northeast. In addition the irregular dark zone east of the bounding lead is a new lead which is not part of the arch structure. Its presence suggests that the weather system driving the formation of the Barrow Arch structure has moved and the arch is becoming inactive. "Arch" indicates the boundary of the arch opposite from the bounding lead. The other symbols are [HB] Hanna Shoal and [PB] Point Barrow.

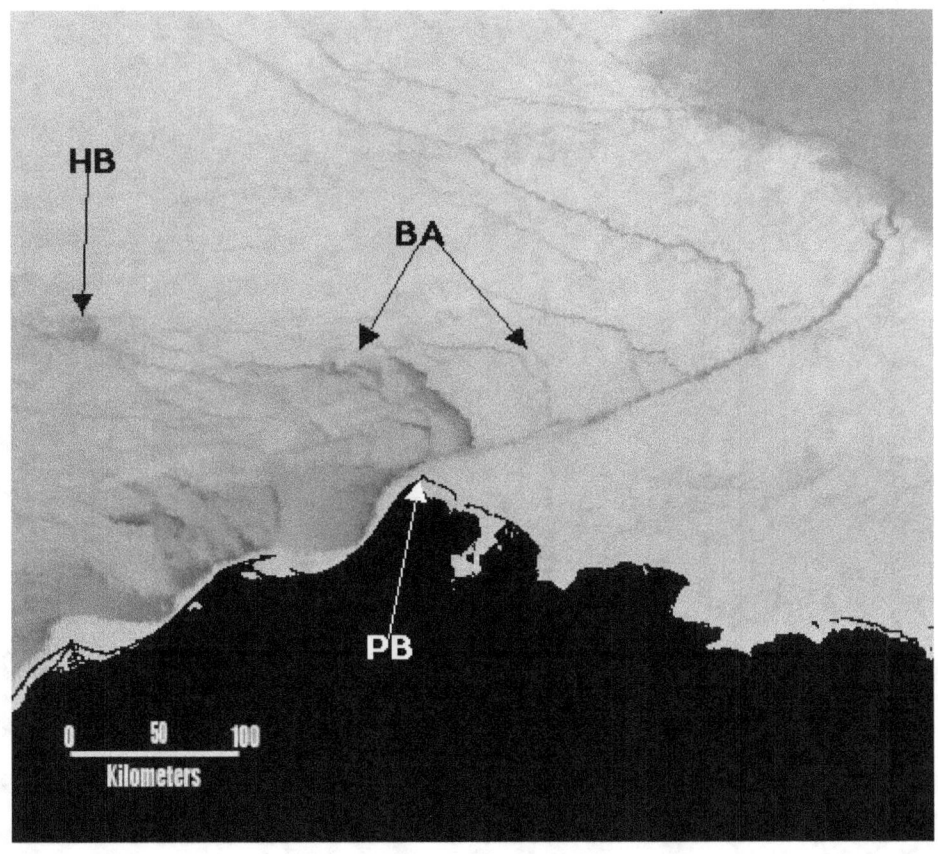

Figure 4.3.8. Another variation of the form and lead spacing of a Barrow Arch bounded on the east by a lead. Note the similarity of the form of the lead to Hanna Shoal to those in Figures 4.3.6 and 4.3.7. This AVHRR image was acquired on February 14, 1997, about one month after that in Figure 4.3.9 below. Symbols are [HB] Hanna Shoal and [PB] Point Barrow. The arrows from [BA] point to the flank and crest of the Barrow Arch structure.

Barrow Arches such as those illustrated above, often occur within wider arches that are made up of a single lead or lead system that extends from near Point Barrow through a broad arc to Hanna Shoal or further west. Figure 4.3.9 is an illustration of that relationship. In that figure, there is grounded ice on Hanna shoal. Figures 4.3.10 and 4.3.11 show similar configurations from other years, but on images acquired before the ice grounded on the shoal. The difference in the pattern of leads that extends across the structure from Point Barrow toward the approximate location of Hanna Shoal is apparent (compare with Figure 5.3.4, Section 5.2.1 (iii)). Note that the wide arches have the same function as the smaller arches in that they enclose pack ice that is breaking into smaller floes. The scale is different, but both types of arches are involved in the process of transporting pack ice from the Beaufort Sea into the Chukchi Sea.

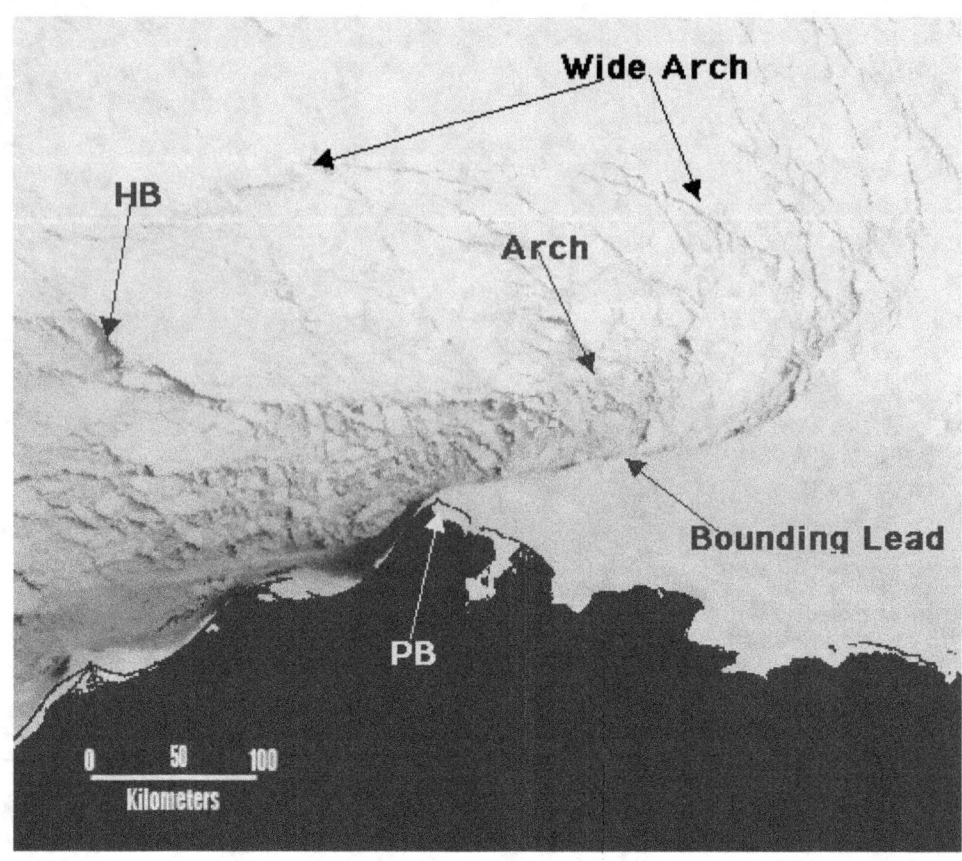

Figure 4.3.9. AVHRR image acquired on January 19, 1997, showing a Barrow Arch bounded on the east by a lead and embedded in a wider arch. The lead from the flank of the Barrow Arch to the grounded ice on Hanna Shoal in this figure is similar to those in the figures above. Note also that the pack ice to the south of the lead is broken into floes and drifting southward. "Arch" indicates the approximate crest of the Barrow Arch structure. Symbols are [HB] Hanna Shoal] and [PB] Point Barrow.

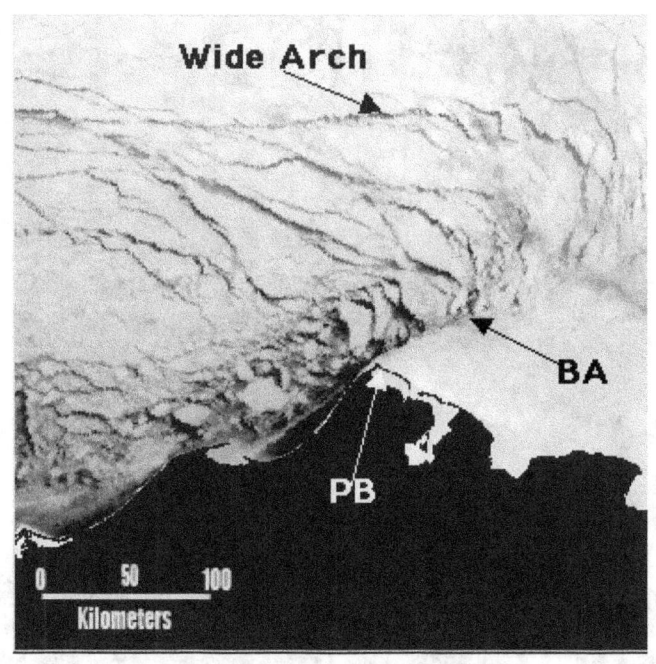

Figure 4.3.10. AVHRR image of a Barrow Arch inside of a wide arch before ice was grounded on Hanna Shoal. The image was acquired on January 8, 1994. The lead marked "Wide Arch" appears to enclose the entire lead complex. [BA] indicates the approximate crest of the smaller Barrow Arch. Symbol [PB] is Point Barrow.

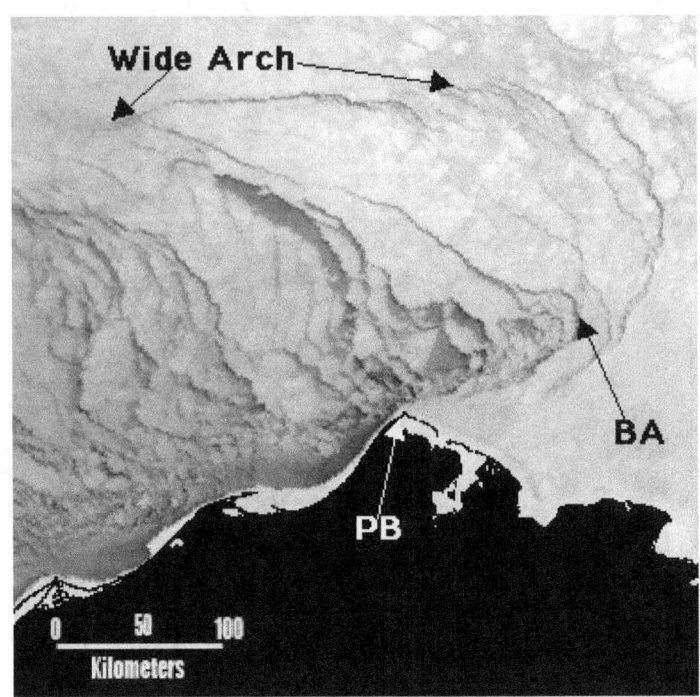

Figure 4.3.11. AVHRR image acquired on December 15, 1995, about one year after that in Figure 4.3.10, showing a Barrow Arch inside of a wide arch before ice is grounded on Hanna Shoal. "Wide Arch" is the bounding lead and [BA] is the crest of the Barrow Arch. Note that there is no lead bounding the east side of the Barrow Arch, and that the wide arch is east of boundary of the Barrow Arch. the symbol [PB] is Point Barrow.

Another structure that might be classified within the group of arch structures described here is shown in Figure 4.3.12. The arch is not as symmetric as those in Figures 4.3.9, 4.3.10, and 4.3.11, and there is no smaller Barrow Arch within it. However, it clearly serves the same function of the structures in those figures. In addition, it illustrates another point discussed below in Section 5.2.1 (*iii*); that is, the role of grounded ice on Hanna Shoal as the source or terminus of leads.

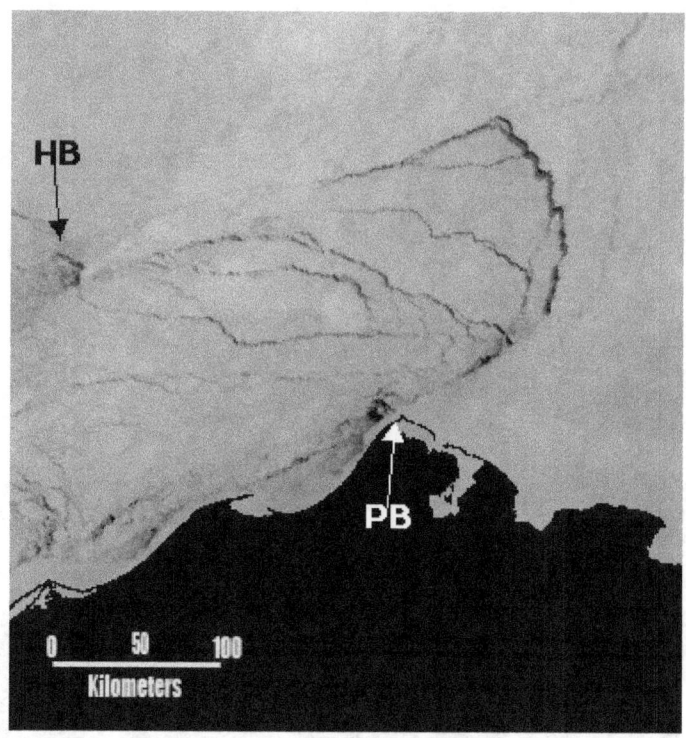

Figure 4.3.12. Leads converging to grounded ice on Hanna Shoal [HB] in late winter. [PB] is Point Barrow shown in an AVHRR image acquired on April 8, 1994. The dark spot at Hanna Shoal is open water or thin ice on the down-drift side of the grounded ice. The arch structure does not continue to curve to the west of Hanna Shoal. Instead, it is truncated by a lead extending straight to the grounded ice at the shoal. (Note that this figure is repeated in the discussion in Section 5.2.1. (iii))

Finally, Barrow Arches form in the absence of other structures as shown in Figure 4.3.13. However, such forms are probably restricted to early winter before there is grounded ice on Hanna Shoal.

73

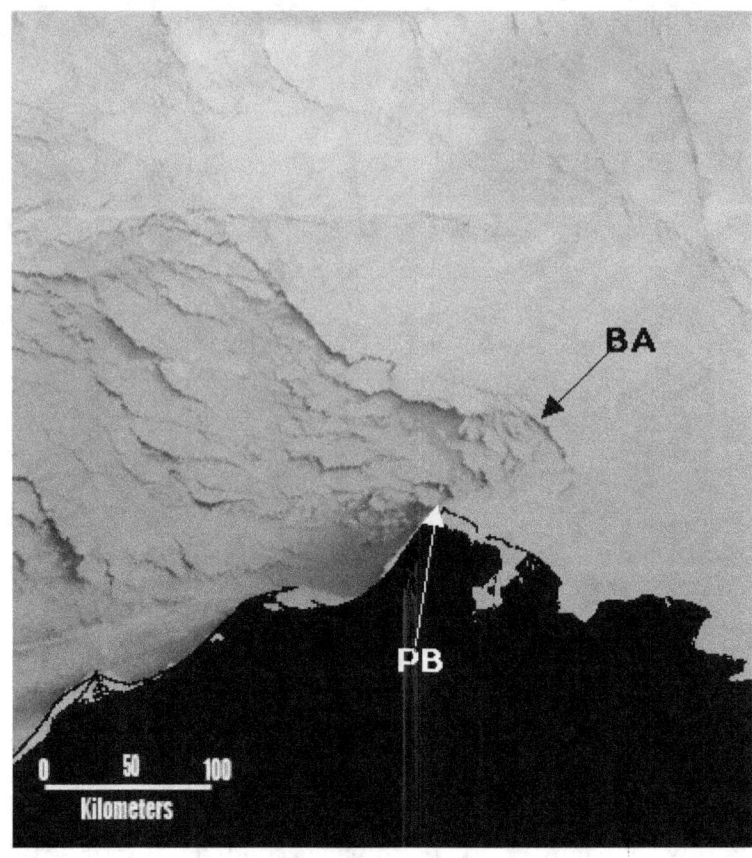

Figure 4.3.13. AVHRR image acquired on December 1, 1999 showing a Barrow Arch with no prominent bounding lead. Note, however that the lead pattern to the northwest of the arch follows the same trend as those in Figures 4.3.6 to 4.3.11 and that the pack ice breaks into floes that drift southward as in those figures. In addition, the Barrow Arch structure may be turning to the east and beginning to progress along the landfast ice edge as a North Slope Arch (see Section 4.3.2. (iii), below) Symbols are [BA] Barrow Arch and [PB] Point Barrow.

It is of interest that in all of the images of Barrow Arches there is a tendency for leads to project toward Hanna Shoal even before there is grounded ice at the shoal. The leads follow the trend of the isobaths so they cross over the highest points on Hanna Shoal approximately along latitude 72°N. Further, the figures show that it is usual for the pack ice to break into large floes along that trend, and to drift away to the south, even when the limit of drifting ice is far to the south. In the imagery examined for this study, the line along which the floes break from the pack in this manner does not appear to extend farther west than about 162°30' W, just outside the study area. The fact that the floes are breaking loose implies that there is space for them to move into. In early winter, the Chukchi Sea closes over later than the Beaufort Sea, while later in the year, the Chukchi Sea pack ice frequently drifts off the Alaska coast. Either of these conditions can provide the space needed to accommodate the floes along that trend.

74

A Barrow Arch in one of the configurations described here is probably the most common ice cover feature observed. As noted, when an arch is present, the pack ice to the east is often relatively stable. However, when the pack ice drift vector turns more westerly, the pattern can change quickly, because the arch creates space for newly broken floes to move into. New patterns can be North Slope Arches (described next) or wide arcs aligned along more easterly trends (see Section 4.3.4. *(iv)* below).

(iii) North Slope Arch

A North Slope Arch is an arch structure that migrates eastward from Point Barrow. The arch is generally narrow and bounded on the south side by the landfast ice edge. The pack ice breaks in the arch as the crest moves eastward so that at times this form resembles a shear zone or flaw zone described above. However, it is probably more limited in extent because the crest must progress eastward, while a flaw or shear zone may form along most of the coast at almost the same time.

As with the Barrow Arch, the mechanism of the formation of a North Slope Arch has not been analyzed. Examples are shown in Figures 4.3.14 and 4.3.15.

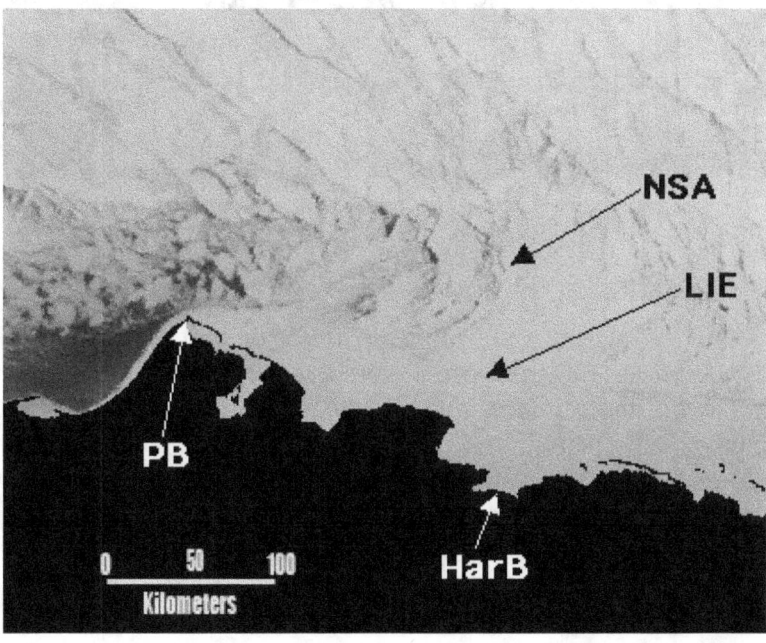

Figure 4.3.14. AVHRR image acquired on December 23, 1993 showing a North Slope Arch which is, in effect, a Barrow Arch that has turned eastward and extended roughly parallel to the coast. Symbols are [LIE] landfast ice edge, [PB] Point Barrow, [HarB] Harrison Bay, and [PrB] Prudhoe Bay.

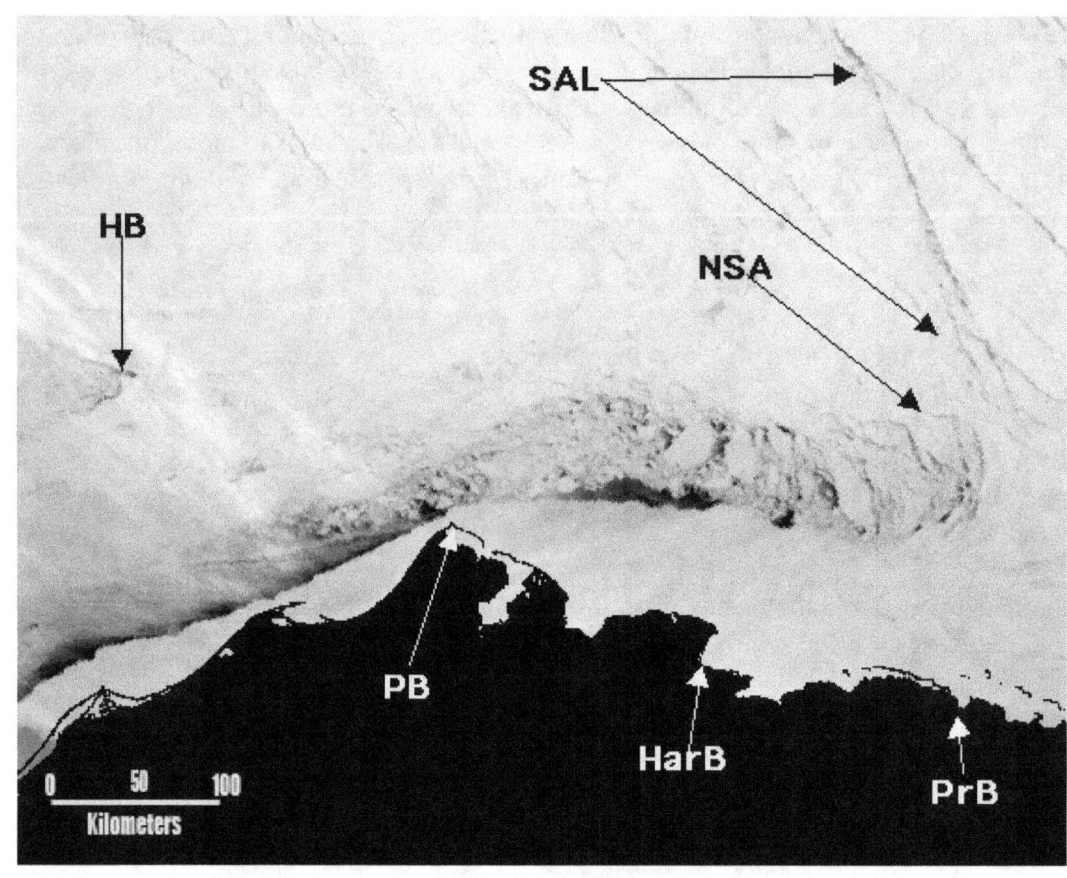

Figure 4.3.15. AVHRR image from March 31, 1995 showing a North Slope Arch that has clearly extended from a Barrow Arch. Note that the latter has been narrowed by southerly movement of the pack ice west of Point Barrow while the North Slope Arch was extending eastward. The notation "SAL" refers to a lead pattern called "Small-Angle" leads. The pattern is discussed in Section 4.3.4. *(vi)* below. Other symbols are [PB] Point Barrow, [HarB] Harrison Bay, [PrB] Prudhoe Bay, [HB] Hanna Shoal and [NSA] the approximate crest of the North Slope Arch.

4.3.4. Lead Patterns

(i). Lead fan

A lead fan is a set of gently arcing leads that radiate from about the same point and have the same sense of concavity. However, they do not curve into arches but, instead remain relatively open. The most common point of origin for lead fans is the edge of the landfast ice north of Point Barrow with the leads concave to the west. However, a lead fan can originate at other promontories along the landfast ice edge. The most shoreward lead of the fan is usually tangent to the edge of the landfast ice, and the sense of ice offset is the same across all the leads in the fan. Figures 4.3.7, 4.3.16, and 4.3.17 show examples of lead fans.

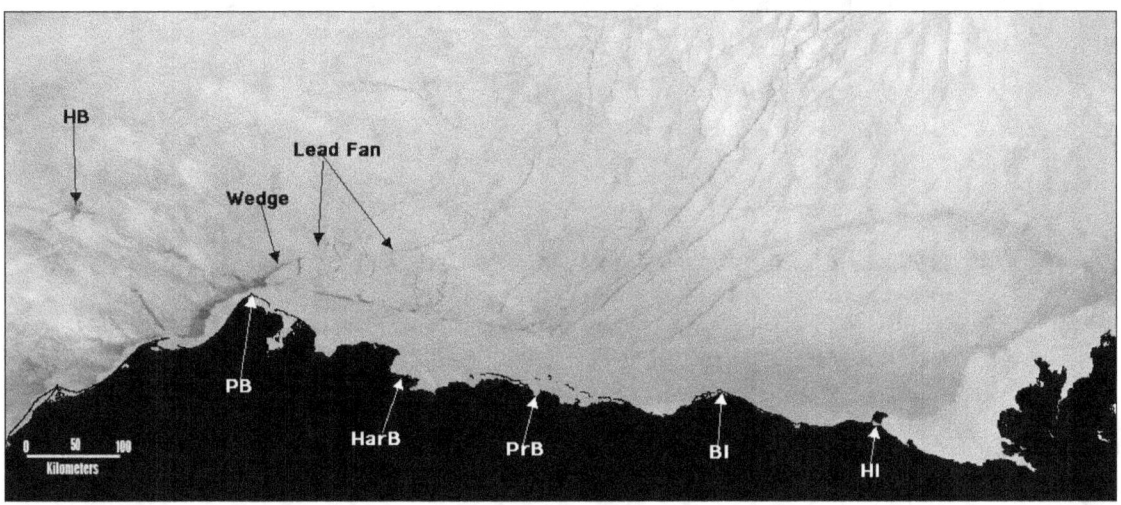

Figure 4.3.16. A lead fan at Point Barrow is shown defining at wedge. This AVHRR image was acquired on March 5, 1998, a day earlier than that in Figure 4.3.4. In this example, the lead fan consists of the two leads indicated in the figure. Comparison with Figure 4.3.4 indicates the speed with which the zone of floes in that figure developed. Symbols are [HB] Hanna Shoal, [PB] Point Barrow, [HarB] Harrison Bay, [PrB] Prudhoe Bay, [BI] Barter Island, and [HI] Herschel Island.

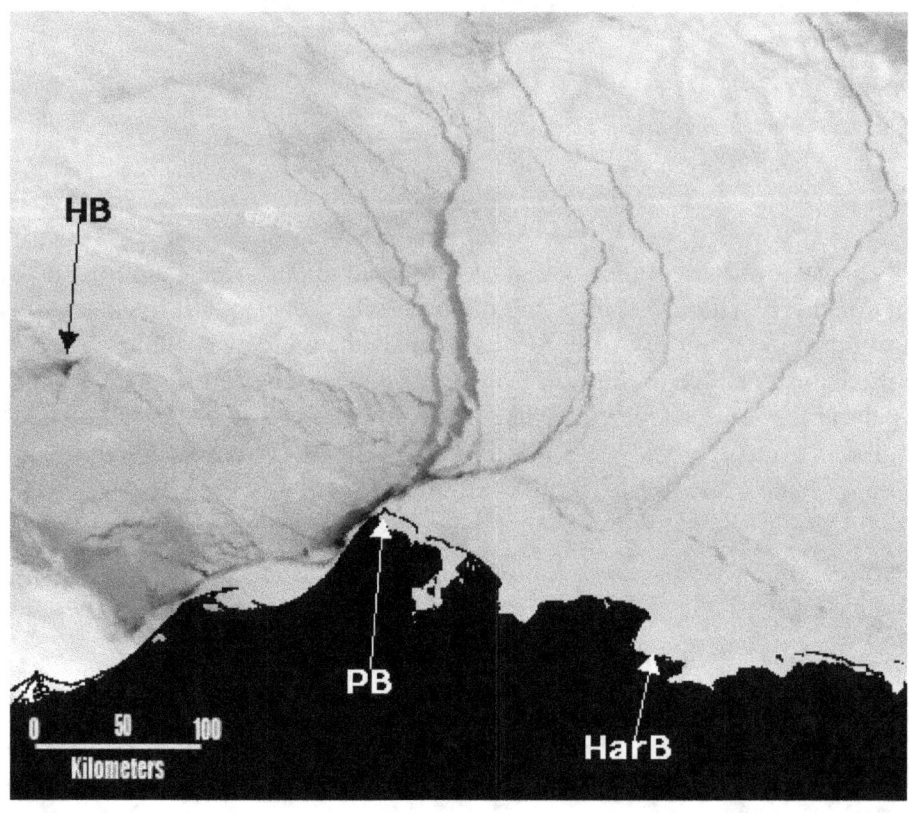

Figure 4.3.17 . AVHRR image acquired on February 9, 2000, showing a lead fan at Point Barrow consisting of arcuate leads with relative displacements approximately normal to the lead trends. Symbols are [HB] Hanna Shoal, [PB] Point Barrow, and [HarB] Harrison Bay.

The sense of offset across all of the leads in the fans at Point Barrow was always observed to be normal to the leads or left-lateral (i.e. pack ice west of the lead moving southward). This implies that lead fans at Point Barrow provide a mechanism for pack ice drifting toward the Alaska coast at a high angle to drift around Point Barrow from the Beaufort into the Chukchi Sea. The shapes of the fans and the sense of drift also suggest that the leads form in sequence from high- to low-angle to the edge of the landfast ice so that the last lead to form is tangent to the landfast ice edge.

(ii). Tangent leads

Tangent leads are gently arcing leads that are tangent to the landfast ice edge, and are not part of a lead fan or a set of wide arcs (see Section 4.3.4 *(iv)* below). Those that form under the same pack ice movement regime are concave in the same direction and have the same sense of relative pack ice displacement across them. Thus, a series of tangent leads permits pack ice motion to be changed from a high angle to nearly parallel to the landfast ice edge, as was the case for lead fans. Figure 4.3.18 shows a tangent lead system associated with an eastward shift of the pack ice.

78

Note the curving en echelon fractures that define the shape of the lead system. The tangent leads in Figures 4.3.19 and 4.3.20 reflect westward movement of the pack ice but with an associated set of leads trending normal to the tangent leads. The similarity of the patterns from two different years (1997 and 2000) is clear but the origin of the secondary leads is uncertain.

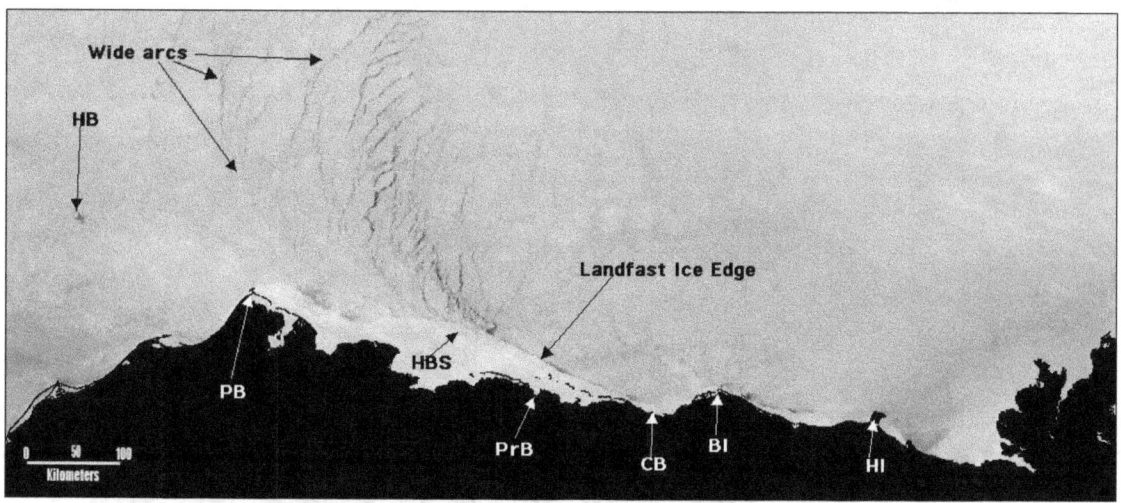

Figure 4.3.18. AVHRR image acquired on March 18, 1996 when the Beaufort Sea pack ice was shifting to the east. Eastward shifts of pack ice are unusual, but not rare. This figure shows a lead zone that is tangent to the landfast ice edge near the site of the grounded ice on the shoal offshore from Harrison Bay. The zone is concave to the east, as are the wide arcing leads west of the zone, indicating displacement in that direction. Note also that the landfast ice edge in this March scene is approximately at the 20 m depth contour in Camden Bay which is unusual so late in the year. Symbols are [HB] Hanna Shoal, [PB] Point Barrow, [HBS] Harrison Bay shoal, [PrB] Prudhoe Bay, [BI] Barter Island, [CB] Camden Bay and [HI] Herschel Island.

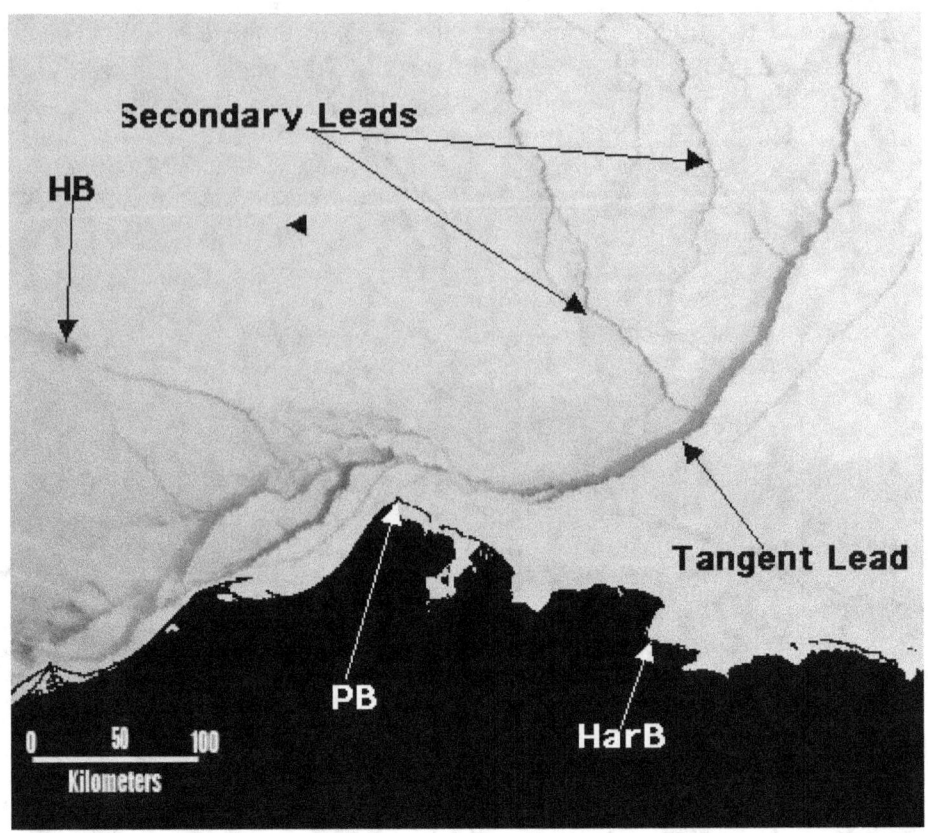

Figure 4.3.19. Tangent lead near Point Barrow formed by westward displacement of the pack ice west of the lead shown on an AVHRR image from April 3, 1997. Note the secondary lead system trending northwest, approximately normal to the tangent lead, and compare them to the similar system in the next figure. Symbols are [HB] Hanna Shoal, [PB] Point Barrow and [HarB] Harrison Bay.

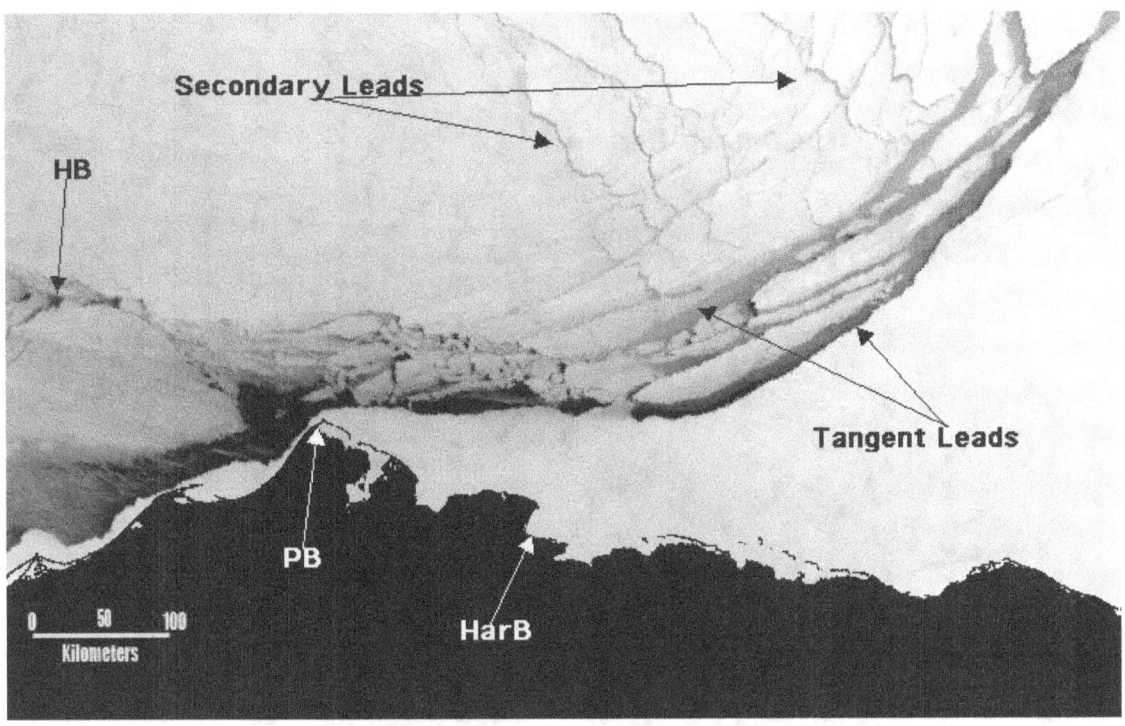

Figure 4.3.20. Tangent lead zone near Point Barrow shown on an AVHRR image from March 10, 2000, The pack ice displacement pattern is similar to that in Figure 4.3.19, as is the secondary lead pattern. Symbols are [HB] Hanna Shoal, [PB] Point Barrow and [HarB] Harrison Bay.

(iii). High-Angle Leads

As the name indicates, high-angle leads form almost normal to the edge of the landfast ice and can extend for up to hundreds of kilometers into the Beaufort Sea. They are often irregular and somewhat jagged, although they may also be gently arched. In addition, some are arced toward tangency to the landfast ice edge over the first few kilometers from the edge, but others show no such arc.

High-angle leads appear to reflect extension of the pack ice parallel to the coast, so the ice displacements are normal to the leads. They form when the pack ice is being compressed to the south at a high-angle to the coast. The mechanism of formation may be similar to fracture in uniaxial compression, in which small samples under axial compression fail in extension across a crack parallel to the compression direction.

Figures 4.3.21 and 4.3.22 show high angle leads in the eastern Beaufort Sea, which is a common location for such leads to form. However, they have been observed elsewhere along the coast.

81

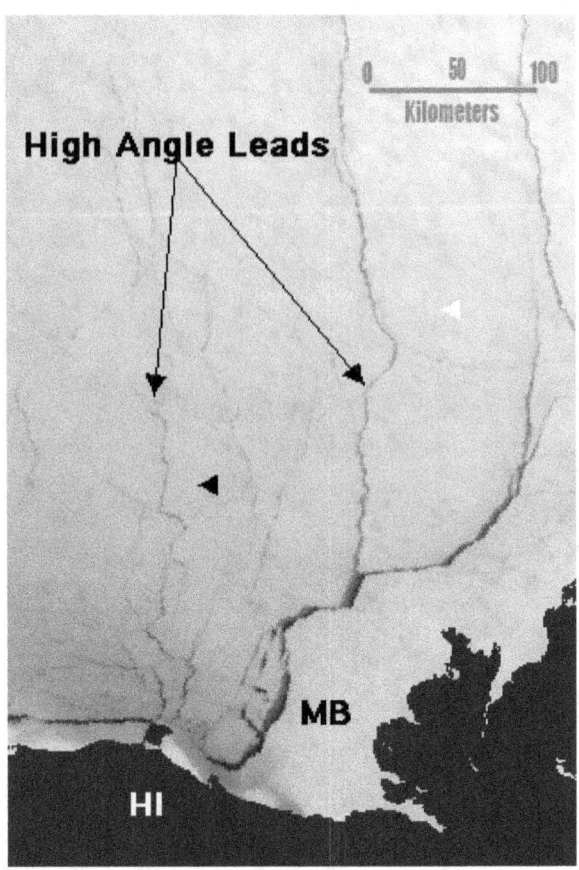

Figure 4.3.21. High angle leads near Mackenzie Bay shown in an AVHRR image acquired on April 20, 1996. The high angle leads project northward from Herschel Island and are offset to the edge of the landfast ice off Mackenzie Bay. The irregular shape, similar degree of opening along their length, and lack of curvature of the leads suggests a failure mechanism similar to extension fracture. In that mode, samples fail across planes parallel to the maximum compressive stress in uniaxial compression. Symbols are [HI] Herschel Island and [MB] Mackenzie Bay.

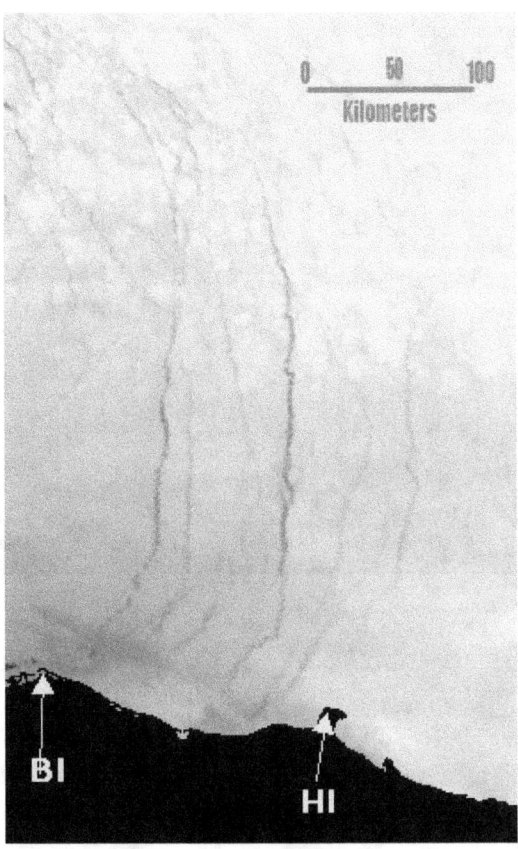

Figure 4.3.22. High angle leads between Barter and Herschel Islands. In this example, the leads tend to curve toward tangency with the edge of the landfast ice, but other characteristics are similar to those in Figure 4.3.21. Symbols are [BI] Barter Island and [HI] Herschel Island. February 14, 2000.

(iv). Wide Arcs

The term "wide arcs" is applied to leads that are curved into the form of one side of a pair of parentheses and may be up to hundreds of kilometers in length. They extend seaward from the landfast ice edge or from other apparent boundaries within the pack ice, and tend to occur in sets, rather than singly. The members of a set are concave in the same direction, and they appear to form sequentially starting from that direction; that is, if concave west, then the leads appear from west to east.

Wide arcs open when the ice on the concave facing side of the lead moves, so that taken together, sets of wide arcing leads imply that the pack ice is diverging in that direction. Figure 5.4.6 (Section 5.2.1 *(iii)*) shows wide arcs enclosing a Barrow Arch. The wide arcs in Figure 4.3.23 formed early in the year when the pack ice was not be continuous enough to sustain long leads. The arcs are therefore somewhat discontinuous, but the trend of the nested arcs is clear from the figure.

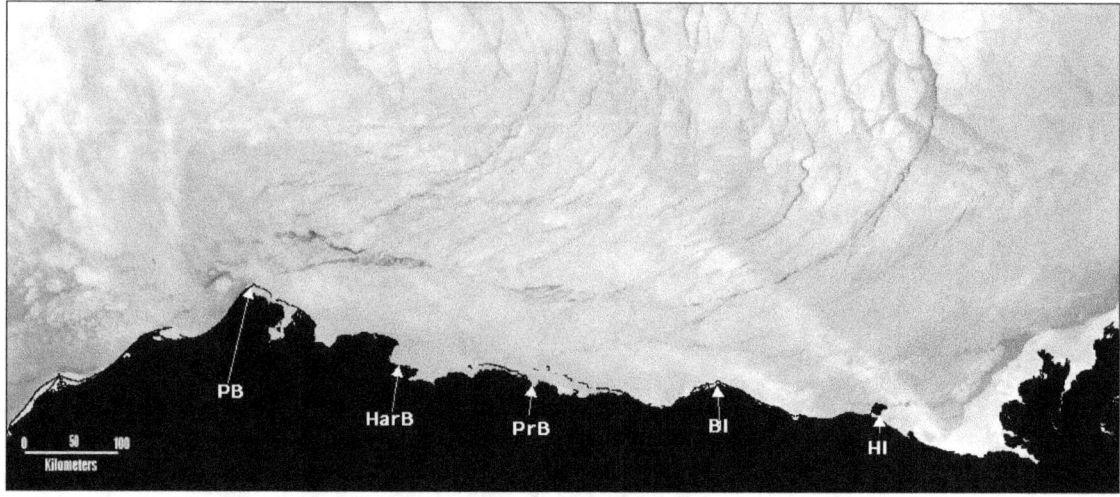

Figure 4.3.23. AVHRR image from December 13, 1999 showing an early winter set of wide arcs formed when the pack ice is not continuous enough to sustain long leads. However, the trends of the nested arcs are clear from the figure. Symbols are [PB] Point Barrow, [HarB] Harrison Bay, [PrB] Prudhoe Bay, [BI] Barter Island, and [HI] Herschel Island.

(v). Chukchi Arcs

Chukchi arcs are arcuate leads that are tangent to the landfast ice along the Chukchi Sea coast of Alaska. They are concave in the direction that the ice is drifting and diverging which, in that area, is most often in a southerly direction. In many cases, the lead pattern originates when ice moves south through Bering Strait, with new arcuate leads forming progressively further north as space is created for the pack ice to displace into. In some cases, the lead pattern results in a feature similar to a North Slope Arch described above, but along the Chukchi Sea coast.

There are few illustrations of these features available because most form outside of our study area. Figure 4.3.24 is a late winter image and shows the effect of the grounded ice on Hanna Shoal on the pattern.

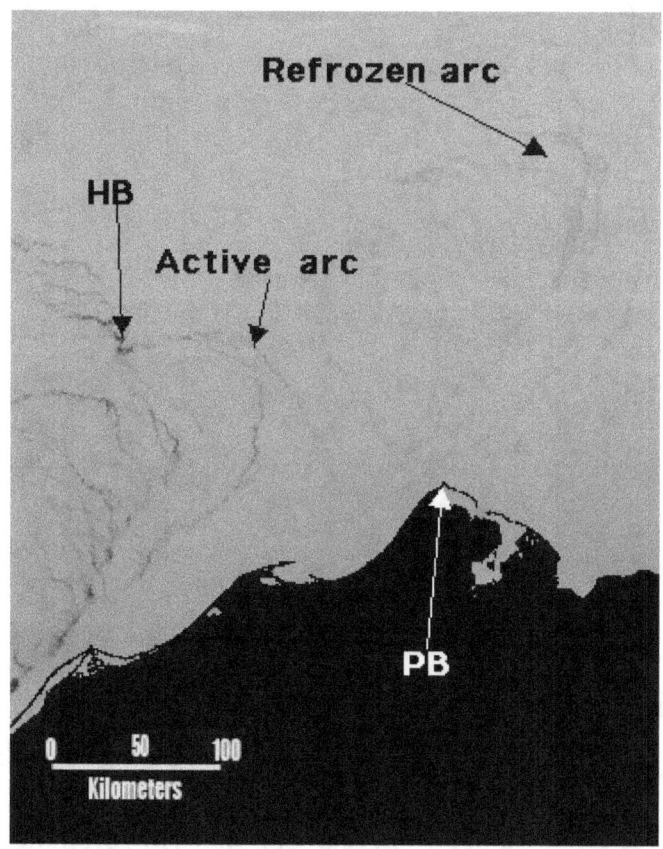

Figure 4.3.24. Chukchi Arcs shown in an AVHRR image from April 11, 1999 when there was grounded ice on Hanna Shoal. The arcs are the northern end of an arch structure that probably extends south to Bering Strait. However, cloud cover south of Cape Lisburne partially obscures the surface so this is not certain. Note that the arch structure is not anchored on the coast north of Icy Cape. Also, note that the north end of the Chukchi Arch is clearly active, as indicated by the dark zones of either thin ice or open water. However, the arch structure that extends further north is probably refrozen. Symbols are [HB] Hanna Shoal and [PB] Point Barrow.

(vi). Small-Angle Leads

The term 'small-angle' leads refers to sets of relatively straight, intersecting leads in which the acute angle between the leads is less than about 60 degrees. They are common at any time of year and, as explained below, they can form anyplace where the pack ice is diverging. The only good example in the processed images is shown in Figure 4.3.15.

In the geologic literature, fractures with this characteristic are called 'joints of small dihedral angle' (Muehlberger, W.R., 1961) in reference to the fact that the angle between the fractures is less than the commonly observed minimum of 60 degrees for brittle fractures formed in

85

compression. The interpretation of the origin of fractures of small dihedral angle in two dimensions is that one of the principal stresses is a true tensile stress, and is aligned to bisect the large dihedral angle while a compressive principal stress direction bisects the small dihedral angle. When applied to small angle leads in pack ice, this implies divergence through extension in the direction of the bisector of the large dihedral angle.

Small angle leads are potentially valuable aids in the interpretation of pack ice motion on AVHRR imagery. They immediately imply that the pack ice is diverging, as well as giving the direction along which the maximum rate of extension is occurring.

4.3.5 Sequences and Trends

(i). Definitions

Individual lead patterns are usually not isolated features in time. Instead, they often appear as steps in sequences in which one pattern predictably follows another. Sequences probably reflect the passage of the weather systems that drive the motion of pack ice, so it seems reasonable to assume that most lead patterns should be part of a sequence. However, the weather systems that cause the sequences are not all of equal effectiveness. They may weaken or pass through the area too rapidly for an entire sequence to form, and then be replaced by another system which changes the sense of motion of the pack ice. Thus, some 'sequences' may not progress past the first pattern before conditions change and, in fact, some patterns may not be part of a sequence. However, regardless of the uncertainties, the idea of sequences of patterns might prove to be useful in the analysis of lead patterns and pack ice deformation in general.

At least some of the features defined below as 'trends' originate from the sequential formation of wide arc leads that are tangent to some line (the trend) that originates near Point Barrow and extends easterly. For that reason, they are included in this section. A more complete discussion and definition is given below.

Over the duration of this project, the two sequences described below were seen often enough to warrant inclusion here. There is evidence that additional sequences could also be identified with time and data from more years than were available for this project.

(ii). Chukchi Offshore Lead (and zone) and Sequences

The term 'Chukchi offshore lead' describes a lead or a zone of leads that reaches from near Icy Cape or Point Franklin and extends northward to beyond the limits of the study area. It generally passes Point Barrow offshore and not along the fast ice edge, but in some cases it may be at that boundary. The pack ice west of the lead (or lead zone) is always displacing southward relative to that east of the lead with the direction indicated by the presence of small en echelon fractures, rotated small floes, or open areas at irregularities along the lead. The pack ice east of the lead (or lead zone) is usually also moving southward. However, it can only advance by closing favorably oriented leads or taking up the motion by ridging, so the magnitude of the displacement is limited. Thus, when a Chukchi offshore lead is present, there are no openings in the southern Beaufort Sea at the scale of the imagery and the lead can be interpreted to represent a shear discontinuity in the southerly drifting pack ice.

A Chukchi offshore lead sequence is shown in Figures 4.3.25 through 4.3.29 from five consecutive days. Figures 4.3.25 and 4.3.26 show the development of a Chukchi offshore lead zone in which the pack ice west of the zone is displaced to the southwest relative to that to the east. The sense of offset across the lead zone is indicated in Figure 4.3.27 by the northerly oriented en echelon fractures along the lead. The offset across the new lead in Figure 4.3.27 is more westerly, but still has a southwest component. Subsequently, the leads develop through the sequence of (1) tangent lead or lead fan at Point Barrow on the fourth day (Figure 4.3.28), and (2) tangent leads along the north slope and (3) high angle leads east of Barter Island or Herschel Island on the fifth day (Figure 4.3.29). The details of the geometry of the lead patterns and the timing at which they appear relative to each other in other sequences of this type may vary. However, the patterns always formed in the order described here, but sometimes over a period of up to a few days.

A total of 8 examples of this sequence of patterns have been identified in the imagery from the years 1993-94 to 2003-04. There were an additional 5 examples in which the sequence appeared to start, but was not completed.

As noted, the formation of the patterns following the Chukchi offshore lead can be interpreted as responding to southward displacement of the Beaufort Sea pack ice. The left-lateral differential motion across the Chukchi offshore lead zone reflects this. The appearance of the tangent lead (or in some cases, a lead fan) at Point Barrow (Figure 4.3.28) begins the process of changing the southerly movement of the pack ice into displacement to the west along shear lines. The tangent leads further east (Figure 4.3.29) continue the westerly transfer of motion. The formation of high angle leads east of Barter Island, rather than tangent leads is interpreted as resulting from a compressive mechanism (see the description of high angle leads above) which is consistent with the southerly displacement of the pack ice. The details of the specific boundary conditions and other variables that control the deformation require analysis.

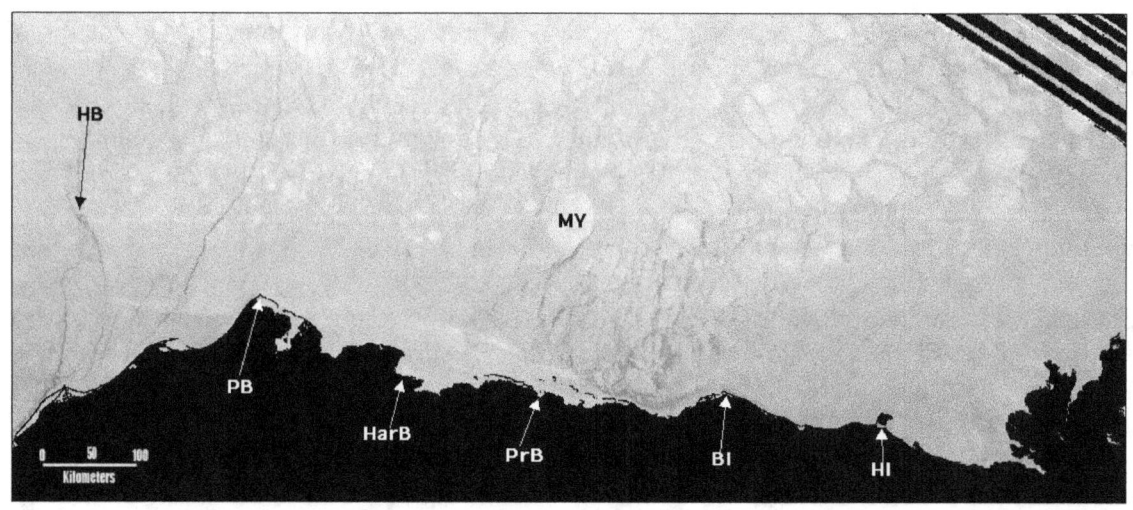

Figure 4.3.25. Start of a sequence of five AVHRR images showing the development of a Chukchi offshore lead sequence beginning on February 17, 1994. The process is described in the text. Note the leads associated with the multiyear floe [MY]. The symbols are [HB] Hanna Shoal, [PB] Point Barrow, [HarB] Harrison Bay, [PrB] Prudhoe Bay, [BI] Barter Island, and [HI] Herschel Island.

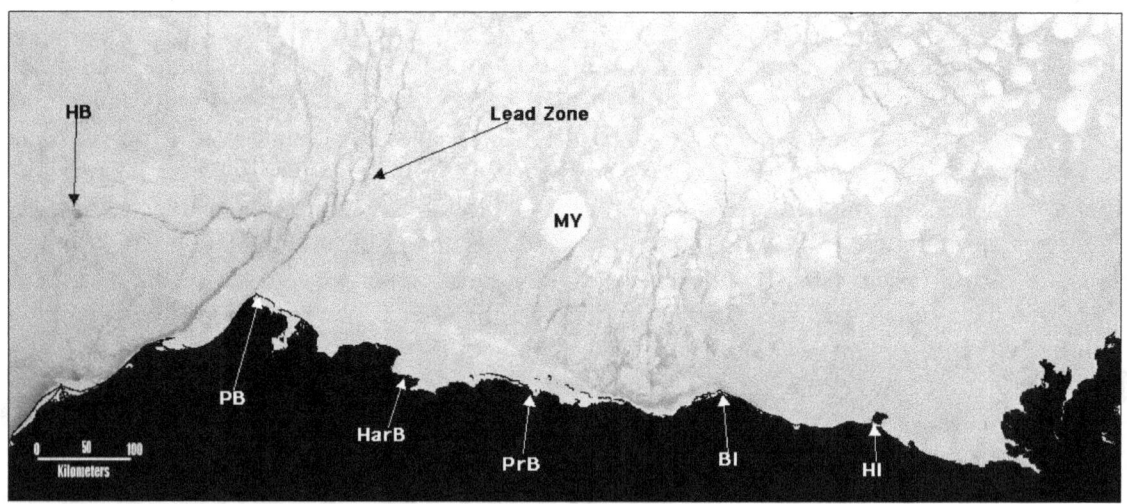

Figure 4.3.26 AVHRR image on February 18, 1994; the second day of the sequence. Symbols are the same as in Figure 4.3.25.

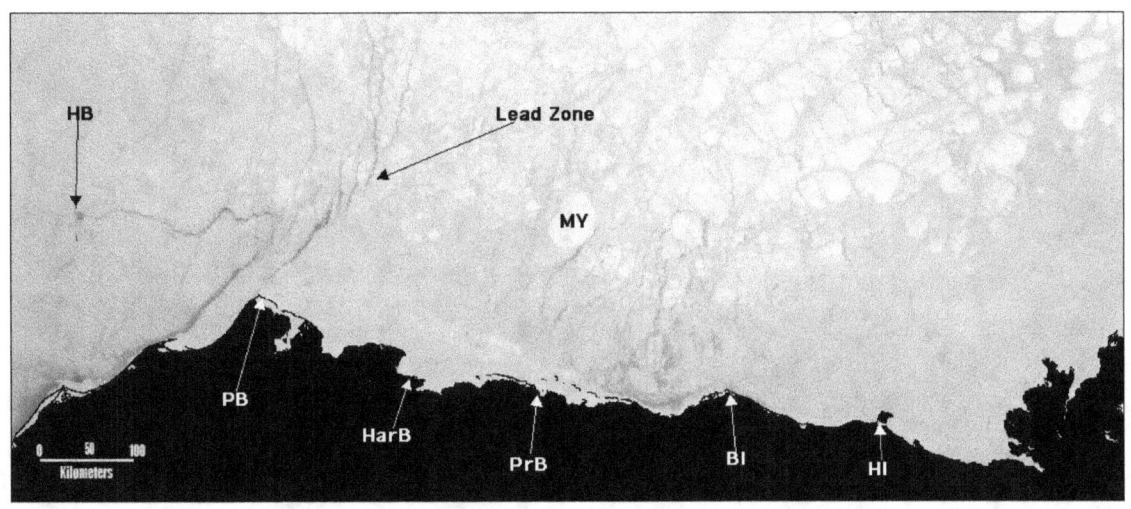

Figure 4.3.27 AVHRR image on February 19, 1994; the third day of the sequence. Symbols are the same as in Figure 4.3.25.

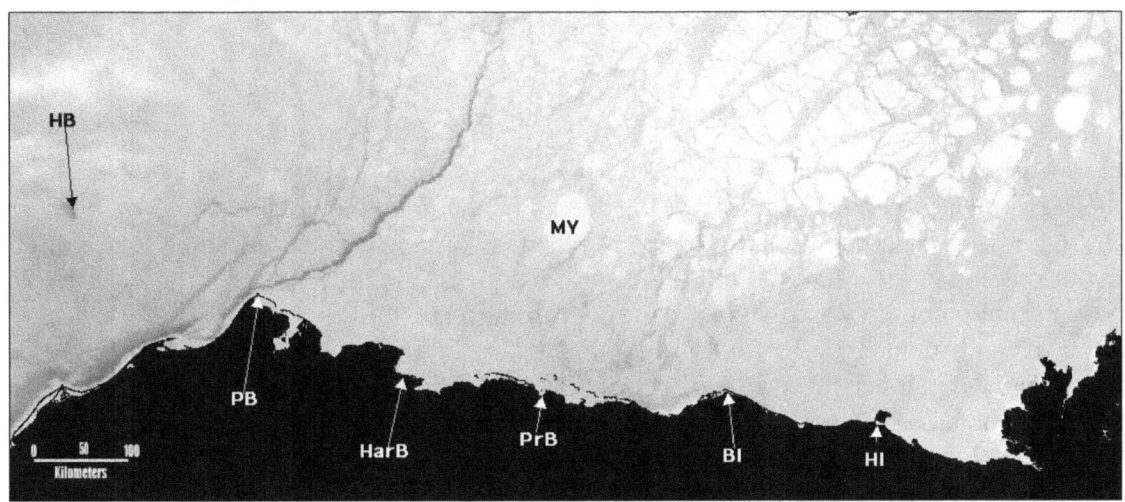

Figure 4.3.28 AVHRR image on February 20, 1994; the fourth day of the sequence. Note that the leads around the multiyear floe [MY} have become less distinct than in the two earlier figures in the sequence. As the ice in the leads thickens, the surface becomes colder, so the leads blend in with the surrounding ice on these thermal IR images. The symbols are the same as in Figure 4.3.25.

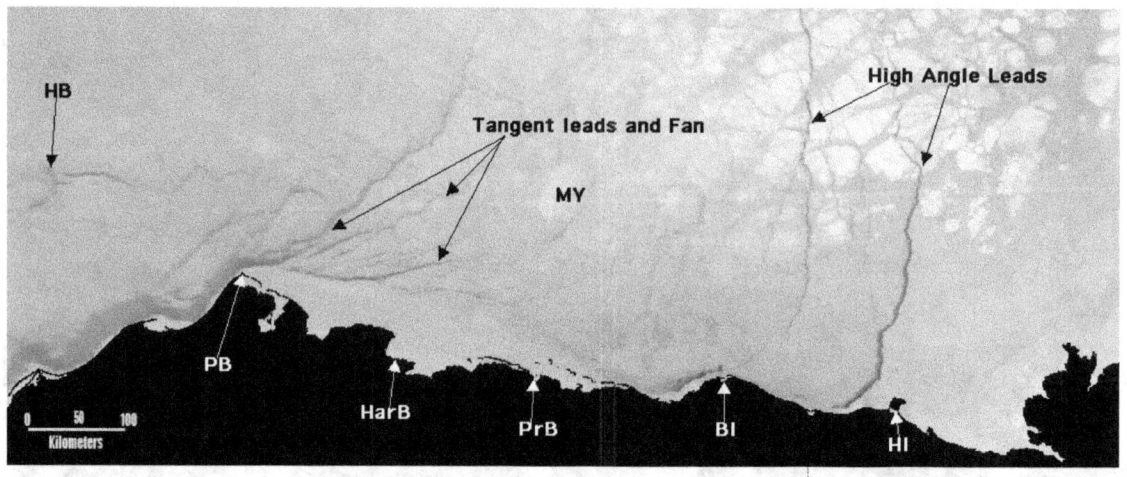

Figure 4.3.29 AVHRR image on February 21, 1994; the fifth and last day of the sequence. Note that the tangent and high angle leads formed within one day. The symbols are the same as in Figure 4.3.25.

(iii). Point Barrow and easterly leads, trends and sequences

Point Barrow is a critical location in the pattern of deformation of the pack ice in the southeastern Beaufort Sea. The reason is that, as noted the main theme of ice deformation in that area is the drift of ice around Point Barrow into the Chukchi Sea. Thus, as can be seen from the earlier discussion in this section, Point Barrow (more precisely, the landfast ice around the Point) is an important point of origin in a number of deformation patterns involved in that process. Linear leads and 'trends" (defined below) originate there and extend toward Banks Island, Camden Bay and points between them. The spread of possible azimuths of these features is about 30 degrees. The more southerly of these extend into Camden Bay or to Barter Island. The remainder lie along azimuths from Point Barrow to points between Cape Dalhousie or Cape Bathurst to the vicinity of Sachs Harbor on Banks Island.

The leads from Point Barrow to Camden Bay generally follow the line of ridges close to the 20 meter depth contour. The ridges are established early in the winter and form the most inshore landfast ice edge. Subsequently, the line of outer ridges may shift to a smooth edge across Camden Bay to the 20m depth contour offshore from Barter Island so the lead crosses deeper water. However, both of these edges are stabilized by grounded ice features and are identified on the AVHRR imagery by the presence of open water or thin ice on their offshore side. Once established, they define the offshore boundary of the most stable landfast ice regime. An example of the landfast ice edge extending into Camden Bay is shown in Figure 4.3.3. Figure 4.3.4 shows a landfast edge projecting across Camden Bay to just offshore from Barter Island.

The term 'trend' as used here refers to a discontinuity in the pack ice deformation field that is defined as (for example) the 'line' to which a series of wide arcs are tangent. They differ from the landfast ice edges because, while these are clearly defined by the presence of grounded ridges,

90

there may be no discernable linear feature at the scale on the imagery that defines the trend. It is clear, however, that there is some property of the deformation field that causes the leads to become tangent to that 'line.' Thus, the 'trend' probably forms as the result of the geometry of the pack ice drift pattern and is analogous to a shear line in a fluid flow field that separates moving from stationary material. In fact, when one of the 'trends' is established, the ice to the south is generally stable with no openings visible at the scale of the AVHRR imagery. In such cases, the trend may represent the offshore boundary of a 'stable extension' of the landfast ice.

About 10 sequences of this type were observed during the years of observation. Questions about the origin and duration of the pattern arise because it can develop over a period of days, and cloud cover can make identification difficult. However, most examples seem to form as extensions of the leads bounding Barrow Arches, as in the following example.

Figures 4.3.30 through 4.3.38 show the development of a trend line from Point Barrow toward the southwest corner of Banks Island. The images cover the days from January 14-17 and 19-23 of 1998. The process starts with a Barrow Arch bounded on the east by a lead which can be seen through the cloud cover in Figure 4.3.30. The lead can be seen more clearly on the following day (Figure 4.3.31), and the Barrow Arch has extended along the lead. However, the pattern changes over the next two days (Figures 4.3.32 and 4.3.33), and the change in the direction of pack ice drift is shown by the appearance of a new lead with a prominent offset point further east and new wide arcing leads. The image for the 5th day in the sequence is missing, but on the 6th day (Figure 4.3.34) a trend is established, and the remainder of the sequence (Figures 4.3.35 through 4.3.38) shows development and displacement of a series of wide arcs that are approximately tangent to the trend. Note that east of the trend there is no indication of motion of the pack ice, while the Barrow Arch becomes narrower as the pack ice west of the trend displaced southward. Thus, at the scale of the AVHRR imagery, the trend line represents a shear boundary between the moving pack ice and the stationary, stable ice southward toward the coast. In that sense, it is analogous to the boundary of the 'dead zone' in the extrusion model discussed in section 5.2.2. The ice within the dead zone is then a stable extension of the landfast ice.

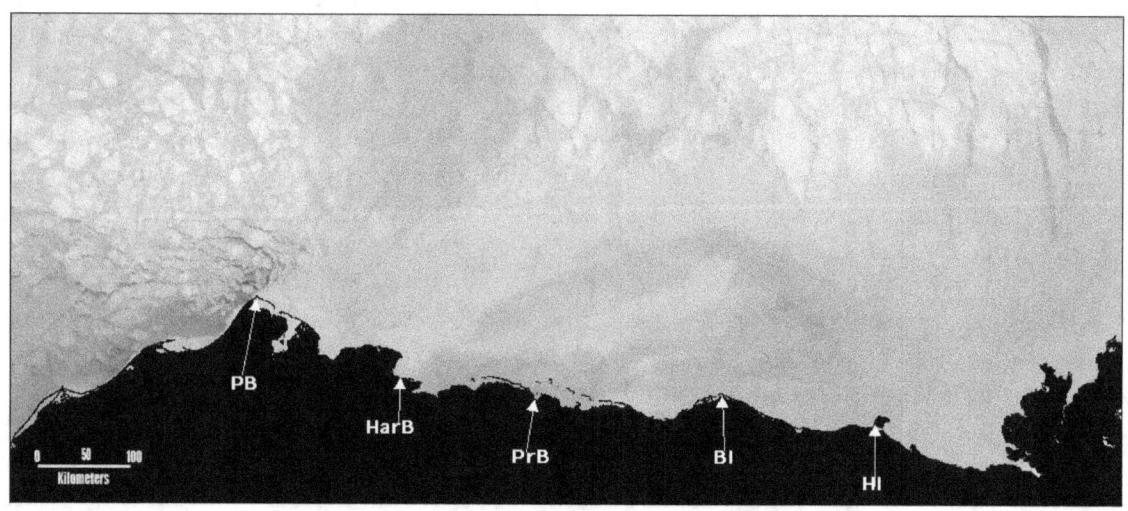

Figure 4.3.30 First AVHRR image of the start of the sequence showing the development of a trend from Point Barrow to southern Banks Island (not shown). The image was acquired on January 14, 1998, and shows a developing Barrow Arch with a lead along its eastern boundary. The lead is just visible through the cloud cover. Symbols are [PB] Point Barrow, [HarB] Harrison Bay, [PrB] Prudhoe Bay, [BI] Barter Island and [HI] Herschel Island.

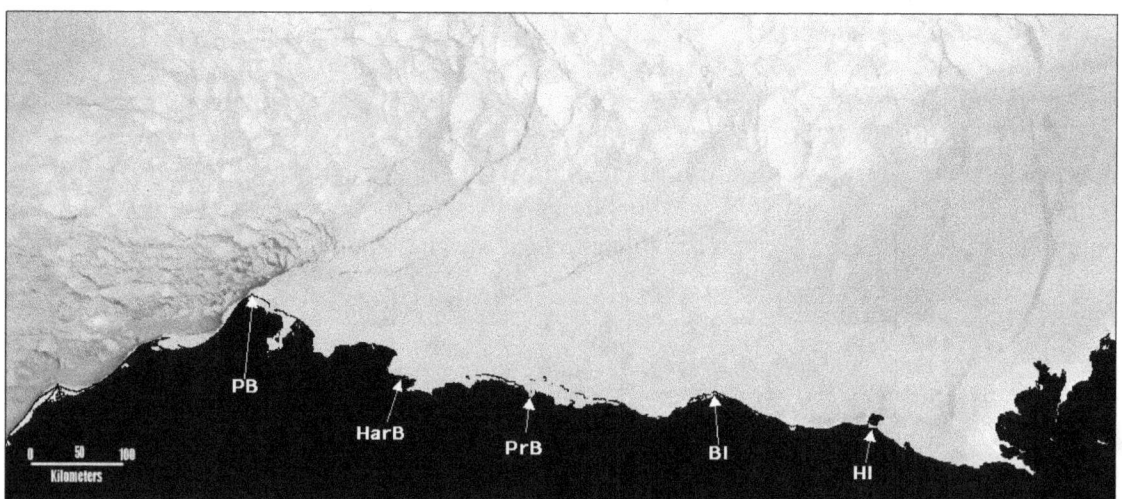

Figure 4.3.31. AVHRR image from the second day of the sequence on January 15, 1998. The Barrow Arch has extended along the bounding lead which is clearer in the absence of cloud cover.

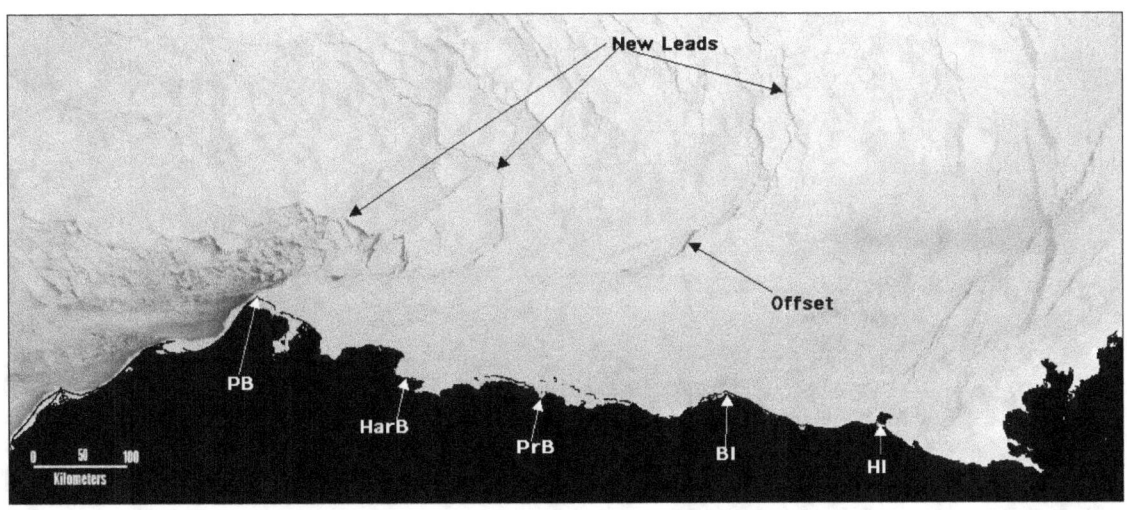

Figure 4.3.32. AVHRR image from the third day of the sequence on January 16, 1998. The Barrow Arch has turned to the east following the change in pack ice drift direction indicated by the new arcing leads and the opening at the offset.

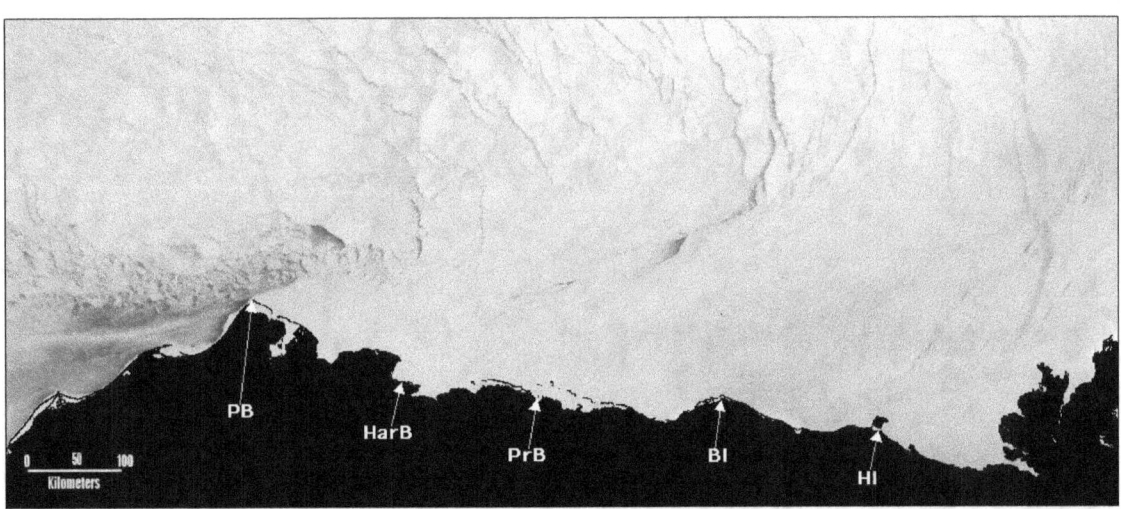

Figure 4.3.33. AVHRR image from the fourth day of the sequence on January 17, 1998 showing that the pattern established on the third day has continued to develop.

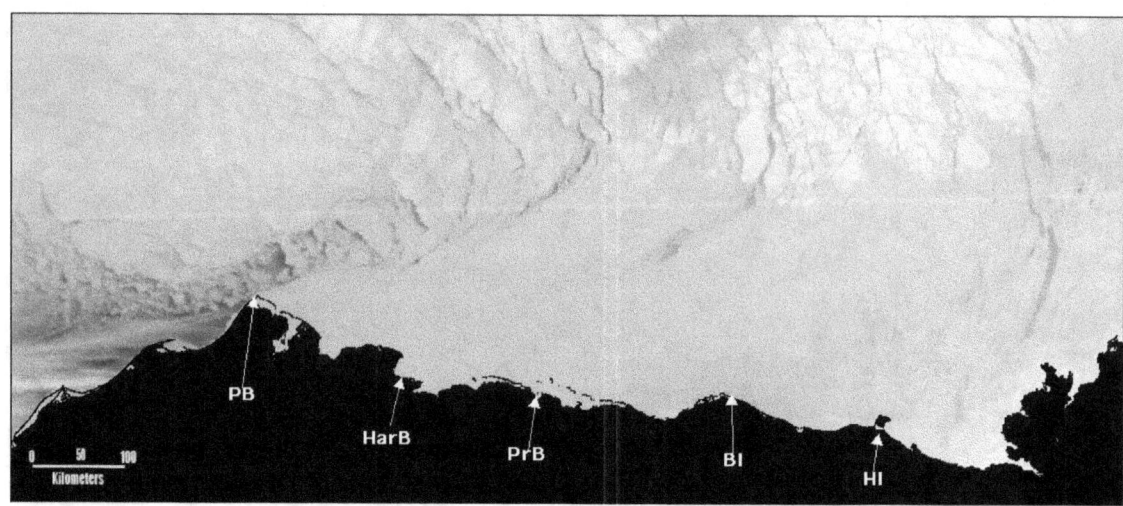

Figure 4.3.34 AVHRR image from the sixth day of the sequence on January 19, 1998. Note that there was no image acquired on the fifth day, January 18, but the image for the sixth day shows that there has been no change in the form of the opening at the offset, and the initial pattern of displacement has been reestablished.

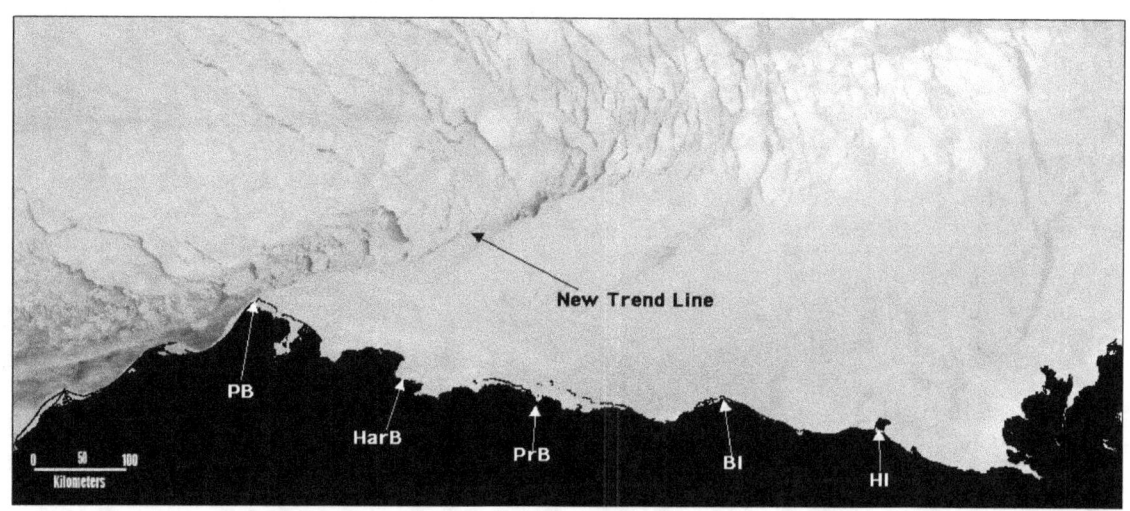

Figure 4.3.35 AVHRR image from the seventh day of the sequence on January 15, 1998. A new trend line has developed, along which the Barrow Arch is extending, and new wide arc leads have appeared that are concave to the southwest. That pattern indicates that the pack ice north of the trend is displacing in that direction. The remaining images in the sequence show the continuation of that process.

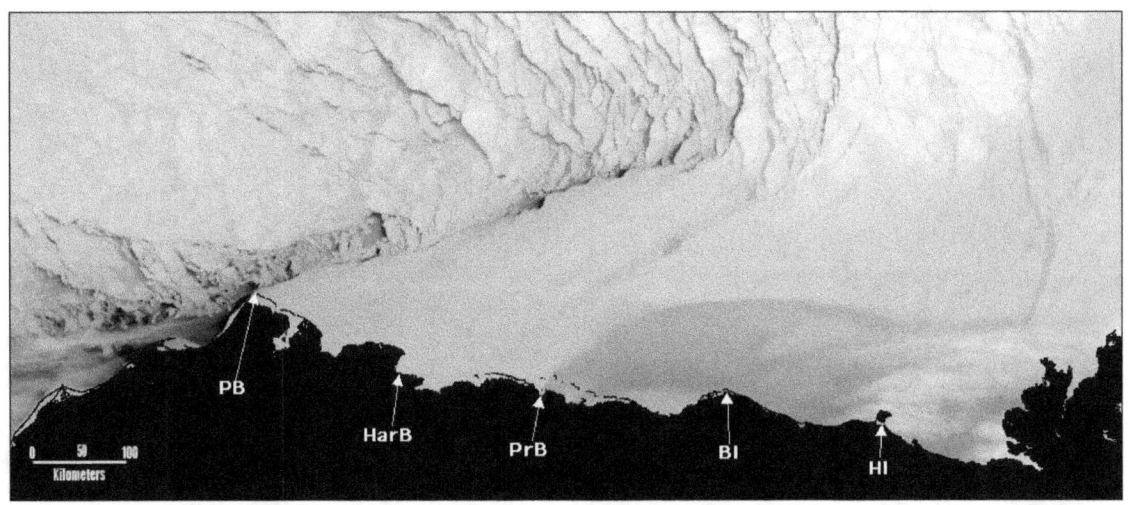

Figure 4.3.36. AVHRR image from the eighth day of the sequence on January 15, 1998

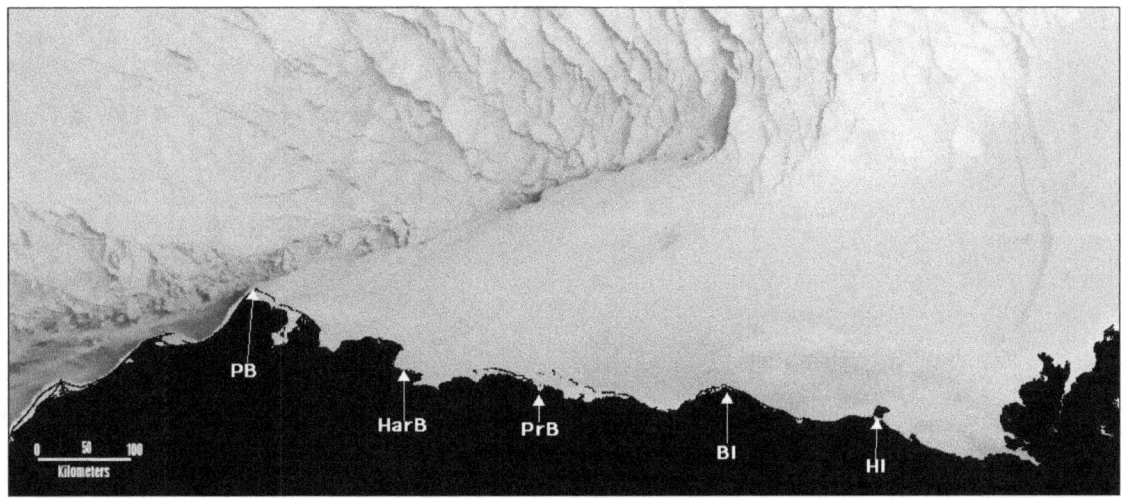

Figure 4.3.37. AVHRR image from the ninth day of the sequence on January 15, 1998

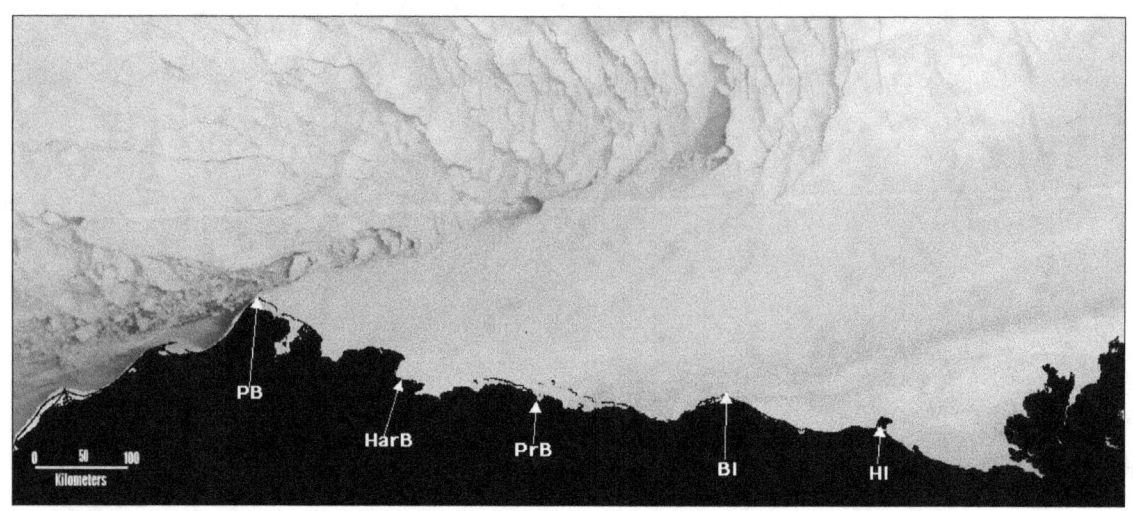

Figure 4.3.38. AVHRR image from the tenth day of the sequence on January 15, 1998

5. Discussion

5.1. Potential analysis errors and biases

The most significant sources and magnitudes of geolocation, detection and classification errors both for landfast ice and leads are described in detail in Section 3.3 and Section 3.2.2. Outside of these, the most important potential source of errors and in particular bias is the limitation of the lead analysis to cloud-free regions and periods. As outlined in previous sections, with limitations in resolution and other problems, AVHRR still remains the most relevant source of data on lead distributions and morphology, at least in the context of studies such as this. Nevertheless, since leads are in significant part driven by atmospheric processes, lack of data on lead morphology and distribution during cloudy periods may result in a bias towards atmospheric conditions favoring cloud-free skies. In the study area, these conditions are associated with a Beaufort Sea high pressure system, with winds predominantly out of the East and Northeast (see also Figure 5.2.2). The penetration of low-pressure systems is associated with winds veering to southerly and westerly sectors. Such weather situations are increasingly common in the summer and fall months (Lynch et al., 2003) and the summer weakening of the Beaufort high pressure system in part explains increasing cloudiness (in turn reducing the number of scenes analyzed in the months of May and June, Figure 3.1.3). In winter, passage of individual storms is typically followed by clearer weather. Since leads have an average lifetime that extends over several days, analysis of the first cloud-free scene available after such periods still contains information about the morphology and size of leads that developed. Furthermore, direct inspection of daily scenes and qualitative comparisons between highly obscured lead patterns and cloud-free conditions suggests that the bias resulting out of this situation is small. A more detailed analysis of this problem would require analysis of SAR (or comparable) data and analysis of the impact of specific weather patterns on lead distributions and cloudiness, which is beyond the scope of this present study.

5.2. Lead patterns

5.2.1. Distribution of leads in the context of large-scale ice motion and deformation: Recurrence of observed patterns

The results of the study clearly show that the basic hypothesis of the recurrence of characteristic patterns and features of the ice cover, including the distribution of leads and landfast ice and their temporal evolution, is valid. Even with the limited number of images available as illustrations for this report, there are enough to show examples of similar patterns in different years, as demonstrated in Section 4.3 of this report. This pattern of recurrence is also apparent in the quantitative data on lead areal fractions and morphology as shown in Figure 4.1.2, Figure 4.1.3 and Table 4.1.1. Sequences also are repeatable in terms of the particular lead patterns and the order in which they form. That fact demonstrates that the weather and oceanographic conditions, and the physical boundary conditions imposed by the geometry of the pack ice/fast ice boundary, are also repeated over the years. However, the rate at which the sequences progress through their patterns appears to be variable, probably reflecting the rate at which weather systems cross the area. Such differences in propagation of weather patterns along with potential changes in the atmospheric circulation regime help explain interannual variability in the seasonal cycle of lead fraction (Figure 4.1.1), lead density (Figure 4.1.5) and other size parameters (Table 4.1.1). This dependence on weather patterns greatly complicates the identification of longer-term variability or potential trends and is discussed in more detail in Section 5.2.4 below.

As in any natural system, variations away from the ideal are expected to occur. An obvious example is the case in which large multiyear floes dominate the near-shore ice pack as they did during the winter of 1993/94 (see Section 4.2 above). In that year, the general drift pattern of the southern Beaufort Sea pack ice was typical, but the lead patterns along the north coast of Alaska did not reflect that. This was mostly due to the generation of open leads around these large floes that moved differentially to the rest of the pack, and thus there were few occasions when new leads needed to form in order for the pack ice to accommodate additional deformation. An example of the effect of the large floes is shown in Figure 5.2.1a. The floe shown was tracked until April when it could no longer be identified on the imagery, and always had leads such as those shown here associated with it. Note that the winter of 1993-94 was the only year in which large multiyear floes with these effects were observed during this study.

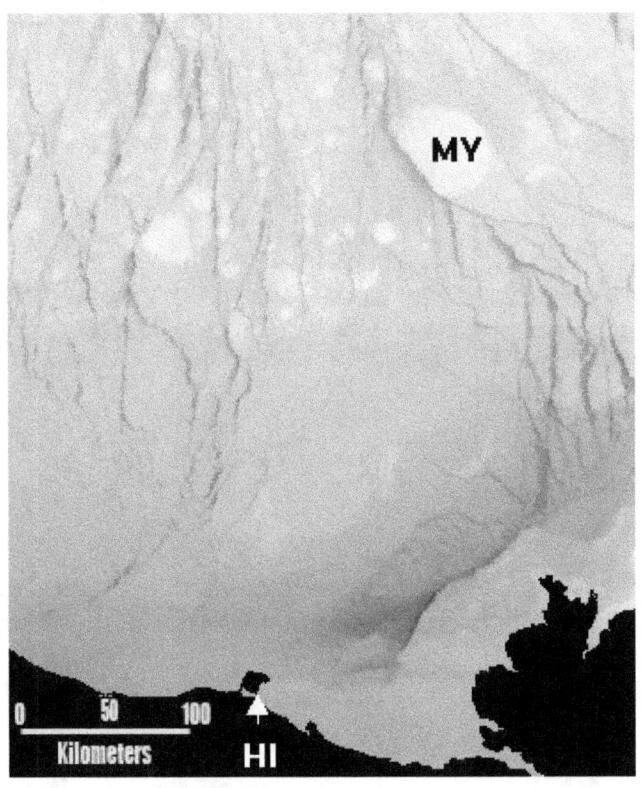

Figure 5.2.1a. AVHRR image from December 23, 1993 showing a large multiyear floe [MY] north of Mackenzie Bay and Herschel Island [HI] with an associated lead system reaching to the coast.

The recurrence of the patterns discussed here warrants a closer examination of average lead distribution fields. This can be achieved by calculating the recurrence probability of leads at a particular location based on the entire data set of AVHRR scenes (with subregions exhibiting partial or total cloud cover removed from the analysis). The resulting mean monthly patterns for December through June are shown in Figure 5.2.1b. Several of the patterns described in more detail in Section 4.3 are apparent in these recurrence maps, with a distinct contrast between the winter/early spring regime prevailing throughout December-March and parts of April and the late spring/early summer regime dominant in May and June. Below, we will discuss the following most prominent and important of these patterns in more detail: (i) Flaw leads and coastal polynyas along the eastern Chukchi Sea coast, off the Mackenzie Delta and off Herschel and (to a lesser extent) Barter Island, (ii) arced leads forming off stable extensions in the central Beaufort Sea, (iii) lead patterns associated with ice grounded on Hanna Shoal, and (iv) the transition between winter/early-spring and late-spring/summer regimes throughout the study area.

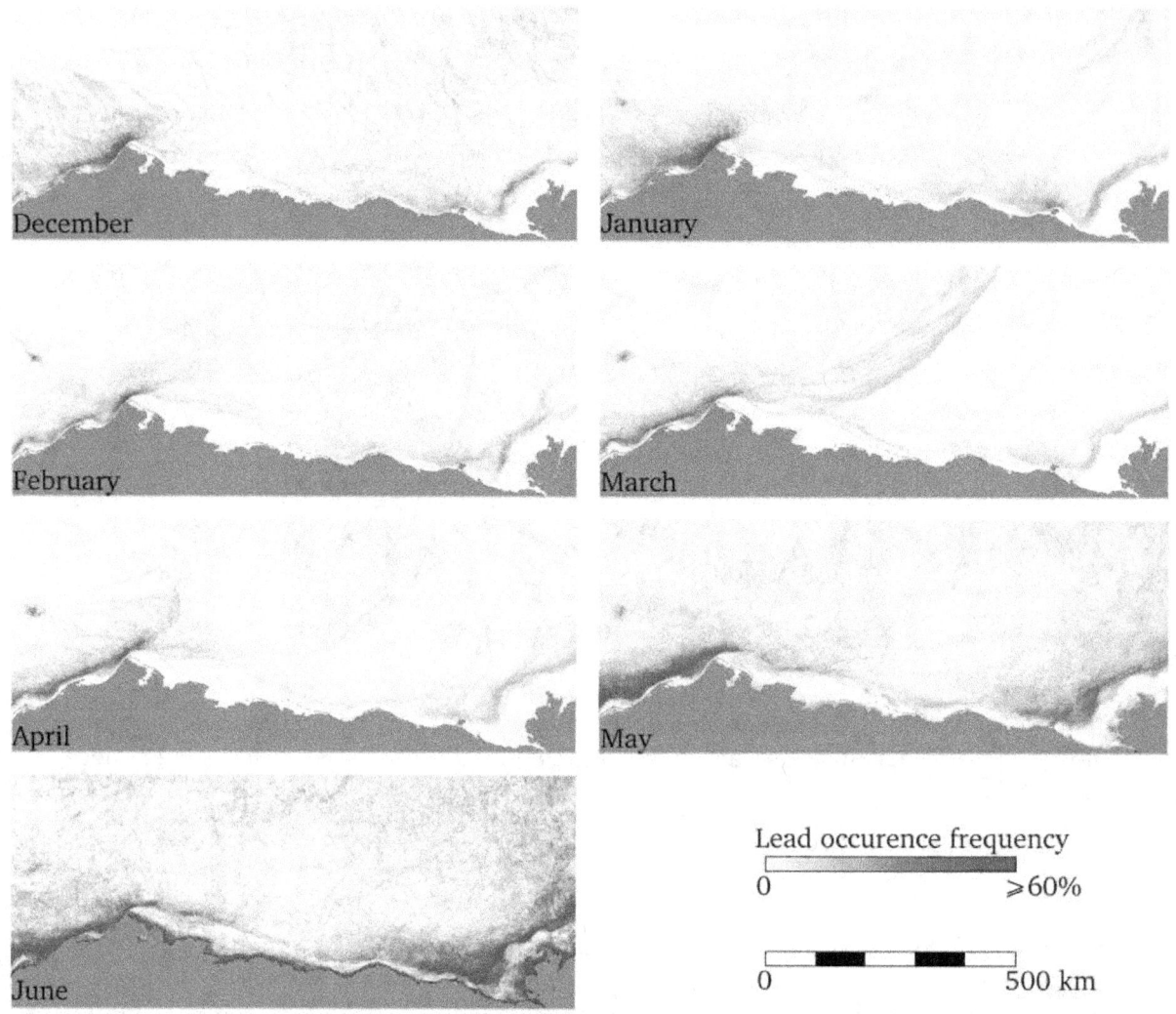

Figure 5.2.1b. Monthly recurrence probability of leads derived from all images for each month during the time period 1993-2004 for each grid cell. Subregions with partial or complete cloud cover have been excluded from the analysis. The significance of different patterns evident in the data is discussed in detail in the text.

(i) Flaw leads and coastal polynyas

The most prominent lead patterns apparent in the recurrence maps for all months are systems of leads or polynyas forming off the eastern Chukchi Sea coast, the Mackenzie Delta and Herschel (and to a lesser extent) Barter Island (Figure 5.2.1b). The WMO Sea Ice Nomenclature (Organization, 1985) defines polynyas as openings in the ice with a non-linear shape and the polynyas occurring adjacent to the fast ice or coast are referred to as flaw or coastal polynyas. According to WMO Sea Ice Nomenclature, the flaw zone is a narrow zone between pack ice and fast ice "where the pieces of ice are in a chaotic state" as a result of (shear) deformation. Norton and Graves Gaylord's (2004) analysis of ice motion in the Barrow region indicates that the flaw zone, as defined by high, shore-parallel ice velocities, can extend several tens of kilometers offshore between March and June. As indicated in Figure 5.2.1b, the extent of the flaw zone as defined by interannual monthly lead recurrence larger than approximately 20 % does in fact range between about 10 km and more than 100 km when it appears at it's widest. Note, however, that the seasonal variation in flaw zone extent based on lead distribution also depends on ice growth rates, as these define the transition between thin lead ice and thicker pack ice. The location of these flaw and coastal leads and polynyas is an indication of their mode of formation, as they a show a clear pattern of preferential occurrence downdrift of promontories or lee coasts as typical of so-called "latent heat" polynyas generated by offshore winds (Gordon and Comiso, 1988). The prevailing winds in the study area are out of ENE at Barrow and E at Barter Island. With a typical turning angle of 20 to 30° to the right of the local wind (Hibler, 1986; Kottmeier et al., 1992), this explains the recurrence patterns of flaw leads or polynyas as well as the absence of such openings in much of the western and central Beaufort Sea. These drift patterns also play an important role in the generation of shear ridges that are of importance in stabilizing the landfast ice edge in the Beaufort Sea (see Sections 4.2 and 5.2).

The winter lead recurrence patterns also demonstrate the impact of large-scale ice-pack/shore interactions. In the Chukchi Sea prevailing ice drift patterns and the presence of thinner ice during the early stages of winter allow for larger mobility of the pack. In contrast, off the Mackenzie Shelf, ice movement is significantly constricted by the orientation of the coastline, in combination with the presence of thicker multiyear ice (Tucker et al., 2001). Correspondingly, the Chukchi flaw zone projects much further out from the coast than the Mackenzie Shelf flaw zone, at least during early winter. At Point Barrow, radiating lead patterns are apparent in some months, reflective of both openings forming to accommodate large-scale strain in the ice pack and in response to changes in wind direction (Figure 5.2.2).

The extent of the flaw zone or the flaw-lead/polynya zone is of significance in the context of potential oil-spill clean-up efforts. The high ice velocities, complex ice motion patterns, and mix of open water, thin ice and highly fragmented ice floes as a result of shear between landfast ice and ice pack result in a challenging environment in the context of oil-spill mitigation. It is notable, however, that in the central portions of the Beaufort Sea, the orientation of the coast with respect to the prevailing wind patterns (Figure 5.2.2) results in very small lead recurrence probabilities and instead favors the formation of shear ridges as described in Section 4.4.

In June, the onset of ice melt has generated larger amounts of open water throughout the ice pack, and part of the landfast ice is starting to retreat (see Section 4.2), both of which are reflected in the recurrence maps. At the same time, the maps also clearly indicate the presence of open water alongshore inside of the landfast ice belt. This reflects both flooding of landfast and in particular bottomfast ice in May (where flooding off the Colville and Mackenzie Rivers is particularly prominent; (Dean et al., 1994; Searcy et al., 1996; Walker, 1973)), as well as actual melt-through and decay of landfast ice in the nearshore regions in late June.

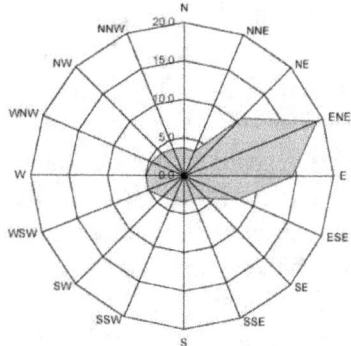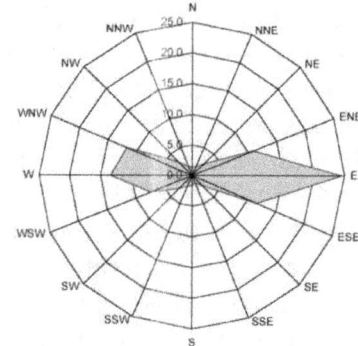

Figure 5.2.2. Frequency distribution of wind directions at Barrow (left) and Barter Island (right) in a wind rose diagram. Plots are based on National Weather Service Observations averaged over 1971-2000 (Barrow) and 1971-1988 (Barter Island) and compiled by the Alaska Climate Research Center (climate.gi.alaska.edu).

(ii) Arced lead patterns

Lead recurrence probability maps for March and April show a distinct pattern of curved or arced leads in the western and west central Beaufort Sea. Some of these leads, in particular shorter ones, are emanating from Point Barrow and associated with accommodation of ice motion and deformation in the vicinity of the Barrow promontory. Some of these leads join with openings emanating from the Hanna Shoal floeberg (see below), making the eastern Chukchi Sea and, in particular, the stretch of coast between Peard Bay and Point Barrow the most active in the entire study region.

The large-scale arcuate leads evident in the monthly recurrence maps for March are dominated by a persistence of these features in March of 2000, accounting for half of all March (16 total) scenes exhibiting this pattern in 7 out of the 11 ice years studied. The leads appear to originate from a shoal off Harrison Bay and trend across the Beaufort Sea towards the Canadian archipelago. Their significance derives from the fact that these are the largest-scale recurring lead patterns studied in the area. They separate a region of stagnant ice that develops in the southeastern corner of the Beaufort Sea from the more mobile pack ice to the West. As described in more detail in Section 4.2 and Section 5.2, motion in the stagnant ice can be diminished to below the detection threshold (based on our analysis of SAR data at sub-kilometer resolution on 10-day scales), with divergence and shear along the edge of this zone that extends from Point Barrow over to Banks Island or the Canadian archipelago, resulting in the lead patterns shown in Figure 5.2.1b for March. As the stagnant ice zone starts to become active again, the lead systems migrate towards the East, on occasion rotating from a NNE-SSW trend into a NE-SW trend (see Figure 5.2.1b). While the pattern is most prominent in 2000 when it gave rise to the longest stable-extension period of more than 44 days observed between 1996 and 2004, such stagnant ice motion is a defining feature of the eastern portions of our study area (see also Section 5.2.2).

It is fortuitous that for the ice season 1999/2000 Radarsat SAR scenes processed with the Radarsat Geophysical Processor System (Kwok, 1998) are available to shed further light on these types of leads and associated ice motion. Figure 5.2.3 shows shear and the magnitude of ice motion as derived from sequences of SAR data for the second week in March of 2000. It is evident that the lead patterns visible in the AVHRR data (Figure 5.2.1b, see also specific examples in Section 4.3) correspond to the zone of localized shear that defines the boundary between stagnant ice in the southeastern Beaufort Sea and the mobile ice pack. The average sea level atmospheric pressure field indicates that at least during this time period, ice motion was driven by a high-pressure system extending throughout much of the Arctic basin (Figure 5.2.3).

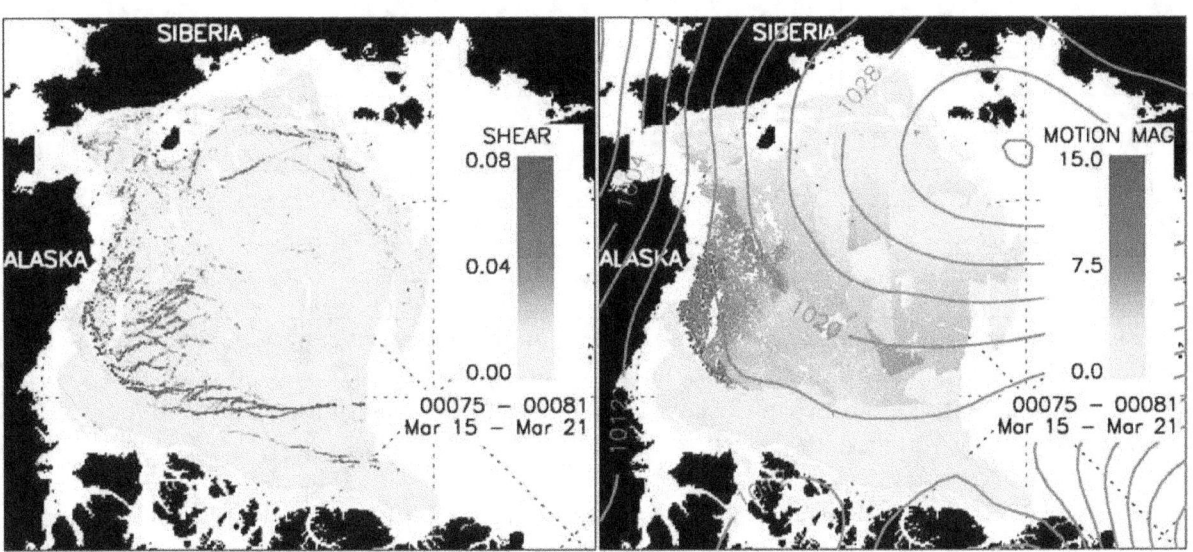

Figure 5.2.3. Shear (left) and the magnitude of ice velocity (right) for the week of March 15 to 21, 2000 as derived from the Radarsat Geophysical Processor System (RGPS; data courtesy of Ron Kwok, Jet Propulsion Laboratory). The sea level atmospheric pressure field is superimposed on the image at right.

(iii) Hanna Shoal and the E-W boundary of the Barrow Arch

The maps of lead recurrence in Figure 5.2.1b. show the effect of the mass of grounded ice that forms annually on Hanna Shoal at approximately 72°N, 162°W. The shallowest bathymetric contour at that location is about 25 m deep over an area with longest dimension of about 15 km. The grounded ice mass itself and its annual evolution have been described by Stringer and Barrett (1975) and Barrett and Stringer (1978) who gave it the unofficial name 'Katie's Floeberg.'

The simple answer to the question of why there is grounded ice on Hanna Shoal is that, at some time in the early winter, a deep-keeled floe or ridge drifts over the shoal where it contacts the

103

bottom and stops. More ice is then added by collisions with the moving pack ice, and that process continues through the winter. If this is correct, then it might be assumed that the time that the ice first grounds would reflect whether the ice cover is typical of a 'heavy' or 'light' ice year. To test this, the dates at which grounded ice could be detected on AVHRR imagery over the duration of this project were determined and the results are shown in Table 5.2.1. The dates agree in general with the lead occurrences shown in Figure 5.2.1b so there are significant increases in the probability of encountering leads in this region (see also Table 5.3.1) after the grounded ice is in place.

Table 5.2.1. Dates of first certain observation of grounded ice on Hanna Shoal

ICE YEAR	FIRST POSITIVE	COMMENTS*
93-94	1/19	
94-95	11/25	Possible 11/17
95-96	1/13	
96-97	1/12	Possible 1/9
97-98	1/9	
98-99	1/26	Possible 1/20; Absent 1/14
99-00	12/23	
00-01	1/28	Cloudy from 1/13
01-02	1/30	
02-03	12/27	Absent 1/19
03-04	1/24	Possible 1/15

* 'Possible' indicates that ice may have been present on that date, but cannot be identified with certainty. 'Absent' is the last day when it could be determined that there was no grounded ice on the shoal; subsequently, cloud cover obscured the area until the date of the first positive identification of the grounded ice.

Observations from AVHRR imagery show that, before the grounded ice is present, there is often an area of open water over Hanna Shoal, even when the Chukchi Sea pack ice edge is far south of that latitude. This appears to be part of a zone of leads that crosses the area in a roughly linear pattern along approximately 72°N latitude and extends westward to about 162°30' W, just outside the study area. The zone sometimes has the appearance of a diverging pack ice edge, where slowly south-drifting Beaufort Sea pack ice breaks into floes that rapidly drift off into the Chukchi Sea. This effect is visible to some degree through the entire winter, and requires that there be space available for the floes to move into. In early winter, the Chukchi Sea closes over later than the Beaufort Sea, while later in the year, the Chukchi Sea pack ice frequently drifts off the Alaska coast shore. Either of these conditions can provide the required space.

The grounded ice itself usually is not visible on the AVHRR imagery because it blends into the surrounding ice cover. However, after grounding has occurred the ice on the shoal acts as a fixed point in the otherwise drifting pack ice. Prominent leads often originate or terminate against the grounded ice, and when leads are absent, the moving pack can leave an opening on the downstream side of the grounded ice providing an excellent indicator of the direction and magnitude of pack ice motion. In some cases the trail of young ice that fills the opening left by the moving pack is visible for several days.

The grounded ice thus influences the deformation of the pack ice by generating leads and, increasing the amount of open water between Hanna Shoal and the Alaska coast. Examples are shown in Figures 5.2.4, 5.2.5 and 5.2.6.

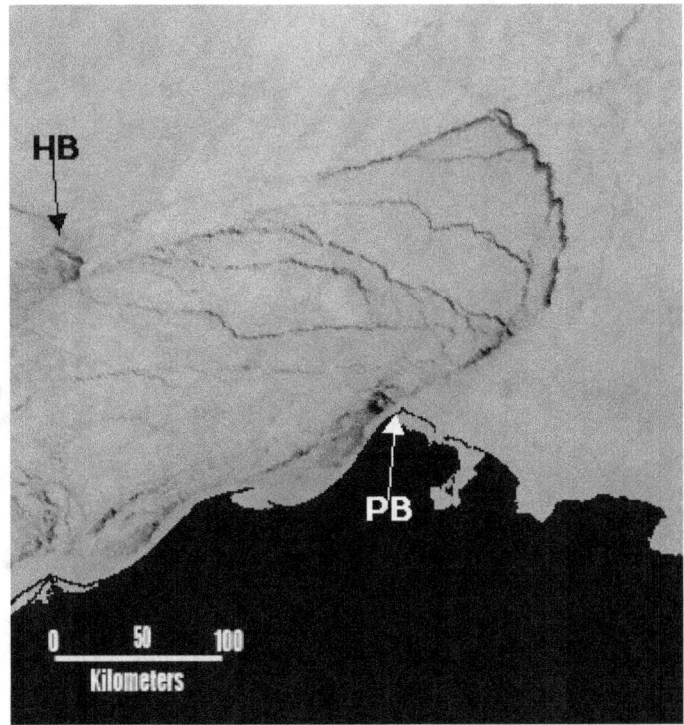

Figure 5.2.4 Leads converging to grounded ice on Hanna Shoal [HB] in late winter. [PB] is Point Barrow shown in an AVHRR image acquired on April 8, 1994. . The dark spot at Hanna Shoal is open water or thin ice on the downdrift side of the grounded ice.

In June, the general opening of the ice pack after the onset of melt has rendered the amount of leads generated by the feature nearly indistinguishable from openings in the remainder of the pack.

It is of interest that, despite its obvious influence, the grounded ice on Hanna Shoal has never been included in models of pack ice drift and deformation. In that context, it might be useful to assemble a catalogue of typical lead patterns that involve this feature as an aid to those modeling deformation patterns in the area.

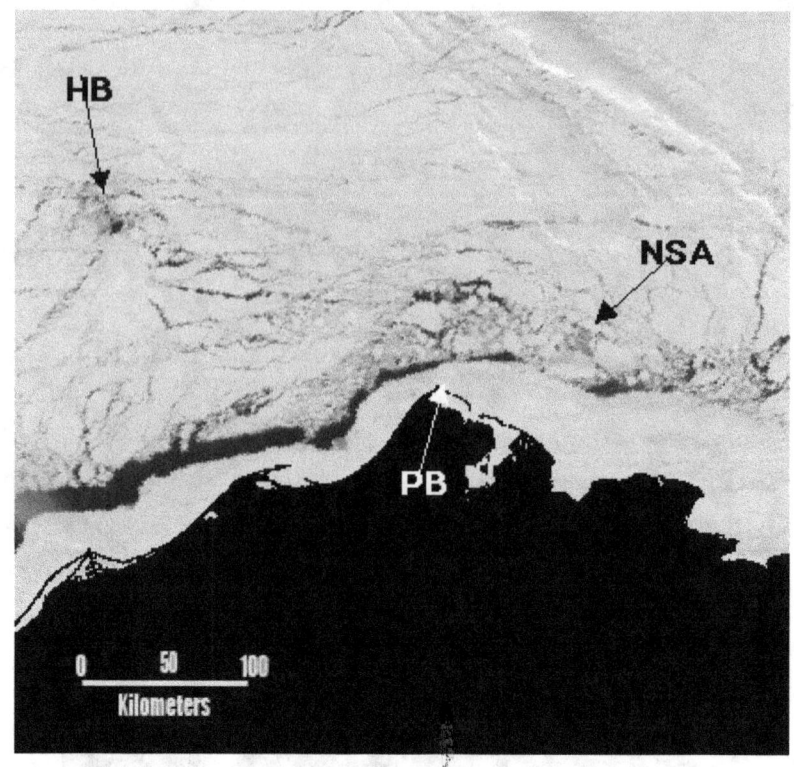

Figure 5.2.5 AVHRR image acquired on May 4, 1977 showing broken floes around the grounded ice on Hanna Shoal [HB] in late winter. [PB] is Point Barrow. The zone of broken floes north of the landfast ice [NSA] is a short North Slope Arch.

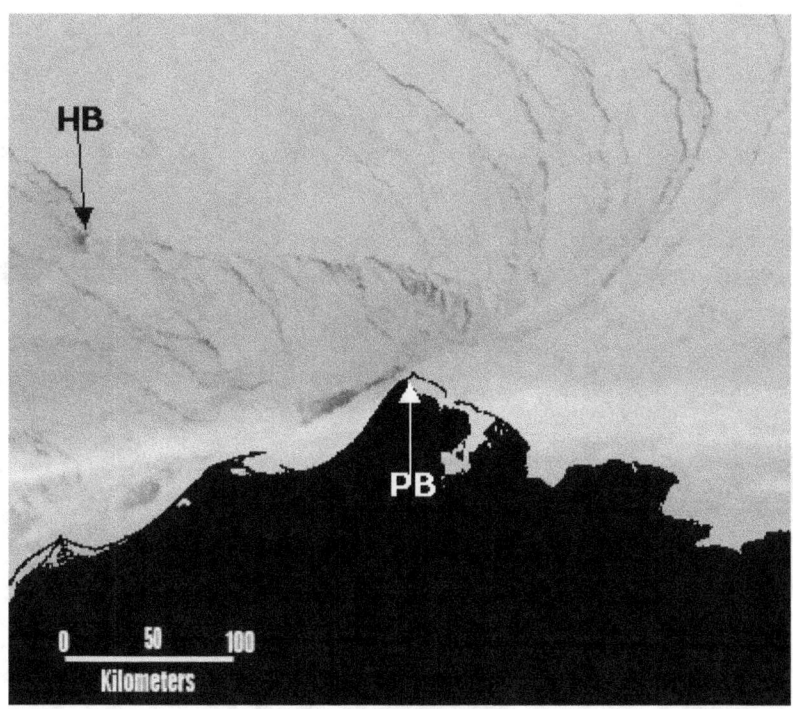

Figure 5.2.6 AVHRR image acquired on February 19, 2000 showing an arcing lead system from near Point Barrow [PB] to the grounded ice on Hanna Shoal [HB]. This is another example of the influence of the grounded ice on the lead pattern in the area of Hanna Shoal.

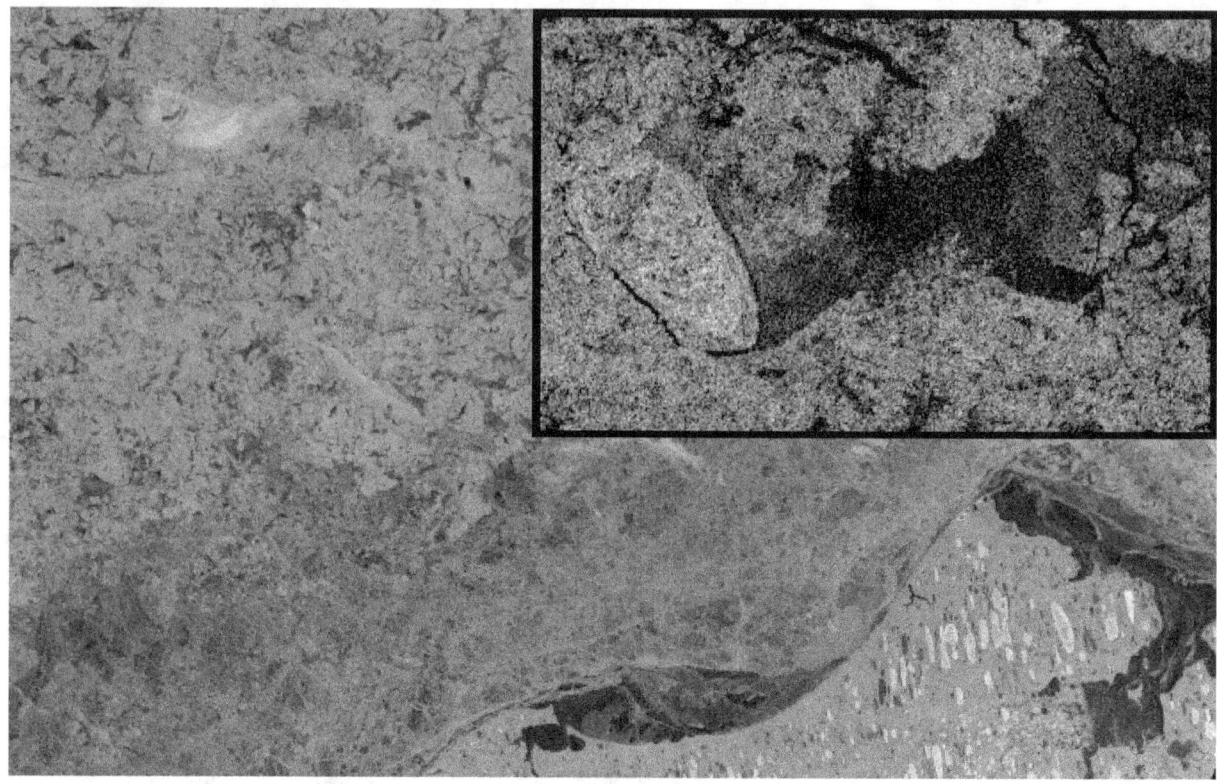

Figure 5.2.7. Radarsat SAR scene (© Canadian Space Agency) showing the location of grounded ice over Hanna Shoal in relation to the eastern Chukchi Sea coastline on March 31, 1997 (North is up). Note the high concentration of deformed ice downstream of the feature. The insert shows the grounded, heavily ridged ice mass on April 24, 1997 with leads delineating part of the feature and thin ice formed as a result of ice drift past the obstacle towards the ENE (size of the feature is approximately 15 km in length).

(iv) Winter-spring ice transition

The lead recurrence probability maps also illustrate the transition between the winter lead regime, characterized by clearly delineated, large-scale lead systems (the March map illustrating the most prominent patterns, Figure 5.2.1b), and the spring ice regime, when the ice pack disintegrates into individual, small-scale floes with open water and new ice mostly distributed in irregular patches (the May map illustrating this pattern well, Figure 5.2.1b). The increase in lead number density indicative of the transition from the winter into the spring ice regime typically occurs some time in April (see Section 4.1.2) and the April lead recurrence probability maps support this finding, with linear lead patterns giving way to a more homogeneous distribution of small-scale lead patterns. The significance of the transition is discussed in more detail in Section 5.2.5 below.

5.2.2. Distribution of leads in the context of large-scale ice motion and deformation: A Beaufort Sea Extrusion Model

There are similarities between the pattern of pack ice drift across the southern Beaufort Sea and southwesterly past Point Barrow, and the geometry of extrusion as in the die casting of metals. That process is described by slip-line field theory which uses the material assumptions of the theory of plasticity to calculate the geometry of flow lines, shear boundaries and stress trajectories in problems involving the flow of materials in two-dimensional problems (see, for example, Johnson and Kudo, 1962). The eastern Beaufort Sea can be visualized as having 'rigid' boundaries represented on the east by Banks Island and islands further north, and on the south by coast of Alaska as modified by landfast ice. When the Beaufort Sea ice pack is driven southward it is constrained by these boundaries but can move into the Chukchi Sea past Point Barrow. The formation of many of the leads and lead patterns described in section 4.3 are the direct result of the process of moving ice from the Beaufort Sea into the Chukchi Sea by that route.

The most common single lead pattern in the study area is the Barrow Arch which takes several forms. It is analogous to the arch structure that that forms when metal is extruded through a die, and is similar to the arch that accompanies the 'extrusion' of pack ice through Bering Strait (Shapiro and Burns, 1974). In that case, the boundaries of the arch define the area in which pack ice fractures into floes which then drift freely through the strait. Examples of similar patterns in the Point Barrow area are given in Section 4.3. However, the mechanisms of arch formation in the two areas differ because at Bering Strait, an arch can be anchored on both its east and west sides, while a Barrow Arch can only have an anchor on its east side. Still, the geometric similarity suggests that there may be some similarity in origin as well.

A second element in the analogy to extrusion processes is the frequent presence of trends from Point Barrow in azimuths directed between Banks Island and Cape Bathurst. These are analogous to shear boundaries separating westerly-moving pack ice from 'dead' material represented by the landfast ice. Stable extensions are then seen as analogous to the dead material in the extrusion process.

Tangent leads (described in Section 4.3.4) also have an analogy in plasticity as lines of shear discontinuity in a plastic material being compressed between two plates with high friction at the interface. The analogy has been noted by Shapiro et al. (1984) and applied to the initial fracture in an ice-push event in which the landfast ice sheet was initially frozen to the beach.

There are obvious differences between the ideal materials used in the calculations and the real pack ice of the Beaufort Sea. However, the similarity in the geometry of both processes, and the fact that plastic materials have been used in models of sea ice deformation, suggests that the analogy could be useful for modeling deformation in the Beaufort Sea under some conditions.

5.2.3. Lead bathymetry linkages

The recurrence of lead patterns evident in Figure 5.2.1b raises the question as to whether lead distributions are in any way linked to seafloor morphology. From the recurrence maps and the merged bathymetric data sets (Section 3.4), the frequency distribution of leads for different water depth intervals has been derived (Figure 5.2.9). Over deeper water, leads appear to follow no distinct distribution pattern (the March peak is a result of the arcuate lead patterns described in detail in Section 5.2.1). Over shallow water, i.e. at depths less than 30 m, the lead distribution appears to follow the seasonal cycle of the landfast ice (see also Section 4.2), with flaw leads sequentially advancing into deeper water. The peak over shallow water (0-5 m) in May and June is a combination of surface flooding in May and decay of nearshore ice in June (see also Section 5.2.1).

The two modes in the distributions in the 20-30 m and 50-100 m interval reflect the distribution of recurring flaw lead and flaw polynya systems. In the eastern Chukchi Sea, most of these leads and polynyas are located over deeper water, which is in large part due to the steep drop-off in the bathymetry associated with Barrow Canyon (Figure 3.4.2). A similar configuration of the landfast ice edge is found off Herschel Island where the Mackenzie channel has incised into the shelf, but the limited areal extent of this feature renders it less important in the context of Figure 5.2.9. The secondary mode at 20-30 m water depth corresponds mostly to the flaw leads in the central and western Beaufort Sea and in particular the Mackenzie Delta system of flaw leads which occurs over shallower water of the Mackenzie submarine sediment fan (Figure. 3.4.2). While oceanographic processes may also be involved in the recurrence of leads over deeper water along the Chukchi coast, this question cannot be examined in the context of this study.

Independent of the origin of these leads, their water depth distribution is of great significance from the perspective of marine ecology. Thus, the lead systems over deeper water in the eastern Chukchi Sea place constraints on their potential benefit for diving ducks and other benthic feeders. At the same time, the Mackenzie flaw lead system is located in waters shallow enough that the euphotic zone may still extend to the benthos.

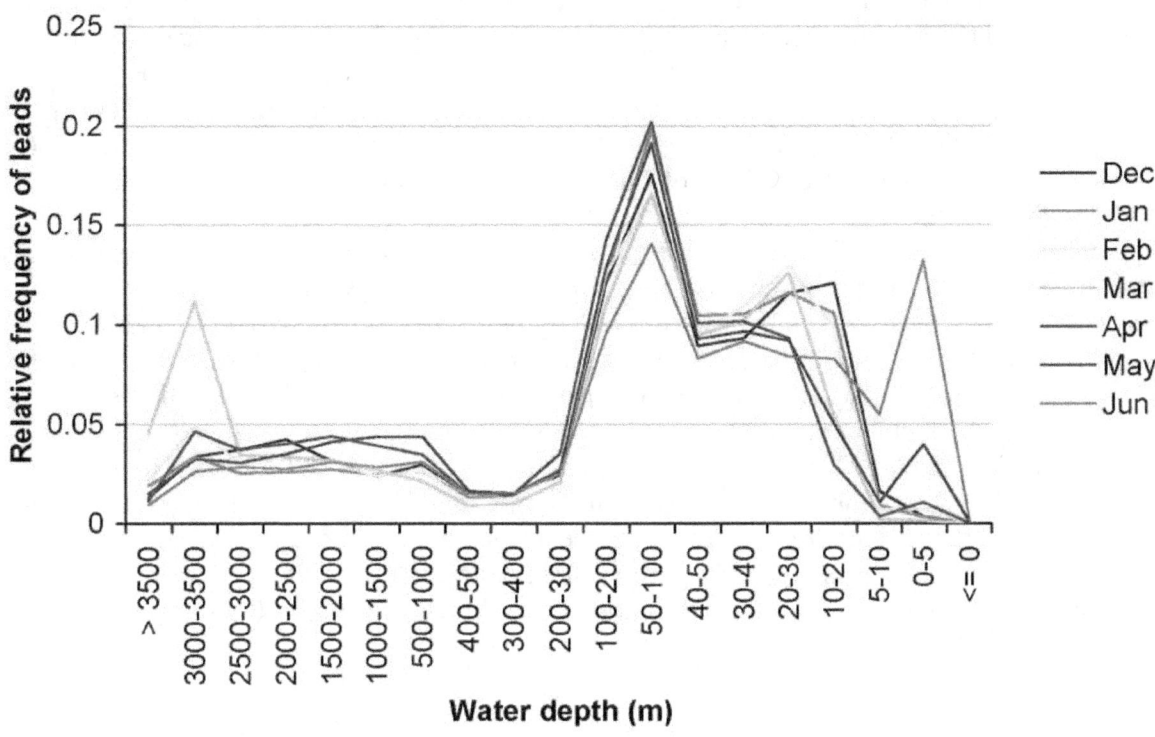

Figure 5.2.8. Frequency distribution of water depth under leads (monthly means for entire study period, 1993-2004).

5.2.4. Long-term variability and change in the context of all available data sets

Lead areal fraction, number density and size exhibit significant variability, both on seasonal and interannual time scales. The seasonal signal is distinct and dominates lead variability in every year examined, as outlined in Section 4.1 and discussed in Section 5.2.5 below. Time series of mean lead areal fraction and number density are shown in Figure 5.2.10 and Figure 5.2.11 averaged over the winter (December-April) and summer months (May-June) for the entire study period. Interannual variability is substantial and no statistically significant trend (at the 90% significance level) is apparent in any of the data. In part, this may be due to the fact that the number of days represented by lead data is small compared to the total length of the study period. Here, we will limit this brief discussion to interannual lead variability in the context of regional air temperature variability, large-scale atmospheric circulation anomalies and changes in the ice thickness regime.

At Barrow, for the time period 1976 to 2004 no significant increase (at the 90% level) has been observed in air temperatures averaged over the December-April and May-June time intervals

(Figure 5.2.12). This lack of a trend in recent decades also holds true for the number of thawing degree days (TDD) and has been discussed in the context of large-scale atmospheric variability (Lynch et al., 2003). The number of freezing degree days (FDD) has been decreasing at the rate of 30 degree-days per year (significant at the 99% level) over the past two decades. However, no significant correlation has been observed between lead area fractions in either season and air temperature or FDD and TDD. The same holds true if we compare only the lead areal fraction of subregion 3 (i.e., the immediate vicinity of Barrow). Thus, it is not clear to what an extent changes in the amount of open water and leads in the area have an effect on surface air temperatures. Moreover, both the open water fraction and air temperature may be independently driven by a variable atmospheric circulation regime, as suggested by a number of studies of large-scale Arctic atmosphere and sea-ice climatology (Deser et al., 2000; Drobot and Maslanik, 2003; Wang and Ikeda, 2000). In our comparatively small study region that is in close vicinity to land (where other factors contribute to climate variability and change) this ambiguity is compounded by the fact that the overall ice thickness appears to have been reduced substantially in the past several decades (Rothrock and Zhang, 2005; Tucker et al., 2001) which in turn is likely to impact surface air temperatures. Examination of the 1993/94 ice season, which was the only one with large concentrations of multiyear ice advected into the coastal region (see Section 5.2.1), indicates that December-April Barrow air temperatures were within the normal range, while May-June temperatures ranked among the lowest three years during the study period.

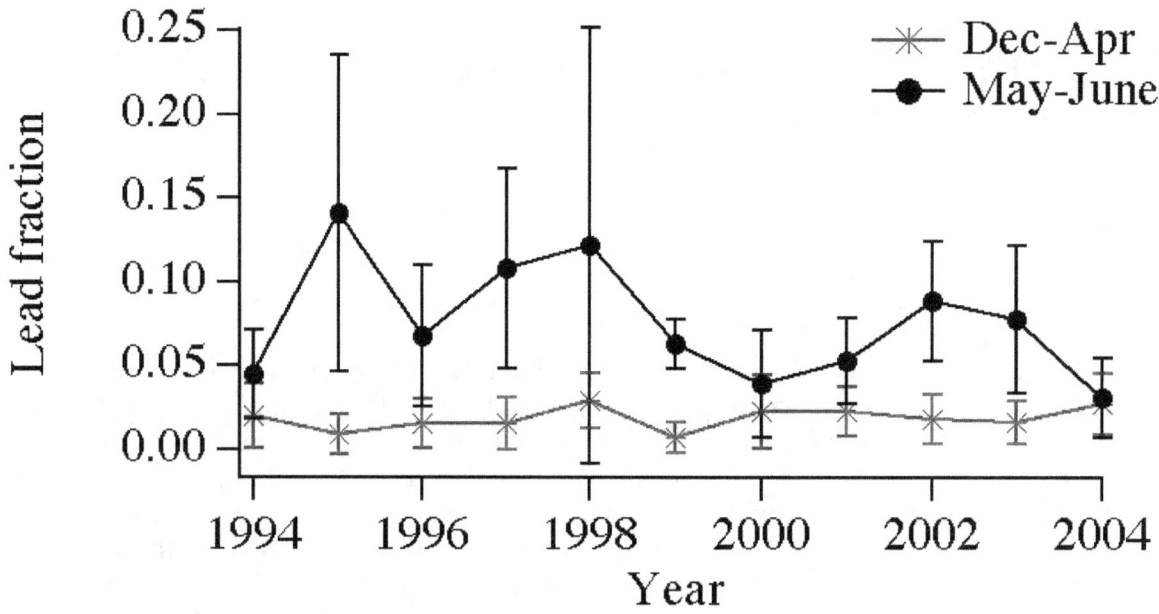

Figure 5.2.9. Mean lead areal fraction averaged over the winter and early spring (December-April) and late spring months (May-June) for the entire study period. (Vertical bars indicate the standard deviation for each year.)

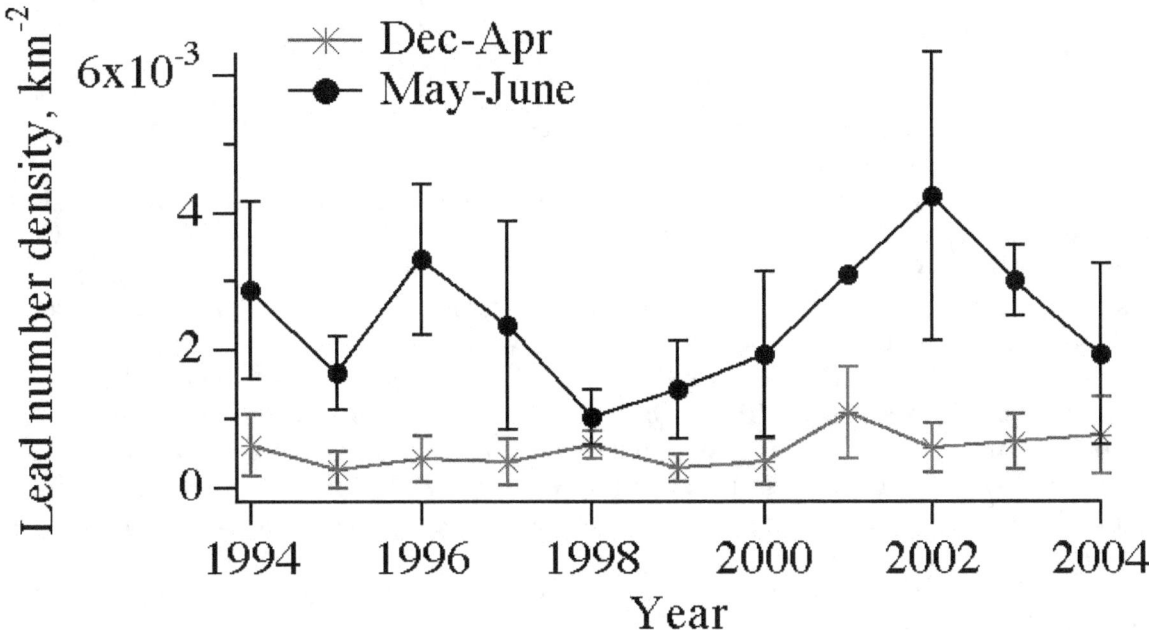

Figure 5.2.10. Mean lead number density averaged over the winter and early spring (December-April) and late spring months (May-June) for the entire study period. (Vertical bars indicate standard deviation for each year.)

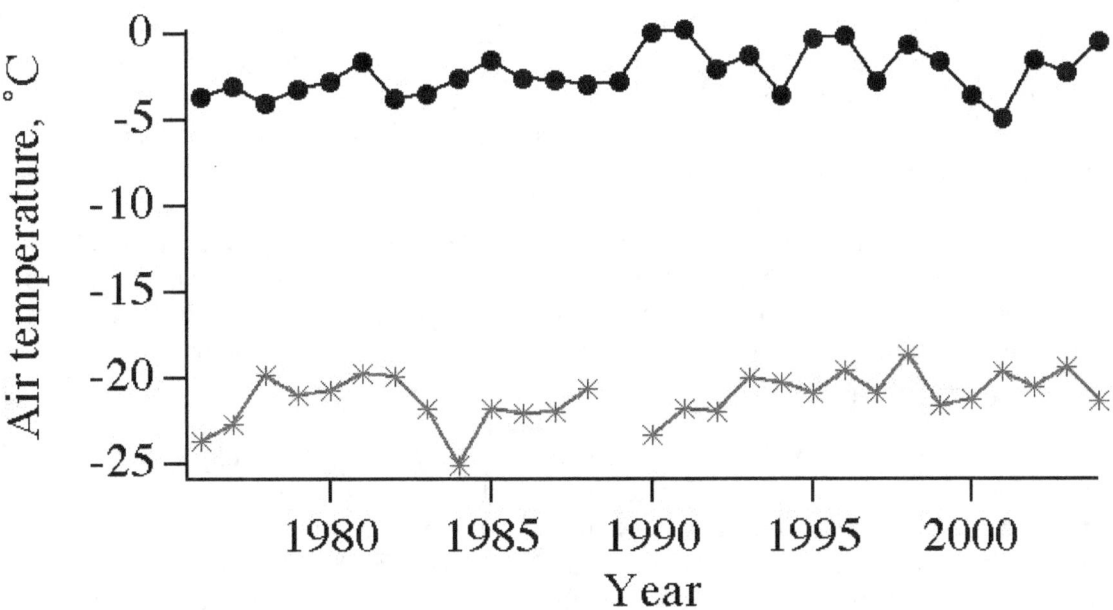

Figure 5.2.11. Mean air temperatures averaged over December-April and May-June as measured at the National Weather Service Station at Barrow for the time period 1976-2004.

To further explore potential linkages between large-scale atmospheric circulation and lead patterns, we have examined the Arctic Oscillation Index (AOI) or Northern Annular Mode (NAM) that describes the prevailing pattern of variability in Arctic atmospheric pressure fields (Thompson and Wallace, 1998). Throughout the 1950s to 1980s high atmospheric pressure was predominant over the Arctic (corresponding to low AOI), resulting in large-scale anticyclonic circulation of sea ice in the Beaufort Gyre that extends over much of the North American Sector of the Arctic Ocean (Proshutinsky and Johnson, 1997), which in turn drove advection of thick multiyear ice into the coastal waters of the Beaufort and to a lesser extent the Chukchi Sea (Rigor et al., 2002; Tucker et al., 2001). With a consistent weakening of sea level pressure throughout the Arctic (Serreze et al., 2000), in the 1990s the AOI reached record high values (Figure 5.2.12), associated with significant surface warming, weakening of the Beaufort Gyre, penetration of low-pressure systems into the Arctic and changes in multiyear ice advection patterns in the study area. In recent years, however, it appears changes in the sea ice regime (and other surface circulation features) are somewhat decoupled from the Arctic Oscillation/Northern Annular Mode (Overland and Wang, 2005).

For the comparatively brief time period under investigation here, we found winter lead fractions to be negatively correlated with the winter AOI, though only marginally so (significant at the 90% level). Lead number densities were also negatively correlated (significant at the 95% level) with the AOI. This finding can likely be explained by a combination of two factors. First, alongshore ice motion in the Beaufort Sea appears to be (inversely) correlated with the AOI (Rigor et al., 2002; Drobot and Maslanik, 2003), such that during low AOI years (relatively high atmospheric pressure over the Beaufort Sea with a well-developed Beaufort Gyre) ice velocities are significantly lower in the study area. Second, during low AOI years, there is a higher likelihood of advection of multiyear ice into the study region (Tucker et al., 2001; Drobot and Maslanik, 2003) leading to generation of open water around multiyear floe aggregates as described in more detail in Section 5.1 and Section 4.3.

For the months of May and June, no significant correlation between lead fractions and number densities and any of the other variables examined here was found. This is to be expected as the Beaufort Gyre as well as the atmospheric circulation patterns driving ice motion typically weaken in summer, with ice decay and production of open water dominated by input of solar radiation and a combination of other factors.

It is possible that much stronger linkages between atmospheric circulation, as expressed in the Arctic Oscillation and Northern Annular Mode, and lead distribution would have become apparent if our time series would have extended further back in time. With limited availability of digital data prior to that point, we have examined hardcopies of AVHRR imagery archived at the Geophysical Institute going back to the 1970s. Qualitative analysis of this imagery indicates that the same types of lead patterns and sequences described in detail in Section 4.3 were present throughout this period and suggest little change between high AOI years in the 1970s and 1980s and conditions in the 1990s, at least based on qualitative analysis.

Quantitative data on lead distributions that cover at least part of the study region is available for 1989, with a winter AOI of 2.60, from Lindsay and Rothrock's (1995) study. While our lead detection approach corresponds to that of Lindsay and Rothrock, and yields comparable results for comparable detection thresholds, their analysis groups data from a range of different regions and focuses mostly on lead morphology and distribution. As apparent from Figure 4.1.6, our lead densities and lead sizes are somewhat below those found by Lindsay and Rothrock, but with differences in the study area extent and methodology of lead size measurements, it is not possible to assign these differences to large-scale circulation changes.

The same holds true when comparing our data with those of a study by Miles and Barry (1998) of lead distributions in the western Arctic between 1979 and 1985. Miles and Barry's analysis is based on tracing of leads on the archived AVHRR hardcopy transparencies. This greatly complicates determination of open water fractions and other size parameters and hence the authors limited their analysis to the number, length and orientation of the linear traces of large lead systems. Without comparative analysis of a subset of these scenes applying our and their approach it is not possible to arrive at any quantitative conclusions or comparisons. However, the large-scale patterns described here appear to correspond well with the findings of Miles and Barry for their somewhat larger study area.

A further potential link between large-scale atmospheric circulation and lead patterns is through the establishment of stable extensions throughout much of the central and eastern Beaufort Sea, as detailed in Section 4.2 and Section 5.2.1. Thus, we note that the year with the most extensive stable-extension episode, well over a month in duration and extending well beyond the study area in March/April 2000, is also the year with the highest AO index between 1993 and 2004. Such episodes may be brought about by a weakened Beaufort Gyre and reduced surface wind forcing, resulting in significantly lower alongshore ice velocities during high-AOI years (Rigor et al., 2002; Drobot and Maslanik, 2003). This interpretation is supported by the fact that in years such as 2000, with a pan-Arctic sea level pressure field and circulation regime representative of the high-AOI, cyclonic circulation regime, stagnation of ice motion is much more widespread and affects the entire "dead space" southeast of a line linking Point Barrow and Northern Greenland (see detailed discussion in Section 4.3, Section 5.2.1 and Figure 5.2.3). Similar conditions prevailed in the winter of 1999 with comparable occurrences of stable extensions in landfast ice extent and the lowest areal lead fractions observed in December-April during the entire study period. At present, however, it is unclear what exactly controls such stable-extension/stagnation episodes, since they have been observed in other, low-AOI years as well.

115

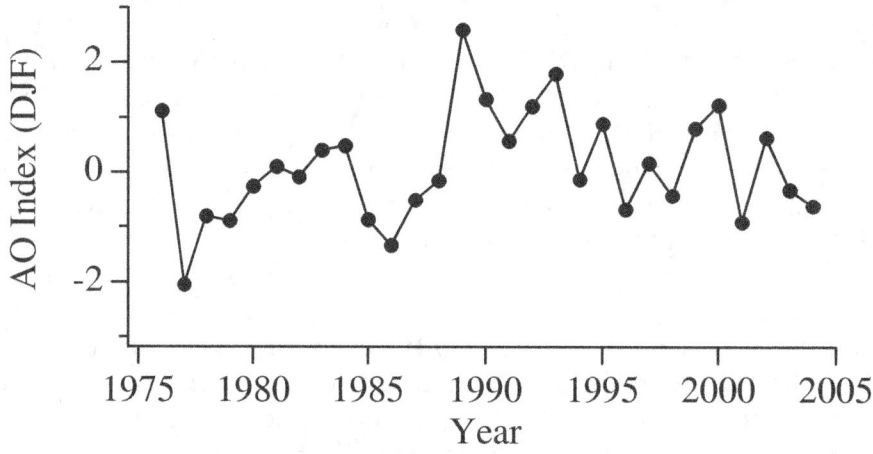

Figure 5.2.12. Time series of the winter Arctic Oscillation Index (DJF) for the time period 1976 to 2004 (data from NOAA's Bering Sea Climate website, www.beringclimate.noaa.gov).

5.2.5. The winter-spring/lead-floe transition

One of the strongest signals in the seasonal cycle is the substantial increase in lead number density in May and June, here termed winter-spring ice transition. It is the result of the increase in the number of isometric (rather than linear) leads appearing throughout the ice pack (Section 4.1.2, Figure 4.1.5). However, the increase is not the result of fracture of the pack ice. Instead it reflects the deterioration of the pack ice into discrete floes so that it can no longer support the propagation of long fractures.

The transition from continuous pack ice with leads that result from fracture, to an aggregate of smaller floes separated by open water or thin ice is important in the context of sea ice geophysics, marine ecology, and operations, particularly with respect to oil-spill clean up.

The term "spring ice" is applied here to pack ice when the season has progressed to the point that little significant refreezing of open water between floes takes place. In that state, at the scale of the AVHRR imagery, the ice has the characteristic appearance of an unconsolidated aggregate. Pack ice with that characteristic tends to develop progressively from south to north in the Chukchi Sea. However, in the Beaufort Sea, 'spring ice' generally forms first off the Mackenzie Delta and further east, and then progresses north and west. Figures 5.2.13a and 13b indicate the progressive expansion of the spring ice regime. Note that despite the fact that spring ice does not support long fractures, arcuate lines of apparent separation can occasionally be seen within the pack. These are often tangent to the coast or the edge of the landfast ice and can be interpreted as analogous to lines of shear in a fluid flow field (Figure 5.2.13c)

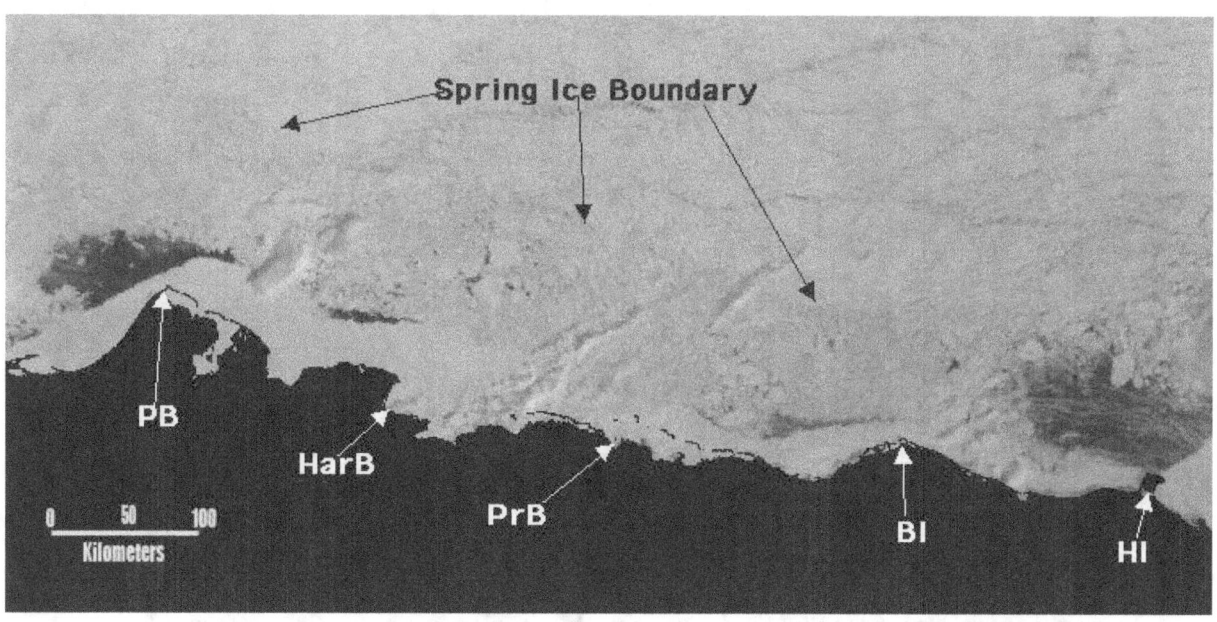

Figure 5.2.13a. 'Spring ice' in the southern Beaufort Sea. The boundary between ice that has deteriorated and pack ice that can still sustain leads is indicated. Other symbols are [HB] Hanna Shoal, [PB] Point Barrow, [PrB] Prudhoe Bay, [BI] Barter Island and [HI] Herschel Island. AVHRR visible band image, May 10, 1995.

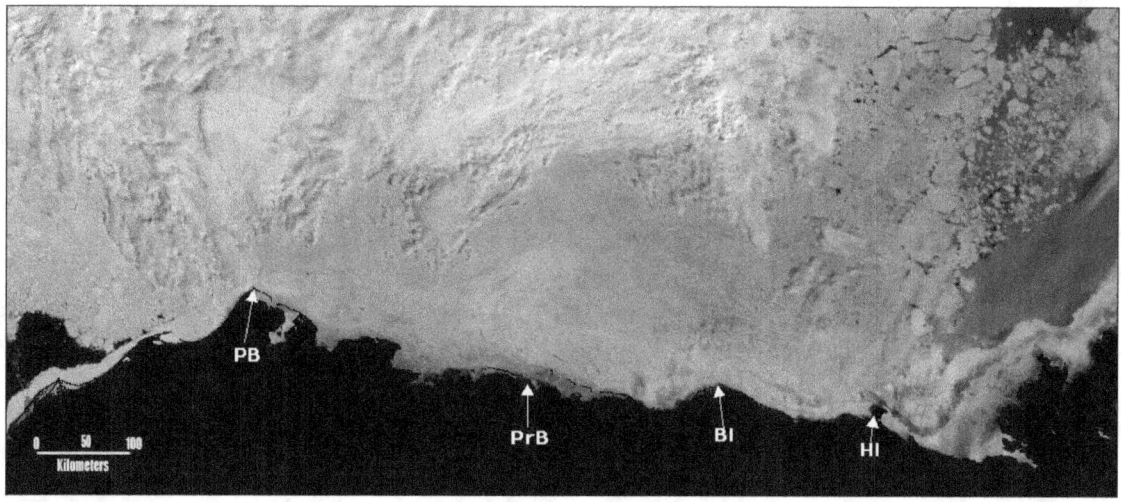

Figure 5.2.13b. AVHRR visible band image of spring ice on June 10, 1995, one month later than the scene in Figure 5.2.13a. The number of large floes is clearly reduced so that, with the exception of the eastern margin, the area occupied by 'Spring Ice' is of uniform texture on the over the entire image. Symbols are the same as in Figure 5.2.13a.

117

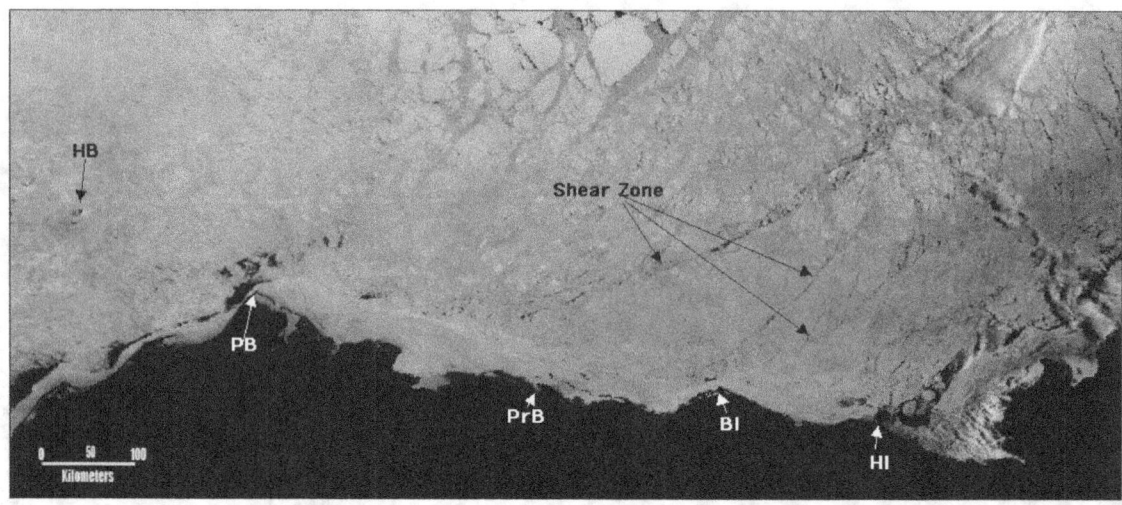

Figure 5.2.13c. AVHRR visible image of spring ice on June 14, 2000 in which the curving lines that appear to be leads are more likely discontinuities in the form of narrow shear zones that pass between discrete floes rather than fractures. Symbols are the same as in Figure 5.2.13a.

There is a possibility that the first recognition of spring ice in various parts of the study area might be used as an indicator of the timing and progress of break up in different years. To examine this, we determined the earliest date for which AVHRR and SAR imagery indicate "spring ice" conditions in Subregion 3 centered on Barrow (Table 5.2.1). Limiting this analysis to a single subregion recognizes the fact that, as noted above, the transition is not a synoptic event. Also, limiting the study to a small region permitted us to study a relatively large number of AVHRR scenes that are at least partially cloud-free. Further because of there is some inherent ambiguity in identifying the "point' at which the transition occurs, the results have an associated error on the order of ±5 days for AVHRR for those years in which cloud cover permitted the transition to be observed. Further, while SAR imagery was available independent of cloud conditions there are uncertainties in the backscatter signatures of different ice types and open water and so the errors are even larger. Both, the combined data and the AVHRR-derived dates exhibit a significant trend (at the 95% significance level) of earlier transition dates over the entire study period.

As to the exact nature and driving forces of this transition, our analysis is inconclusive. Thus, the transition typically occurs well (on average 21 days) before the onset of melt in the study region. The transition date does not correlate with any of the atmospheric or temperature variables determined for this study, other than the number of thawing degree days, for which a marginally significant (at the 90% level for the combined data sets) positive correlation was found. This would indicate that a later spring ice transition is paralleled by a larger number of thawing degree days which is counterintuitive if we consider the transition driven by thermodynamic, rather than dynamic forcing. However, field observations (see Section 4.1) confirm that the transition typically occurs at a time where significant amounts of new ice form in leads. An intriguing possibility would be that the transition is a result of dynamic and thermodynamic processes and

118

ultimately driven by the absorption of solar energy in leads. Several studies have indicated substantial absorption and sub-ice heating of surface waters well before the onset of surface melt (Kadko and Swart, 2004) and there are indications of a general oceanic warming trend in the study area (McPhee et al., 1998). At this point it is pure speculation whether these processes play any role in the context of the spring ice transition, however.

Table 5.2.2. Earliest appearance of "spring ice" conditions as derived from AVHRR and Radarsat SAR imagery for subregion 3 centered on Barrow

Year	Spring ice transition (AVHRR)	Spring ice transition (Radarsat SAR)
1994	129	n.d.
1995	126	n.d.
1996	n.d.	n.d.
1997	124	118
1998	124	130
1999	123	125
2000	124	117
2001	110	111
2002	114	123
2003	115	113
2004	n.d.	120

5.3. Landfast ice

5.3.1. Linkages with coastal morphology and bathymetry

From our analysis of Radarsat imagery between October 1996 and July 2004, we have characterized the landfast ice of northern Alaska and northwest Canada in terms of its width, the water depth at its seaward edge and the timing of key events during its annual cycle. In doing so, we have observed spatial variability in the character of the landfast ice at different scales and will now examine the relationship of this with different aspects of coastal morphology and nearshore bathymetry. To begin, it is informative to consider the study area as a whole with regard to typical sea ice drift patterns. In this context Point Barrow is the most important feature of the coast, acting as an obstacle which westward drifting pack ice in the Beaufort Sea must pass. This places the entire Alaska Chukchi coast in the lee of such drift, while other smaller coastal promontories such as Herschel and Barter Islands have similar effects on sections of the Beaufort Sea Coast.

119

The leeward aspect of a coastline results in the recurring presence of an expanse of open water, in the form of polynyas and shore leads, between the landfast and pack ice. During spring, when these open water areas are most common, typical incoming shortwave radiation provides approximately 270 Wm^{-2} to the Earth's surface at Barrow (data obtained from the North Slope Atmospheric Radiation Measurement Program). Some simple calculations show that over a 12-hour period, this can deliver 250 MJ per linear km of a 1 km wide lead. This is sufficient to melt approximately 50,000 m^3 of sea ice or 1 m of ice from a 50 m wide ridge at the SLIE. Therefore, although mechanisms for transferring upper ocean heat to the landfast ice are not well quantified, the presence of open water at the SLIE could promote more rapid break-up of landfast ice and result in the accumulation of fewer TDDs prior to break-up.

Open water also increases the exposure of the landfast ice to wind waves and swell, the latter of which can penetrate into ice covers causing them to break-up (Fox and Squire, 1990; 1991; Langhorne et al., 1998; Squire, 1993). Although the waves formed in polynyas are typically of much shorter period than are required for this (Biggs and Willmott, 2004), observations on the landfast ice near Barrow show that sections can break off following the passage of a long period wave across a large expanse of mostly open water.

At smaller scales, there are embayments and lagoons, which provide shelter from wind, waves and drifting ice and therefore promote the more rapid formation of continuous landfast ice. There are also river mouths located in many of these embayments, the effects of which can be complex. In the Siberian Arctic, the discharge of these rivers is thought to partly control the location of the SLIE (Dmitrenko et al., 1999), though as we observe below, their effect is not so far-reaching along the coastlines studied here. Instead, their most noticeable effect appears to be flooding of the landfast ice and promotion of melt in spring. This may explain why fewer TDDs are accrued prior to break-up in embayments in zone 2 than headlands (Figure 4.2.8). River in-flow can also freshen the surface waters and therefore enhance ice production in the fall. However, despite having more rivers than other zones, the difference between headlands and embayments in FDDs acquired prior to ice formation is less pronounced than in other zones (Figure 4.2.7). Part of the reason for this may be that Admiralty Bay and other deeply convoluted areas of the coast are excluded by the transects along which landfast ice width is measured (Section 3.3.7).

As observed in Section 4.2.3, stabilization of the landfast ice is strongly related to the water depth at the SLIE. Consequently, spatial variability of landfast ice extent also corresponds well with that of the distance from the coast to the isobaths around 20m. Thus, the steepness of the nearshore bathymetry can modulate the effect that the coastal morphology has on the behavior of landfast ice. Furthermore, isolated shoals can create leeward regions in a similar fashion to coastal promontories as discussed above.

There are also differences in the weather experienced by different sections of coast in the study area. In particular, that of zone 1 is influenced by the proximity of the Bering Sea to the south. The effects of weather and climate will be addressed in Section 5.3.2, but here we propose that much of the differences in landfast behavior that distinguish the 4 zones identified in this study (Figure 4.2.2, Figure 4.2.4, Figure 4.2.5 and Figure 4.2.7) can be related to three elements of the configuration of coast and bathymetry.

In zone 1, with the exception of Peard Bay, the landfast ice is among the latest to form each year and acquires more FDDs before it does so. In part, this can be ascribed to sparsity of sheltered locations in which sea ice can form without being broken up by wind and waves or large drifting floes. The only such feature of the coast is Peard Bay, in which ice forms significantly earlier than on the rest of the coast, although it is unclear whether the inflow of Kugrua River has any impact on this. Also in this zone, the SLIE is typically closest to shore and exhibits the smallest range in width, which is explained by the steepness of the offshore topography that leaves only a narrow band close to the shore in which ice floes may become grounded.

Also, in zone 1 except in the north near Point Barrow, the landfast ice achieves stability later in the year than in other zones and breaks up earlier (Figure 4.2.7, Table 4.2.3). We propose here that both are related to the leeward aspect of the coastline. First, this is probably the reason the Alaska Chukchi Sea coast has fewer ridges and less ridging intensity than the Beaufort Sea (Tucker et al., 1979). For the landfast ice, this means fewer potential floes to anchor the landfast ice, which together with a smaller area in which to ground them would lead to a later onset of stability. This is supported by Figure 4.2.7, which shows that stabilization occurs progressively later on the leeward side of other features apart from Point Barrow such as Barter Island and the shoals north of Prudhoe Bay and the Colville Delta. The leeward aspect of the coast in zone 1 also leads to the more frequent presence of open water at the SLIE. Grounded ice on Hanna Shoal (Section 4.3) may also lead to open water during periods of southward ice drift in the Chukchi Sea. This may explain the earlier date of break up and ice free coasts and fewer TDDs accrued beforehand, via exchange of heat to the ice from solar heated open water, as described above.

Zone 2 is distinguished from the others by a more gently sloping seabed and presence of shoals in less than 20m of water up to 35 km from shore (Figure 3.4.2). Both these features of the bathymetry coupled with of a greater supply of deep-keeled ridges (Tucker et al., 1979) explain the greater mean width of landfast ice in this zone. There are also many bays and lagoons, but there is less landfast ice variability associated with them and overall the behavior of the landfast ice is more uniform than in other zones. We attribute this to the buffering effect of the broader landfast ice belt in zone 2, where the characteristics of landfast ice appear to be dominated by the shallow bathymetry offshore rather than the shape of the coastline. However we also note that by discounting sea ice attached to barrier islands but not contiguous with the mainland (Section 3.3.1) the observed effect of barrier islands may be lessened, particularly in the spring. In addition, the rivers that can be seen to flow over the landfast ice in spring do not seem to affect the behavior of the landfast ice that we have measured here.

In coastal morphology and bathymetry, zone 3 resembles zone 1 and except during large stable extension episodes, the landfast ice belt is similarly narrow. However, its location and aspect are such that it has a similar intensity of ridging as zone 2 (Tucker et al., 1979), to which it has a similar date of stabilization. Although the coastline of zone 3 does not have a leeward aspect, its proximity to the Mackenzie Delta means that open water appears at the SLIE shortly after it does so in zone 4. As a result, the dates of break-up and ice-free coasts are slightly later than in zone 4 and earlier than zone 2.

121

In zone 4, the landfast ice is stable in the deepest waters of any zone when it bridges the Mackenzie Channel (Figure 4.2.7). We deem it unlikely that grounded ridges are holding the landfast ice in place on such occasions and it is therefore the involution of the coastline that shapes the SLIE in this case. The leeward aspect of the coastline results in a region of open water at the SLIE in spring that expands to the west. In flow from the Mackenzie River is also certain to influence this region and can be seen to overflow on the landfast ice in spring. It is therefore unclear which of these is responsible for the early break-up in this zone. Freshening of the nearshore seawater by Mackenzie discharge is likely to explain the earlier formation of landfast ice, which may in turn explain the earlier stabilization despite the leeward aspect of the coast.

In each zone the landfast ice appears to stabilize at a slightly different depth, though at this stage we are unable to explain the reasons why this is so. However, it may be more important to examine the similarities between the zones and understand the processes that lead to the landfast ice terminating in such a narrow range of water depths close to 20 m. The manner in which the SLIE advances into deeper water, with the discrete sections advancing first, followed by surrounding sections (Figure 4.2.5), indicates that the SLIE is pinned discontinuously by grounded ridges. However, it is not clear how many grounded ridges are required to stabilize landfast ice. Upward looking sonar measurements in waters beyond the landfast ice off of the Mackenzie Delta suggest that ridges with a draft greater than 20 m occupy only 0.1% of the ice surface (Melling et al., 1995). If a typical ridge section is assumed to be on the order of 100 m wide, this corresponds to approximately one such ridge per 100 km of ice. Melling et al (1995) observed a net drift of pack ice approximately 300 km over the course of the winter, which is sufficient to transport 3 deep-keeled ridges over any potential grounding location. If we assume that only one of these grounds, then grounded ridges would be located every 33 km along the SLIE. Although this corresponds approximately with the spacing of some nodes identified in Figure 4.2.1 and Figure 4.2.2, field observations at Barrow suggest such features are more closely spaced (Mahoney et al. in prep.). Therefore it seems likely that more grounded features are required to hold the landfast ice in place and therefore *in situ* deformation of ice is important in creating grounded ridges to stabilize the landfast ice.

This leaves the question of why the landfast ice terminates so frequently in waters around 20 m deep. It is possible that this is purely determined by the limited abundance of ridges with deeper keels. However, although the abundance decreases rapidly with increasing keel draft (Melling et al., 1995), ice gouges in the sea bed testify to the existence of keels as deep as 64 m (Gilbert and Pederson, 1987; Reimnitz and Barnes, 1985; Reimnitz et al., 1977). It is therefore also possible that ridges grounded in greater than 20 m are less capable of stabilizing the SLIE. Hibler (personal communication, 2005) suggests that drag exerted by the sea bed on the boundary layer beneath the sea ice may reduce ocean drag on ridge keels in shallow water. However, (Reimnitz et al., 1977) note an absence of hydraulic bedforms, which would be expected to be present if the boundary layer was interacting with the sea bed in such a manner.

Through a detailed analysis of the spatial variability of landfast ice behavior we have identified 3 elements of the coastal and bathymetric configuration that control the mean extent and annual cycle of landfast ice in a given area. However, in any given year the landfast ice will deviate from this mean behavior according to the atmospheric (and to a lesser extent oceanic) forcing it experiences. We must therefore also examine the temporal variability in the landfast ice and the environmental factors to which it responds.

5.3.2. Linkages with atmospheric circulation and air temperature

There are 3 different timescales relevant for observations of landfast ice behavior in this study. We can observe intra-annual episodic events as well as interannual variability between the 8 annual cycles between 1996 and 2004. Furthermore, results of this work can be compared to earlier, detailed studies completed in the 1970's to address potential change on decadal timescales. As brief episodic events are the subject of other ongoing research (Mahoney et al., in prep.), in this study we will address just the latter two timescales.

Mahoney et al. (2005) compared the locations of the SLIE from studies in the 1970's (Barry et al., 1979b; Stringer et al., 1980) and found that there was little difference in the end-of-season locations of the SLIE. However, in this study we have noted significant changes in the timing and duration of the annual landfast ice cycle between the periods 1973-76 (Barry, 1979; Barry et al., 1979b) and 1996-2004 (Section 4.2.4). We have also noted long-term changes in the onsets of freezing and thawing temperatures (Section 4.2.7) and significant differences in these between the two study periods. However, in order to elucidate the processes driving the timing of the landfast ice cycle, we will first examine interannual variability between 1996 and 2004 to shed light on the processes driving the timing of the landfast sea ice cycle.

From Figure 4.2.2, it is apparent that interannual variability in maximum landfast ice extent is dominated by the presence or absence of large stable extensions. It also appears that the position to which the SLIE retreats after the extension breaks up is farther offshore than the typical end of cycle maximum position in other years. However, their occurrence has little correlation with the timing of the final break-up of the landfast ice. We also find nothing in our analysis of sea level pressure patterns that corresponds to the occurrences of stable extensions.

If stable extensions are excluded, as by others (Barry et al., 1979b; Stringer et al., 1980), landfast ice extent does not appear to vary significantly on an interannual basis. It is noteworthy that this is different to observations in other Arctic marginal seas. In the Russian Artic, landfast ice extent has been correlated with the discharge of Ob', Yenisei, Lena and Kolyma rivers (Dmitrenko et al., 1999) Also, although they observe no significant long-term trends, Polyakov et al. (2003) note that variability in landfast ice extent in the Laptev, East Siberian and eastern Chukchi Seas correlates with both dynamic and thermodynamic forcing. In the Kara Sea, they suggest that thermodynamic forcing is more important, which differs from the findings of Divine et al. (2005), who note that there are modes of Kara Sea landfast ice extent, which are controlled by atmospheric circulation. However, probably due to steeper bathymetric gradients that in the Russian Arctic, Alaska landfast ice extent appears more narrowly confined by bathymetry and less dependent on climatic forcing. Also little change is observed over a longer timescale, and so we will instead focus on interannual variability in the timing of the landfast ice cycle.

Although we do not see any significant correlations between the timing of landfast ice events and the occurrence frequencies of individual CPs there is a seasonal cycle in the ratio of winter to summer patterns over a running 90-day period. Estimates of the dates of each year's spring transitions were derived by identifying the day of year on which the winter:summer ratio dropped below 0.5. Similarly the dates when the ratio rose back above 0.5 were used to estimate the fall transition. This provides a way to compare the key landfast ice events with the seasonality of sea level pressure patterns to complement similar comparisons with air temperature (Section 3.4.3).

As mentioned in Section 1, landfast ice does not exclusively form in-situ, but relies upon the advection of pack ice to stabilize and increase in area. To include interannual variability of pack ice interaction, Defense Meteorological Satellite Program (DMSP) Special Scanner Microwave/Imager (SSM/I) Daily Polar Gridded Sea Ice Concentrations (Cavalieri et al., 1990) were acquired for the 8 annual cycles of our study period. From these data, we derived estimates of the timing of the appearance and disappearance of pack ice from the nearshore zone. These dates were defined according to the mean daily sea ice concentration (SIC) in grid cells between 50km and 200km of the coast rose above and dropped below a threshold. A threshold of 80% concentration was found to yield the strongest correlations with landfast ice behavior.

Table 5.3.1. Correlation and lags between key landfast ice events (Sections 3.3.8 and 4.2.4) and measures of interannual variability in the temperature and atmospheric circulation.

| | | Correlation R^2 | Lag (days) | | | |
			Mean	σ	Min	Max
Onset of freeze	First landfast ice*	0.08	60	10.4	47	3
	Stabilization	0.02	147	16.3	128	173
Fall CP Transition	First landfast ice*	0.16	60	10.3	45	73
	Stabilization	0.23	143	13.3	130	170
Fall 80% nearshore SIC	First landfast ice*	0.72	29	13.1	15	59
	Stabilization	0.07	112	18.4	91	144
Onset of thaw	Break up	0.68	18	4.6	11	24
	Ice-free coasts	0.72	29	3.7	24	34
Spring CP transition	Break up	0.34	11	9.8	-4	24
	Ice-free coasts	0.38	23	10.1	9	35
Spring 80% nearshore SIC	Break up	0.45	-36	15.0	-54	-9
	Ice-free coasts	0.08	-25	15.5	-42	2

*1996-1998 omitted from analysis (see Section 3.3.8)

The start of the landfast ice cycle does not correlate strongly with either of the measures of interannual variability in the climate (Table 5.3.1). Furthermore, there is great variability in FDDs acquired prior to the presence of landfast ice (Figure 4.2.9). However there is a strong correlation ($R^2 = 0.72$) between the mean date of the first appearance of landfast ice and the date at which the mean sea ice concentration in the nearshore rose above 80%. Although this analysis is only based upon dates from 5 annual cycles due to Radarsat data availability (Section 3.3.8) this suggests that the strongest direct effect upon landfast ice formation is the presence of significant concentrations of pack ice in the near shore zone. Clearly, however, the pack ice is also responding to atmospheric circulation and the accumulation of freezing degree days.

The patterns of events in spring are more clearly correlated (Table 5.3.1), with the mean date of onset of thawing temperatures being the strongest corollary for events at the end of the landfast ice season. In addition, the mean annual dates of break-up correlate very strongly with those of ice-free coastlines ($R^2 = 0.91$). On average, over the 8 years of the study period, the onset of thawing temperature occurred 18 and 29 days prior to break up and ice free coasts, respectively. However, despite the relatively small standard deviations in lag intervals, the predictive usefulness of this date is limited since lag periods are also small and only slightly larger than the window of time used to calculate onset of thaw (Section 3.4.3). The correlations of break up and ice free coasts with the springtime transition from winter to summer CPs are considerably weaker, which suggests that the end of the annual landfast ice cycle is controlled more by thermodynamics than atmospheric dynamics. In addition, there is less variability in the TDDs required for break-up and ice free conditions as compared with FDDs required for the formation of landfast ice (Figure 4.2.8). The TDD totals for each event are within the same range as those determined by Barry (1978) and Barry et al. (1979b). However, no correlation could be found that might suggest an underlying cause for interannual variability in the number of TDDs acquired prior to break-up and ice-free conditions.

In the above analysis, we have identified the main variables that explain the interannual variability in the timing of landfast ice events between 1996 and 2004. This has been achieved through correlation of mean annual measures of atmospheric circulation, pack ice concentration and air temperature with mean dates of landfast ice events. However, in doing so we have neglected differences in climate across the study area. This may explain the weak correlations found at the beginning of the landfast ice cycle. Although additional correlations were performed on individual zones, with no significant improvement in the correlations, the CP analysis cannot be broken down in this way and so does not take into account differences between zones. In particular, the Chukchi Sea coast experiences the influence of the Bering Sea to the south more directly than the Beaufort Coast experiences more frequent and stronger storms than the Beaufort Sea (Atkinson, 2005). Furthermore, such storms are not well captured by the CP analysis. The differing climate of the Chukchi Sea probably explains one half of the u- and n-shaped date curves in Figure 4.2.6 and the greater level of interannual variability (Table 4.2.2)

In the examination of differences between the dates of key events identified in this study (Section 4.2.4) and those of the period 1973-77 (Barry et al., 1979b), we take into account some of these regional differences. According to a comparison of the mean dates, landfast ice formation occurs up to 1 month later in zone 1, while zone 2 shows little change from the earlier period. However, these mean standard deviations of dates in zone 1 are significantly larger than in zone 2, such that the difference between study periods is within the range of uncertainty. Furthermore, it is unclear what may be responsible for such a change due to weak correlations with the date of landfast ice formation. Thus, although Figure 4.2.10 and Figure 4.2.11 show trends toward more summer-like Septembers and later onsets of freezing temperatures, respectively, it is not clear whether these are related to any change in the landfast ice season.

In spring, it is in the Beaufort Sea that the greatest differences are seen between study periods, though both zone 1 and 2 show earlier break up and ice-free conditions in recent years, particularly if the first dates of break-up within each zone are used (Section 4.2.4). In agreement with Barry (1979; 1978), the results of this study show that the timing of landfast ice break-up is most closely correlated with air temperature and thawing degree days. However, this is not to say that turbulent heat flux from the atmosphere is the main driving mechanism behind melting and break-up since the other processes in the surface energy balance also control the accumulation of thawing degree days. Hence, the breaking-up of ice can be a positive feedback on air temperature since increasing open water fractions will increase the shortwave flux and therefore lead to increased surface air temperature. We therefore suggest that the long term trend towards an earlier onset of thawing (Figure 4.2.11) is evidence that the shortening of the landfast ice year in spring is also part of a longer term trend.

6. Conclusions

A major conclusion from this study of lead distribution patterns and landfast ice extent along the northern Alaska and Northwestern Canadian coast between 1993 and 2004 is the fact that throughout these years (and earlier time periods examined in a qualitative fashion or by consulting datasets published in previous studies) major lead patterns and landfast ice patterns are repeated and recurring and appear to conform to consistent seasonal and spatial patterns of variability. These patterns are controlled to a large extent by a combination of topographic (or bathymetric) constraints, atmospheric forcing and large-scale ice dynamics, as summarized in a simplistic fashion in Figure 6.1. Thus, the prevailing direction of ice motion with the Beaufort Gyre results in import of ice from the Canada Basin and north of Greenland into the study area. Despite an overall ice thinning trend in the region (Tucker et al., 2001), at least for some years substantial fractions of multiyear ice have been observed in the study area (see Section 4.3). During periods with significant onshore motion components, this ice circulation pattern creates a "dead space" in the southeastern Beaufort Sea that may extend well up along the coast towards the Canadian archipelago and possibly northern Greenland. As a result, we find a significantly lower lead fraction in the eastern part of the study area during such stagnation episodes (see detailed discussion in Section 4.2 and 5.2). Furthermore, the landfast ice extent, once it has attained its stable minimum near the 20-m isobath also responds to such stagnation episodes, resulting in several stable extension periods where the SLIE was shifted far to the North (see also further discussion below). The prevailing circulation regime hence also results in a more stable landfast ice cover in the eastern and central stretches of the Beaufort Sea. The local production of grounded ridges due to shear along the WNW-ESE trending stretches of coastline contributes to the stabilization of the landfast ice. At the same time, the prevailing wind regime favors production of open water and flaw leads or polynyas off the Mackenzie Delta and Herschel and Barter Islands during periods where atmospheric forcing and ice dynamics work in concert to clear ice out of the southeastern Beaufort Sea.

Transiting out of the Beaufort 'dead space" further towards the West, ice conditions become much more dynamic, with lead patterns radiating out of Point Barrow throughout the year. Furthermore, the orientation of the coastline in the eastern Chukchi Sea results in the highest recurrence probabilities of leads anywhere in the study area during all months of the year. A further set of lead systems of importance originates with ice grounded on Hanna Shoal. The higher areal lead fractions and higher lead densities in this region are due to a combination of two factors. First, both Hanna Shoal grounded ice as well as the Point Barrow landmass jutting out into the Chukchi and Beaufort Seas generate leads for a wide range of ice drift conditions. Second, the stagnation of ice movement in the eastern Beaufort Sea actually concentrates shear deformation into the eastern Chukchi and Western Beaufort Sea. This fosters the formation of long, arcuate leads that originate from Point Barrow or slightly further East and extend well up into the Canada Basin and off towards the coast of northern Greenland. These lead systems are also apparent in a couple of year's worth of Radarsat Geophysical Processor System data that determine the amount of shear for larger grid cells throughout the Arctic. The stagnating ice also acts as an anchor point that furthers the development of arches, including stacked lead systems that develop as ice clears out between the pinned ice in the East and more mobile (or partially pinned, in particular on Hanna Shoal) ice in the West.

These processes lead to characteristic sequences of lead evolution, with arch patterns propagating towards the NNE as the ice becomes more mobile and is cleared out. Large arcuate leads that parallel the lines of maximum shear between stagnant ice in the East and mobile ice in the West can also progress eastward, either through multiplication along progressive shear lines or through the development of separate arch systems that are capable of fragmenting the entire stretch of coastal ice between Point Barrow and the Mackenzie Delta in a few days. Such episodic events also impact the landfast ice edge, in particular in areas where it extends beyond this stable minimum position. The fact that winter break-out events are more frequent in the eastern Chukchi and western Beaufort Sea than the eastern half of the study area reflects the large-scale offshore pack-ice regime.

The large-scale sea-ice characteristics and recurrence of characteristic spatial and temporal patterns of variability are of importance both from a short- and long-term planning perspective. The regional and local contrasts in parameters such as lead recurrence probability or between lead number density and progression of the transition season can aid in planning of industrial development and assessment of ecological impacts of development. The temporal sequence of lead propagation, which depends largely on the passage of weather systems, may hold predictive power on operationally relevant time scales of days (development of arch patterns) and possibly even weeks (stable extensions). The data compiled in this study and the detailed description and discussion of characteristic patterns and associated quantitative information on SLIE or lead locations and morphology can furthermore aid in the validation and improvement of high-resolution sea-ice/ocean models operational in the Western Arctic sector.

Understanding the controlling factors of interannual variability in these landfast ice and lead patterns appears to be much more of a challenge, however. The development of leads in particular is highly dependent on the passage of individual weather systems. With sampling rates of such processes dictated by cloud conditions in the case of AVHRR, only a few promising leads worthy of further pursuit emerge. Thus, lead patterns appear to be linked to the prevailing atmospheric circulation regime, albeit only marginally. However, in combination with quantitative estimates of the distribution of multiyear ice advected into the study area, atmospheric circulation indices may hold some promise as potential predictors of lead patterns. With significant interannual variability dominating lead patterns, only one variable, the first appearance of "spring ice" characterized by an increase in the number density of leads and the lack of linear leads, appears to show some significant trend during the study period. The importance of this transition from the perspective of marine ecology, solar heating of the upper ocean and lateral melting of ice floes as well as from an operational viewpoint (e.g., for oil spill clean-up efforts) is significant. However, at this point, it is far from clear what exactly drives the timing of this transition and how these processes are related to more tangible measures such as the onset of surface melt.

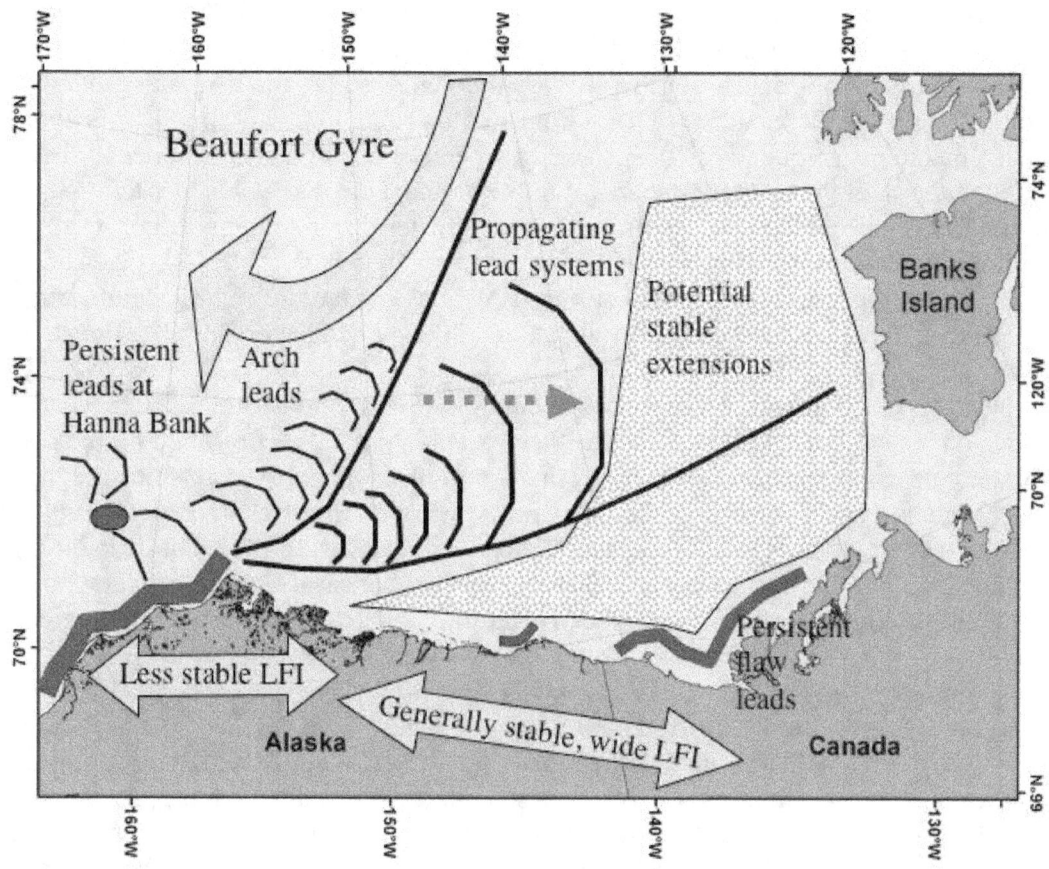

Figure 6.1. Schematic depiction of the dominant features and processes driving lead and landfast ice variability patterns in the study area. The red arrow designates the propagation of lead systems into the central and eastern Beaufort Sea. The dark blue areas indicate recurring flaw leads or polynyas. The big arrow shows the general trend of ice drift in the Beaufort Gyre, with shore-parallel drift dominating on average along the Beaufort coasts.

By examining the spatial variability in landfast ice extent and stability at higher spatial resolution, we were able to identify 4 distinct zones of contrasting landfast ice behavior (eastern Chukchi, west-central Beaufort, east-central Beaufort and Mackenzie Shelf region). Furthermore, we have identified 3 elements of the coastal and bathymetric configuration that differ between these zones and can be used to explain the differences in behavior. These elements are:

(1) The width and slope of the shallow inner shelf,
(2) The convexity and convolution of the coastline,
(3) The coastline orientation with respect to mean pack ice drift direction.

Despite the differences between zones, the landfast ice terminates at approximately 20 m of water in each one. This observation has been made by many authors (Stringer, 1980; Kovacs, 1976; Shapiro, 1975, 1976; Reimnitz, 1974) but in this study we have quantified the relationship and its spatial and temporal variability. Furthermore we show that reaching an isobath near 20 m is a critical event in the annual cycle allowing the advance of neighboring landfast ice to this depth and in turn the subsequent advance of the SLIE into deeper water. However, although the data indicate that grounded ridges are important in stabilizing the landfast ice, questions remain regarding why the SLIE is apparently stabilized so much less frequently in deeper water when there is evidence that deeper keels exist. It seems likely either there is an abrupt decrease in the abundance of keels deeper than 20 m, as suggested by Melling (1995), or that the ridge keels experience greater ocean drag in deeper water (Hibler, 2005 personal communication). Understanding the mechanisms by which grounded ridges hold sea ice fast to the coast is likely to be important in predicting the response of landfast ice to the observed changes in the Arctic sea ice in recent years (e.g. Perovich et al., 2003; e.g. Tucker et al., 2001).

We have also examined temporal variability of landfast sea ice on interannual and decadal timescales. In doing so we have noted that while the landfast ice extent is typically controlled by the configuration of the coast and bathymetry as discussed above, the occurrences of stable extensions are the cause of large interannual variability. No corollary to these events was found in the characteristic sea level pressure patterns. While these extensions are not usually considered as part of the landfast ice from an operational standpoint, they represent a persistent physical barrier isolating the waters beneath from the atmosphere above, which we expect would have significant oceanographic and ecological implications.

To examine variability in the timing of the annual cycle, we defined 4 key events that could be determined objectively from the SLIE data. Figure 4.2.7 shows the detailed spatial variability of these dates across the study area and the means of these dates over the study period for all coast points in each zone are given in Table 4.2.2. These data represent the most recent description of the annual cycle of Alaska landfast ice. In comparison with dates reported by (Barry et al., 1979b) for the period 1973-77, we observe a significant shortening of the landfast ice cycle. Along the northern Alaska Chukchi Sea coast the first landfast ice formed approximately 1 month later, though this is approaching the range of uncertainty. Along the western Beaufort Sea coast, there was no appreciable difference in these dates. Break-up occurred earlier on average by 6 and 19 days along the Chukchi and Beaufort coasts respectively. Although the difference for the Chukchi coast is less than the typical interannual variability, we feel that our dates are conservative since we calculate a mean date for each zone instead of the date of the first observance, which occurs approximately 3 weeks earlier. The greatest differences we observed in the mean dates of ice-free coasts, which occur 17 and 37 days later in the Chukchi and Beaufort Seas respectively.

By examining interannual variability of the timing of key landfast ice events within the study period, we found that the timing of pack ice incursion into coastal water was the best corollary for the timing of landfast ice formation, suggesting that later formation in recent years may be related to the more northward retreat of the perennial ice edge in recent years ([*Serreze, et al.*, 2003; *Stroeve, et al.*, 2005]). However, due to weak interannual correlation, we were unable to conclude whether any progressive delay of landfast ice formation was related to observations of summer-like Septembers (Figure 4.2.10 and later onsets of freezing temperatures (Figure 4.2.11). However, in spring we found a strong correlation between the timing of break-up and ice free coastlines and the onset of thawing temperatures. This leads us to the conclusion that the shortening of the landfast ice cycle in spring is related to the earlier onset of thawing temperatures in recent years (Figure 4.2.11).

7. Recommended New Research

The purpose of this study was to attempt to identify and classify features and lead patterns in the pack ice of the Beaufort Sea. With that information available, it is possible to suggest studies of a more analytical and quantitative nature that can be used to improve modeling of pack ice deformation, distribution of openings in the ice pack and the establishment and persistence of a seasonal landfast ice cover. In addition, several features and parameters have been identified that might be indicators of environmental change, if their times of origin can be determined. These are discussed in the following sections. Note that while this study relied almost exclusively on AVHRR and Radarsat SAR imagery, the availability of MODIS and high-resolution passive microwave imagery in the most recent years should not be overlooked as additional sources of data. Based on the present work, we have identified a number of areas requiring further research in the future. Listed in topical order (i.e., not by priority) these are:

1. The sequences of lead patterns identified and described here provide a basis for case history studies in which climate data is used to drive models to attempt to recreate the observations. Lead orientations can be deduced from the calculated displacement patterns and, alternatively, the observed patterns provide the opportunity to experiment with fracture criteria in the models. However, in general, models of pack ice deformation do not include the nearshore areas because of the need to know the boundary conditions at the pack ice – landfast ice interface. These are variable depending upon the configuration of the landfast ice edge, the direction of pack ice motion, bulk mechanical properties of the pack ice and the adhesion, or lack of it, at the boundary. For some of the lead patterns and sequences described here, the sense of motion of the pack ice at the time the leads formed can be found. Then, because many leads either originate or terminate at the boundary, it should be possible to test likely boundary conditions to reproduce the observed lead patterns. This is a reasonable approach to obtaining this type of information, given the scale of the problem.

2. The formation and persistence of leads along the pack ice-landfast ice boundary (i.e. flaw polynyas or flaw leads) depends on the movement of the pack ice and the configuration of the landfast ice edge. Displacements roughly parallel to the boundary leave openings on the downstream sides of nodes at the landfast ice edge. The length of the openings and the area of open water produced depend on the shape of the boundary and the duration of the movement episode. If the movements are limited in time, then the openings will probably remain narrow. However, with larger displacements, leads project into the pack ice, and eventually produce a Pack Ice Edge Zone (Section 4.3). The frequency of occurrence of open water along parts of the boundary, and the area it occupies, could be determined from satellite imagery and could be useful in considerations of possible oil dispersion.

3. Operationally, the flaw zone (as discussed in detail in Section 5.2) presents a particular challenge in the context of oil and gas production and oil-spill response and mitigation. The present study identified the extent of the flaw zone based on lead recurrence maps and data on the variability of the outer landfast ice edge. Further work could focus on a more in-depth

examination of ice drift and deformation patterns in this zone that may not be well described by large-scale forcing or ice motion fields.

4. The first appearance of one or more specific features in both early and late winter might be useful as indicators of the timing of the limits of the ice year. As a test, a catalogue of these could be assembled from the available satellite imagery.

The problem of identifying the day of the first appearance of the grounded ice on Hanna Shoal from AVHRR imagery was described in the text. However, other possibilities are (1) the grounding of ice on the shoal off Harrison Bay, (2) the formation of the line of ridges along the 20 m depth contour into Camden Bay, (3) the first occurrence of the line of ridges to offshore Barter Island, and (4) the smoothing of the landfast ice edge across the mouth of Mackenzie Bay.

The transition to warmer conditions might be marked by the first recognition of "spring ice", followed by the rate at which it spreads across the southern Beaufort Sea. Spring ice appears as a phenomenon that is largely unstudied yet of substantial importance in a variety of contexts. A more detailed examination, in particular, of its exact nature and potential trends in its timing may aid describing and predicting a range of important seasonal transitions. In addition, the first appearance of a lead deep into Mackenzie Bay (the 'fishhook') might serve as another indicator.

5. Analysis of the mechanics of formation of several features observed in this study could be useful for improving our ability to model pack ice deformation in the southern Beaufort Sea. The similarities and differences between the arch that forms in the Bering Strait as ice is extruded southward, and the Barrow and North Slope Arches was commented on in the text. The fact that those arches are present so much of the time indicates that they are important elements in the deformation pattern of the Beaufort Sea. Similar observations apply to other patterns and features described in Section 4.3, including the lead fans at Point Barrow, tangent and high-angle leads along the landfast ice edge, the relationship between wide arcs and the northeasterly trends from Point Barrow, and leads that originate or terminate at the grounded ice on Hanna Shoal. Thus, there is a wealth of isolated problems in the mechanics of pack ice deformation that requires study, and the data provided here supplies case histories for that effort.

6. In looking for the first day of the ice year when there was grounded ice present on Hanna Shoal, it was noted that in early winter, it was common at that location to find areas of open water surrounded by large floes broken from the pack ice, even though the edge of the pack ice was farther south. A similar observation was noted in describing the Barrow Arch with leads aligned near 72°N. In that case, the emphasis was on the fact that the broken floes are in a linear zone that extends westward from an arch to about 162°30'W. The zone appears to coincide with the area in which the water depth has decreased to less than about 50 m as the Chukchi shelf is approached from the north. This estimate of the depth is approximate, because of the difficulty in transferring locations of points on the SWATHVIEW images to a map of the bathymetry on a much larger scale. The apparent influence of the change in depth on the fracturing within the pack ice is an observation that might be of interest to oceanographers concerned with near-shore phenomena. Note also that in describing Barrow Arches with leads bounding their east sides it was noted that many of the bounding leads are aligned along the trend of the shallower depth contours on the east flank of Barrow Canyon. It is possible (perhaps likely) that the lead over the

east flank of Barrow Canyon is more the result of the drift pattern of the pack ice in that area than the change in water depth, but the point could still be investigated.

7. By combining our observations of the location of the SLIE with a bathymetric DEM compiled for this study, we found strong evidence that the landfast ice is pinned at discrete locations by grounded deep-keeled ice. Furthermore, there is an apparent limit at around 20 m to the depth at which such keels can effectively stabilize the surrounding floating ice. However, we are unable to conclude whether this is due to a decrease in abundance of ridges with deeper keels or a change in the oceanic drag at this depth. A further problem in this context is the lack of a consolidated, up-to-date bathymetric data set in the depth range between 0 and 50 m. A study examining the quality of existing bathymetric data and consolidating various data sources into a single, high-quality data set appears to be in order.

Also, although we identified some likely areas where the landfast ice well grounded, it is not clear what fraction of the SLIE is grounded. This is not only important for stabilizing the ice, but also in determining the nature of the SLIE as a boundary between current regimes. Deep, continuous ridges at the SLIE could make an effective barrier to prevent the spread of oil spilled beneath the ice, where as gaps in such ridges would represent areas where oil could be dispersed beneath moving pack ice. Addressing these questions would likely require an intensive program of ice-based field observations coupled with mooring data and high-resolution altimetry of the ice cover.

8. The importance of stable extensions and vast sectors of stagnant ice devoid of leads appears to have gone largely unnoticed, despite their great importance for atmosphere-ocean exchange of heat and momentum. Ecologically, stable extension episodes of more than a month can have a substantial impact on marine birds and mammals. The SAR data and SLIE locations as well as the lead patterns compiled for this study could help guide a dedicated study of such events. For some years, availability of SAR-derived deformation maps would add substantially to such an effort.

9. We observed a strong correlation between the timing of the onset of thawing temperatures and the subsequent break-up of the ice. However, although this suggests that warming and melting of ice are important in weakening the ice, it does not address the role of mechanical breakage of the ice, which may be responsible for mid-winter breakouts. Also, we speculated that solar heat absorbed by open water in spring could be transferred to adjacent landfast ice and promote an early onset of break-up. The exchange of water across the SLIE also has implications for the fate of spilled oil and ties in with the questions regarding the nature of keels beneath the landfast ice. Hence, any research program intending to address one ought to address the other.

10. A concerted effort was put forth to compile useful bathymetry for analyzing both the lead and landfast ice characteristics, but it is clear that additional work could be conducted to develop an improved data set. The concentration of depth sounding data is in the nearshore area (less than 20 meters). Much less concentrated sounding data exist for offshore areas. Data mining the archives from ship cruises (such as the USCGC *HEALY*) with onboard multibeam instrumentation could be incorporated to supplement these offshore areas. In addition, new industry data sources should be included. Opportunities for MMS to develop improved

bathymetry may be accomplished through increased collaboration with other regional efforts with similar needs, such as the Alaska Ocean Observation System, the Arctic Observing Network and the Barrow Coastal Observatory. The Hawaii Mapping Research Group based out of the University of Hawaii at Manoa is currently processing multibeam surveys conducted from the 2005 USCGC *HEALY* cruise, plus other data sources in an effort to create an improved bathymetry grid (personal communication with Margo Edwards and Paul Johnson.) Such efforts should eventually yield an improved data set.

8. References Cited

Alam, A. and J.A. Curry, 1998. Evolution of new ice and turbulent heat fluxes over freezing winter leads. J. Geophys. Res., 103(C8): 15783-15802.

Atkinson, D.E., 2005. Observed storminess patterns and trends in the circum-Arctic coastal regime. Geo-Marine Letters, 25(2 - 3): 98.

Barber, D.G., T.N. Papakyriakou, E.F. LeDrew and M.E. Shokr, 1995. An examination of the relation between the spring period evolution of the scattering coefficient (s°) and radiative fluxes over landfast sea-ice. Int. J. Remote Sens., 16(17): 3343-3363.

Barnett, D., 1991. Sea ice distribution in the Soviet Arctic. In: L.W. Brigham (Editor). Belhaven Press, London, pp. 47-62.

Barrett, S.A. and W.J. Stringer, 1978. Growth mechanisms of "Katie's Floeberg". Arctic and Alpine Research, 10(4): p.775-783.

Barry, R., 1976. Study of climatic effects on fast ice extent and its seasonal decay along the Beaufort-Chukchi coasts. Environmental Assessment of the Alaskan Continental Shelf. Annual Report, Research Unit #244, 15 March 1976: 58-113.

Barry, R., 1979. Study of climatic effects on fast ice extent and its seasonal decay along the Beaufort-Chukchi coasts, Environmental Assessment of the Alaskan Continental Shelf, vol.2 : Physical Science Studies, final report, pp. 272-375.

Barry, R.G., 1978. Energy budget studies in relation to fast-ice breakup processes in Davis Strait : A climatological overview. Occasional paper (Institute of Arctic and Alpine Research). University of Colorado, Institute of Arctic and Alpine Research, Boulder, CO.

Barry, R.G., R.E. Moritz and J.C. Rogers, 1979a. The fast ice regimes of the Beaufort and Chukchi Sea coasts, Alaska. Cold Reg. Sci. Technol., 1: 129-152.

Barry, R.G., R.E. Moritz and J.C. Rogers, 1979b. The fast ice regimes of the Beaufort and Chukchi Sea coasts, Alaska. Cold Regions Science and Technology, 1(2): 129-152.

Bauer, J. and S. Martin, 1983. A model of grease ice growth in small leads. J. Geophys. Res., 88(C5): 2917-2925.

Belchansky, G.I., D.C. Douglas, I.V. Alpatsky and N.G. Platonov, 2004. Spatial and temporal multiyear sea ice distributions in the Arctic: A neural network analysis of SSM/I data, 1988–2001. J. Geophys. Res., 109: C10017, doi:10.1029/2004JC002388.

Biggs, N.R.T. and A.J. Willmott, 2004. Steady apply flux model solutions incorporating a parameterization for the collection thickness of consolidated new ice. Ocean Modelling, 7: 343-361.

Blazey, B., A. Mahoney and H. Eicken, 2005. Landfast Ice Breakouts on the Northern Alaskan coast, AGU Fall Meeting. American Geophysical Union, San Francisco.

Braham, H.W., M.A. Fraker and B.D. Krogman, 1980. Spring migration of the western arctic population of Bowhead whales. Marine Fisheries Rev., 42 (9-10): 36-46.

Bump, J.K. and J.R. Lovvorn, 2004. Effects of lead structure in Bering Sea pack ice on the flight costs of wintering spectacled eiders. J. Mar. Sys., 50: 113-139.

Burns, J.J., L.H. Shapiro and F.H. Fay, 1980. The relationship of marine mammal distributions, densities and activities to sea ice conditions. In: OCSEAP, Final Reports of Investigators, Vol. 2, Biological Sciences, RU 248, 1981.

Cavalieri, D.J., P. Gloersen and H.J. Zwally, 1990. updated current year, DMSP SSM/I daily polar gridded sea ice concentrations. In: J. Maslanik and J. Stroeve (Editors). National Snow and Ice Data Center, pp. Digital Media.

Comiso, J.C., 2002. A rapidly declining perennial sea ice cover in the Arctic. Geophys. Res. Lett., 29(20): 1956, doi:10.1029/2002GL015650.

Dean, K.G., W.J. Stringer, K. Ahlnäs, C. Searcy and T. Weingartner, 1994. The influence of river discharge on the thawing of sea ice, Mackenzie River Delta: albedo and temperature analyses. Polar Res., 13: 83-94.

Deser, C., J.E. Walsh and M.S. Timlin, 2000. Arctic sea ice variability in the context of recent atmospheric circulation trends. J. Climate, 13: 617-633.

Divine, D.V., R. Korsnes and A.P. Makshtas, 2004. Temporal and spatial variation of shore-fast ice in the Kara Sea. Cont. Shelf Res., 24: 1717-1736.

Divine, D.V., R. Korsnes, A.P. Makshtas and F. Godtliebsen, 2005. Atmospheric-driven state transfer of shore-fast ice in the northeastern Kara Sea. J. Geophys. Res., 110: C09013, doi:10.1029/2004JC002706.

Dmitrenko, I.A., V.A. Gribanov, D.L. Volkov, H. Kassens and H. Eicken, 1999. Impact of river discharge on the fast ice extension in the Russian Arctic shelf area. Proceedings of the 15th International Conference on Port and Ocean

Engineering under Arctic Conditions (POAC99), Helsinki, 23-27 August, 1999, vol. 1: 311-321.

Drobot, S.D. and J.A. Maslanik, 2003. Interannual variability in summer Beaufort Sea ice conditions: Relationship to winter and summer surface and atmospheric variability. J. Geophys. Res., 108(C7): 3233, doi:10.1029/2002JC001537.

Eicken, H., I. Dmitrenko, K. Tyshko, A. Darovskikh, W. Dierking, U. Blahak, J. Groves and H. Kassens, 2005. Zonation of the Laptev Sea landfast ice cover and its importance in a frozen estuary. Global Planet. Change, 48: 55-83.

Eicken, H., R. Gradinger, A. Graves, A. Mahoney, I. Rigor and H. Melling, 2006. Sediment transport by sea ice in the Chukchi and Beaufort Seas: Increasing importance due to changing ice conditions? Deep-Sea Res.

Fett, R.W., R.E. Englebretson and S.D. Burk, 1997. Techniques for analyzing lead condition in visible, infrared and microwave satellite imagery. Journal of Geophysical Research, 102(D12): 13657-13671.

Fetterer, F., D. Generis and R. Kwok, 1994. Sea ice type maps from the Alaska Synthetic Aperture Radar Facility imagery: an assessment. Jour. Geophys. Res., 99(C11): 22,443,22,458.

Fox, C. and V. Squire, 1990. Reflection and transmission characteristics at the edge of shore fast sea ice. J. Geophys. Res, 95(C7): 11629-11639.

Fox, C. and V. Squire, 1991. Strain in shore fast ice due to incoming ocean waves and swell. J. Geophys. Res, 96(C3): 4531-4547.

Fraker, M.A. and J.R. Bockstoce, 1980. Summer distribution of Bowhead whales in the eastern Beaufort Sea. Marine Fisheries Rev. 42 (9-10): 46-51.

George, J.C., H.P. Huntington, K. Brewster, H. Eicken, D.W. Norton and R. Glenn, 2004. Observations on Shorefast Ice Dynamics in Arctic Alaska and the Responses of the Iñupiat Hunting Community. Arctic.

GEODAS, http://www.ngdc.noaa.gov/mgg/geodas/geodas.html, National Geophysical Data Center.

Gilbert, G. and K. Pederson, 1987. Ice scour database for the Beaufort Sea, Report No. 055. Environmental Studies Revolving Funds, Ottawa, 99 pp.

Gordon, A.L. and J.C. Comiso, 1988. Polynyas in the southern ocean. Scientific American, 256: 90-97.

Grants, A. and M.W. Mullen, 1992. Bathymetric map of the Chukchi and Beaufort Seas and adjacent arctic oceans. US Geological Survey Misc. investigations series, Map I-1182.

Hallikainen, M. and D.P. Winebrenner, 1992. The physical basis for sea ice remote sensing. In: F.D. Carsey (Editor). Geophysical Monograph 68, American Geophysical Union, Washington, pp. 29-46.

Hibler, W.D.I., 1986. Ice dynamics. In: N. Untersteiner (Editor). Plenum Press, New York (NATO ASI B146), pp. 577-640.

Hibler, W.D., S.F. Ackley, W.K. Crowder, H.L. McKin and D.M. Anderson, 1974. Analysis of shear zone ice deformation in the Beaufort Sea using satellite imagery. In: J.C. Reed and J.E. Sater, eds, The coast and shelf of the Beaufort Sea, Arctic Institute of North America, pp. 285-296.

Holt, B. and S. Digby, 1985. Processes and Imagery of First-Year Fast Sea Ice During the Melt Season. J. Geophys. Res., 90(C3): 5045-5062.

Horowitz, W.L., 2002. Evaluation of sub-sea physical environmental data for the Beaufort Sea OCS and incorporation into a Geographic Information System database. Minerals Management Service Outer Continental Shelf Study, Anchorage, AK.

Huntington, H., 2000. Native observations capture impacts of sea ice changes. Witness the Arctic, 8(1): 1-2.

Jacobs, J.D., R.G. Barry and R.L. Weaver, 1975. Fast ice characteristics, with special reference to the eastern Canadian Arctic. Polar Record, 110(17): 521-536.

Kadko, D. and P. Swart, 2004. The source of the high heat and freshwater content of the upper ocean at the SHEBA site in the Beaufort Sea in 1997. J. Geophys. Res., 109(C01022): doi:10.1029/2002JC001734.

Key, J.R., R. Stone, J.A. Maslanik and E. Ellefsen, 1993. The detectability of sea-ice leads in satellite data as a function of atmospheric conditions and measurement scale. Annals of Glaciology, 17: 227-232.

Kirchhofer, W., 1974. Classification of European 500 mb patterns;. 43: 1-16.

Kottmeier, C., J. Olf, W. Frieden and R. Roth, 1992. Wind forcing and ice motion in the Weddell Sea region. J. Geophys. Res., 97: 20373-20383.

Kovacs, A., 1976. Grounded ice in the fast ice zone along the Beaufort Sea coast of Alaska. CRREL Report, 76-32.

Kovacs, A. and M. Mellor, 1974. Sea ice geomorphology and ice as a geologic agent in the northern Beaufort Sea. In: J.C. Reed and J.E. Sater (Editors), The Coast and Shelf of the Beaufort Sea. Arctic Institute of North America, Arlington, VA.

Krupnik, I. and D. Jolly, 2002. The Earth is Faster Now: Indigenous Observations of Arctic Environmental Change. Arctic Research Consortium of the United States, Fairbanks, Alaska.

Kwok, R., 1998. The RADARSAT Geophysical Processor System. In: C. Tsatsoulis and R. Kwok (Editors). Springer Verlag, Berlin, pp. 235-257.

Kwok, R. and G.F. Cunningham, 1994. Use of time series SAR data to resolve ice type ambiguities in newly opened leads, IGARSS'94; International Geoscience and Remote Sensing Symposium. Surface and Atmospheric Remote Sensing: Technologies, Data

Analysis and Interpretation. Institute of Electrical and Electronic Engineers, Pasadena, California, pp. 1024-1026.

Kwok, R. and G.F. Cunningham, 2002. Seasonal ice area and volume production of the Arctic Ocean: November 1996 through April 1997. J. Geophys. Res., 107(C10): doi:10.1029/2000JC000469.

Langhorne, P., V. Squire, C. Fox and T.G. Haskell, 1998. Break-up of sea ice by ocean waves. Annals Glaciol., 27: 439-442.

Lestak, L.R., W.F. Manley and J.A. Maslanik, 2003. Point Barrow and vicinity bathymetry. National Snow and Ice Data Center, http://nsidc.org/data/arcss031.html.

Lindsay, R.W. and D.A. Rothrock, 1994. Arctic sea ice albedo from AVHRR. J. Climate, 7(11): 1737-1749.

Lindsay, R.W. and D.A. Rothrock, 1995. Arctic sea ice leads from advanced very high resolution radiometer images. J. Geophys. Res., 100(C3): 4533-4544.

Lynch, A.H., E.N. Cassano, J.J. Cassano and L.R. Lestak, 2003. Case studies of high wind events in Barrow, Alaska: Climatological context and development processes. Month. Weather Rev., 131: 719-732.

Mahoney, A., H. Eicken, L. Shapiro and A. Graves, 2005. Defining and locating the seaward landfast ice edge in northern Alaska. In: J.P. Dempsey (Editor), 18th International Conference on Port and Ocean Engineering under Arctic Conditions,. POAC '05, Potsdam, N.Y.

Martin, S. and R. Drucker, 1997. The effect of possible Taylor columns on the summer ice retreat in the Chukchi Sea. J. Geophys. Res., 102(C5): 10473-10482.

Martin, S., R. Drucker, R. Kwok and B. Holt, 2004. Estimation of the thin ice thickness and heat flux for the Chukchi Sea Alaskan coast polynya from Special Sensor Microwave/Image data, 1990-2001. J. Geophys. Res., 109(C10012): doi:10.1029/2004JC002428.

Maykut, G.A., 1986. The surface heat and mass balance. In: N. Untersteiner (Editor). Martinus Nijhoff Publ., Dordrecht (NATO ASI B146), pp. 395-463.

McPhee, M.G., T.P. Stanton, J.H. Morison and D.G. Martinson, 1998. Freshening of the upper ocean in the central Arctic: Is perennial sea ice disappearing? Geophys. Res. Lett., 25(10): 1729-1732.

Melling, H., P.H. Johnston and D.A. Riedel, 1995. Measurements of the Underside Topography of Sea Ice by Moored Subsea Sonar. J. Atmosph. Ocean Technol., 12: 589-602.

Melnikov, I.A., 1997. The Arctic sea ice ecosystem. Gordon Breach Sci. Publ., Amsterdam.

Miles, M.W. and R.G. Barry, 1998. A 5-year satellite climatology of winter sea ice leads in the western Arctic. Journal of Geophysical Research. C. Oceans, 103(C10): 21723-21734.

Nautical Data International. Digital Ocean Chart 7662, Mackenzie Bay, http://digitalocean.ca/.

Nautical Data International. Digital Ocean Chart 7662, Demarcation Bay to Philips Bay, http://digitalocean.ca/.

NOAA, 2001. International Bathymetric Chart of the Arctic Ocean (IBCAO), Version 1, Sheet 3, National Geophysical Data Center, http://www.ngdc.noaa.gov/mgg/bathymetry/arctic/arctic.html.

NOAA. Electronic Navigational Chart 16004, Barrow to Herschel Island, Office of Coast Survey, http://nauticalcharts.noaa.gov/mcd/enc/index.htm.

NOAA. Electronic Navigational Chart 16005, Cape Prince of Wales to Point Barrow, Office of Coast Survey, http://nauticalcharts.noaa.gov/mcd/enc/index.htm.

NOAA, 1990. Chart 16082, Point Barrow and vicinity.

Norton, D.W. and A. Graves Gaylord, 2004. Drift velocities of ice floes in Alaska's northern Chukchi Sea flaw zone: Determinants of success by spring subsistence whalers in 2000 and 2001. Arctic, 57(4): 347-362.

Onstott, R.G., 1992. SAR and scatterometer signatures of sea ice. In: F.D. Carsey (Editor). Geophysical Monograph 68, American Geophysical Union, Washington, pp. 73-104.

Organization, W.M., 1985. WMO sea-ice nomenclature, terminology, codes and illustrated glossary. WMO/DMM/BMO 259-TP-145, Secretariat of the WMO, Geneva.

Overland, J.E. and M. Wang, 2005. The Arctic climate paradox: The recent decrease of the Arctic Oscillation. Geophys. Res. Lett., 32: L06701, doi:10.1029/2004GL021752.

Pegau, W.S. and C.A. Paulson, 2001. The albedo of Arctic leads in summer. Ann. Glaciol., 33: 221-224.

Perovich, D.K., 1990. Theoretical estimates of light reflection and transmission by spatially complex and temporally varying sea ice covers. J. Geophys. Res., 95: 9557-9567.

Perovich, D.K., 1998. Optical properties of sea ice. In: M. Leppäranta (Editor). University of Helsinki, Helsinki, pp. 195-230.

Polyakov, I., G.V. Alekseev, R.V. Bekryaev, U.S. Bhatt, R.L. Colony, M.A. Johnson, V.P. Karklin, D. Walsh and A.V. Yulin, 2003. Long-term ice variability in Arctic marginal seas. J. Climate, 16(12): 2078-2085.

Proshutinsky, A.Y. and M.A. Johnson, 1997. Two circulation regimes of the wind-driven Arctic Ocean. J. Geophys. Res., 102: 12493-12514.

Reimnitz, E., 2000. Interactions of river discharge with sea ice in proximity of Arctic Deltas: A review. Polarforschung, 70: 123-134.

Reimnitz, E. and E.W. Kempema, 1974. Pack ice interaction with Stamukhi Shoal, Beaufort Sea, Alaska. In: Barnes, P., D.M. Schell and E. Reimnitz, eds., The Alaskan Beaufort Sea, Ecosystems and Environments, Academic Press, pp. 159-183.

Reimnitz, E. and P. Barnes, 1974. Sea ice as a geologic agent on the Beaufort Sea shelf of Alaska. In: J.C. Reed and A.G. Slater (Editors), The Coast and Shelf of the Beaufort Sea (proceedings of a Symposium on Beaufort Sea Coast and Shelf Research). Arctic Institute of North America, Arlington, VA.

Reimnitz, E. and P. Barnes, 1985. Determining the maximum keel depth in the Arctic Ocean, Arctic Energy Technologies Conference, Proceedings. U.S. Dept. Energy, Morgantown Energy Technology Center, WV.

Reimnitz, E., P.W. Barnes, L.J. Toimil and J. Melchior, 1977. Ice gouge recurrence and rates of sediment reworking, Beaufort Sea, Alaska. Geology, 5: 405-408.

Rigor, I.G., J.M. Wallace and R.L. Colony, 2002. Response of sea ice to the Arctic Oscillation. J. Climate, 15(18): 2648-2663.

Rodionov, S.N., 2004. A sequential algorithm for testing climate regime shifts. Geophys. Res. Let., 31(L09204, doi:10.1029/2004GL019448).

Rothrock, D.A. and J. Zhang, 2005. Arctic Ocean sea ice volume: What explains its recent depletion? J. Geophys. Res., 110: C01002, doi:10.1029/2004JC002282.

Schulson, E.M., 2004. Compressive shear faults within arctic sea ice: Fracture on scales large and small. J. Geophys. Res., 109(C07016): doi:10.1029/2003JC002108.

Searcy, C., K. Dean and W. Stringer, 1996. A river-coastal sea ice interaction model: Mackenzie River Delta. J. Geophys. Res., 101(C4): 8885-8894.

Serreze, M.C. and A. Etringer, 2003. Precipitation characteristics of the Eurasian Arctic drainage system. International Journal of Climatology, 23(11): 1267-1291.

Serreze, M.C., J.E. Walsh, F.S. Chapin III, T. Osterkamp, M. Dyurgerov, V. Romanovsky, W.C. Oechel, J. Morison, T. Zhang and R.G. Barry, 2000. Observational evidence of recent change in the northern high-latitude environment. Climatic Change, 46: 159-207.

Service, C.H., 1968. Pilot of Arctic Canada. Canadian Hydrographic Service, Surveys and Mapping Branch, Department of Mines and Technical Surveys, Ottawa.

Shapiro, L.H. and J.J. Burns, 1973. Satellite observations of sea ice movement in the Bering Strait region. In: Weller, G. and S.A. Bowling, eds., Climate of the Arctic, Proceedings of the 24th Alaska Science Conference, Fairbanks, AK, August, 1973.

Shapiro, L., 1975. A preliminary study of the formation of landfast ice at Barrow, Alaska. Winter 1973-74. UAG R-235, Geophysical Institute, Fairbanks.

Solomon, S., G. Manson, D. Monita, T. Hirose and D. Power, 2004. Synthetic Aperture Radar remote sensing of bottom-fast ice in the Mackenzie Delta region, Northwest Territories, Canada, American Geophysical Union spring meeting, 2004, abstract #$43A.

Squire, V.A., 1993. The breakup of shore fast sea ice. Cold Regions Science and Technology, 21(3): 211-218.

Stirling, I., 1997. The importance of polynyas, ice edges, and leads to marine mammals and birds. J. Mar. Sys., 10: 9-27.

Stringer, W.J., 1974. Morphology of the Beaufort Sea shorefast ice. In: J.C. Reed and J.E. Sater (Editors), The Coast and Shelf of the Beaufort Sea. Arctic Institute of North America, Arlington, VA, pp. 165-172.

Stringer, W.J., 1978. Morphology of Beaufort, Chukchi and Bering Seas nearshore ice conditions by means of satellite and aerial remote sensing, Environmental assessment of the Alaskan continental shelf, Vol.10, Transport. Principal investigators' annual reports for the year ending March 1978, pp. 1-220. Outer Continental Shelf Environmental Assessment Program, Boulder, Colorado.

Stringer, W.J., S.A. Barrett and L.K. Schreurs, 1980. Nearshore ice conditions and hazards in the Beaufort, Chukchi and Bering Seas. Geophysical Institute report. Geophysical Institute, University of Alaska, Fairbanks, AK.

Stroeve, J.C., Serreze, M. C. , F. Fetterer, T. Arbetter, W. Meier, J. Maslanik and K. Knowles, 2005. Tracking the Arctic's shrinking ice cover: Another extreme September minimum in 2004. Geophys. Res. Lett., 32: L04501, doi:10.1029/2004GL021810.

Thompson, D.W.J. and J.M. Wallace, 1998. Arctic Oscillation signature in the wintertime geopotential height and temperature fields. Geophys. Res. Lett., 25(9): 1297-1300.

Thorndike, A.S. and R. Colony, 1982. Sea ice motion in response to geostrophic winds. J. Geophys. Res., 87(C8): 5845-5852.

Tschudi, M.A., J.A. Curry and J.A. Maslanik, 2002. Characterization of springtime leads in the Beaufort/Chukchi Seas from airborne and satellite observations during FIRE/SHEBA. Journal of Geophysical Research, 107(C10): SHE9.1-SHE9.14.

Tucker, W.B., W.F. Weeks and M. Frank, 1979. Sea ice ridging over the Alaska continental shelf. J. Geophys. Res., 84(C8): 4885-4897.

Tucker, W.B.I., J.W. Weatherly, D.T. Eppler, D. Farmer and D.L. Bentley, 2001. Evidence for the rapid thinning of sea ice in the western Arctic Ocean at the end of the 1980s. Geophys. Res. Lett., 28(14): 2851-2854.

United States Geological Survey, 1997. Bering and Chukchi Sea bathymetry, http://www.absc.usgs.gov/research/walrus/bering/bathy/berchuk.htm.

Wadhams, P., 1981. Sea-ice topography of the Arctic Ocean in the region 70° W to 25° E. Phil. Trans. R. Soc. Lond. A, 302: 45-85.

Wadhams, P., A.S. McLaren and R. Weintraub, 1985. Ice thickness distribution in Davis Strait in February from submarine sonar profiles. J. Geophys. Res., 90: 1069-1077.

Walker, H.J., 1973. The nature of the seawater-freshwater interface during breakup in the Colville River Delta, Alaska. Permafrost: The North American Contribution to the Second International Conference: 473-476.

Wang, J. and M. Ikeda, 2000. Arctic Oscillation and Arctic Sea-Ice Oscillation. Geophys. Res. Lett., 27(9): 1287-1290.

Weaver, J.C., 1951. The sea ice in the North American Arctic. Encyclopedia Arctica. The Stefansson Library, New York.

Weeks, W.F. and S.F. Ackley, 1986. The growth, structure and properties of sea ice. In: N. Untersteiner (Editor). Plenum Press, New York(NATO ASI B146), pp. 9-164.

Weeks, W.F., A. Kovacs, S.J. Mock, W.B. Tucker, W.D. Hibler, III and A.J. Gow, 1977. Studies of the movement of coastal sea ice near Prudhoe Bay, Alaska, U.S.A. J. Glaciol., 19(81): 533-546.

Zubov, N.N., 1945. Arctic ice. Izd. Glavsevmorputi, Moscow.

Appendix A.   Publications and presentations resulting from this project

A.1. Presentations

Mahoney, A., H. Eicken, L. Shapiro, A. Graves and P. Cotter, Landfast sea ice extent and variability in the Alaskan Arctic derived from SAR imagery, IEEE International Geoscience and Remote Sensing Symposium, 2004. IGARSS '04. Proceedings, 20-24 Sept. Anchorage, Alaska, Vol. 3, p 2146 - 2149

Eicken, H., L. Shapiro, A. Graves, P. Cotter, 2005. Mapping and characterization of recurring spring leads and landfast ice in the Beaufort and Chukchi Seas. MMS Information Transfer Meeting, Anchorage, March 2005.

Mahoney, A., Eicken, H., Shapiro, L. and Graves, A., 2005, Defining and locating the seaward landfast ice edge in northern Alaska, 18th International Conference on Port and Ocean Engineering under Arctic Conditions. POAC '05, Potsdam, N.Y. June 26-30, 2005

Mahoney, A., 2005, Alaskan Landfast Sea Ice: Links with Bathymetry and Climate, Cooperative Institute for Research in Environmental Sciences, Boulder, CO, July 7, 2005.

A.2. Papers

Eicken, H., R. Gradinger, A. Graves, A. Mahoney, I. Rigor, H. Melling, 2005. Sediment transport by sea ice in the Chukchi and Beaufort Seas: Increasing importance due to changing ice conditions? Deep-Sea Res. II, 52, 3281-3302.

Mahoney, A., H. Eicken, L. Shapiro, A. Graves and P. Cotter, Landfast sea ice extent and variability in the Alaskan Arctic derived from SAR imagery, IEEE International Geoscience and Remote Sensing Symposium, 2004. IGARSS '04. Proceedings, 20-24 Sept. Anchorage, Alaska, Vol. 3, p 2146 - 2149

Mahoney, A., Eicken, H., Shapiro, L. and Graves, A., 2005, Defining and locating the seaward landfast ice edge in northern Alaska. In: J.P. Dempsey (Editor), 18th International Conference on Port and Ocean Engineering under Arctic Conditions. POAC '05, Proceedings, Volume 3, Potsdam, N.Y. June 26-30, 2005

Appendix B.   Bibliography on landfast ice and sea-ice leads

Agerton, D. J. Large winter ice movements in the nearshore Alaskan Beaufort Sea. Proceedings of the 6th International Conference on Port and Ocean Engineering under Arctic Conditions. 599-608. 81. Quebec, Canada, Universite Laval.

Agerton, D. J. and Kreider, J. R. Correlation of storms and major ice movements in the nearshore Alaskan Beaufort Sea. Proceedings of the 5th International Conference on Port and Ocean Engineering under Arctic Conditions (POAC 79). 1, 177-189. 79. Trondheim, Norway, Norwegian Institute of Technology.

Agnew, T. A., H. Le, and M. Shokr, Characteristics of Large Winter Leads over the Arctic Basin from 85.5 GHz DMSP SSM/I and NOAA/AVHRR Imagery, *Canadian Journal of Remote Sensing*, 25, 12-20, 1999.

Ahlnas, K. and Wendler, G. Sea Ice Observations by Satellite in the Bering, Chukchi and Beaufort Sea. Proceedings of the 5th International Conference on Port and Ocean Engineering Under Arctic Conditions. v.1, pp. 313-328. 79. Trondheim, Norway, University.

Allen, W. T. R. and B. S. V. Cudbird, Freeze-up, break-up and ice thickness in Canada = Embacle, debacle et epaisseur de la glace au Canada, Fisheries and Environment Canada, Atmospheric Environment Service, Downsview, Ontario, 1977.

Andreas, E. L. Environment of wintertime leads and polynyas. Richter-Menge, W. B., Tucker, W. B., III, and Kleinerman, M. M. Proceedings, Arctic Technology Workshop. 273-288. 89. Washington, DC, USGPO. Special Report (U.S. Army Cold Regions Research and Engineering Laboratory).

Anonymous, Landfast ice movement -- Mackenzie Delta 1972, 1973, 1974, *A.P.O.A. Review*, 3, 10-11, 1980.

Anonymous, Landfast ice zone explored in paper re Beaufort Sea, *Offshore Resources*, 2, 34, 1984.

Arikainen, A. I., Salinity and thermal state of Bering Sea waters as indices of development of the Chukchi flaw lead in June, *Problems of the Arctic and the Antarctic : Collection of articles = Problemy Arktiki i Antarktiki, Sbornik Statei*, 48, 75-82, 1976.

Arikainen, A. I., Method of calculating the state of the Chukchi flaw lead in June, *Problems of the Arctic and the Antarctic : Collection of articles = Problemy Arktiki i Antarktiki, Sbornik Statei*, 49, 39-51, 1977.

Arikainen, A. I., Using mean-weighted criteria in forecasting leads beyond fast ice in the Chukchi Sea = Ispol'zovanie srednevzveshennykh kriteriev dlia prognoza chukotskoi zapripainoi progaliny, *Trudy (Arkticheskii i antarkticheskii nauchno-issledovatel'skii institut)*, 372, 69-72, 1981.

Arikainen, A. I., Possibilities of long-range forecast of the state of the Chukchi flaw polynya in spring = Vozmozhnosti dolgosrochnogo prognozirovaniya sostoyaniya Chukotskoy zapripaynoy polyn'i vesnoy, *Problems of the Arctic and the Antarctic : Collection of articles = Problemy Arktiki i Antarktiki, Sbornik Statei*, 51, 51-56, 1984.

Atwater, R. K. Ice characteristics of the Alaskan Arctic. Proceedings of the 1st Arctic Offshore Drilling Platform Symposium. 8-1 to 8-26. 83. Newport Beach, CA, Global Marine Development Inc.

Banfield, J., Skeletal modeling of ice leads, *IEEE Transactions on Geoscience and Remote Sensing*, 30, 918-923, 1992.

Barnes, P. W. and E. Reimnitz, Geologic processes and hazards of the Beaufort Sea shelf and coastal regions, in *Environmental assessment of the Alaskan continental shelf : Quarterly reports of principal investigators, April-December 1979, vol.II*, pp. 189-192.

Barnes, P. W. and E. Reimnitz, New insights into the influence of ice on the coastal marine environment of the Beaufort Sea, Alaska, in *Symposium on Significant Results Obtained From the Earth Resources Technology Satellite, v.1*, pp. 1307-1314, NASA, New Carrollton, Md., 1973.

Barnes, P. W., E. Reimnitz, and D. Drake, Shoal migration under the influence of ice: a comparison study 1950-1975, in *Environmental Assessment of the Alaskan Continental Shelf : Annual Reports of Principal Investigators for the Year Ending March 1976. vol.XII : Geology*, pp. 583-590, 1976.

Barnes, P. W., E. Reimnitz, and Environmental Research Laboratories, Marine environmental problems in the ice covered Beaufort Sea shelf and coastal regions, in *Environmental Assessment of the Alaskan Continental Shelf. Annual Reports of Principal Investigators for the Year Ending March 1978. vol.XI, Hazards*, pp. 148-299, 1978.

Barnes, P. W., Reimnitz, E., and Rearic, D. M. Ice gouge characteristics related to sea-ice zonation, Beaufort Sea, Alaska. Workshop on Ice Scouring. 185-219. 85. Ottawa, National Research Council of Canada, Associate Committee on Geotechnical Research. Technical memorandum/ National Research Council of Canada, Associate Committee on Geotechnical Research ; no.136.

Fast-ice thickness and snow depth in relation to oil entrapment potential, Prudhoe Bay, Alaska. Barnes, P. W., Reimnitz, E., Toimil, L. J., and Hill, H. R. Open-File report (United States Geological Survey) ; 79-539. 79. Menlo Park, CA, USGS.

Barnes, P. W., Reimnitz, E., Toimil, L. J., and Hill, H. R. Fast ice thickness and snow depth relationships related to oil entrapment potential, Prudhoe Bay, Alaska. Proceedings of the 5th International Conference on Port and Ocean Engineering under Arctic Conditions (POAC 79). 2, 1205-1225. 79. Trondheim, Norway, Norwegian Institute of Technology.

Barnes, P. W., Effects of elevated temperatures and rising sea level on Arctic coast, *Journal of Cold Regions Engineering*, 4, 21-28, 1990.

Barnes, Peter W. and Asbury, Jeffrey L. Detailed morphology of the seafloor at the inner edge of the stamukhi zone, Beaufort Sea, Alaska. Proceedings of the Arctic Energy Technologies

Workshop. 68-78. 85. Morgantown, WV, U.S. Department of Energy, Office of Fossil Energy, Morgantown Energy Technology Center (DOE/METC-85/6014).

Barnes, P. W., J. L. Asbury, D. M. Rearic, and C. R. Ross, Ice erosion of a sea-floor knickpoint at the inner edge of the stamukhi zone, Beaufort Sea, Alaska, *Marine Geology*, 76, 207-222, 1987.

Barrett, S. A. and Stringer, W. J. Growth and decay of "Katie's Floeberg". 78. Fairbanks, AK, Geophysical Institute, University of Alaska Fairbanks.

Barrett, S. A. and W. J. Stringer, Growth mechanisms of "Katie's Floeberg", *Arctic and Alpine Research*, 10, p.775-783, 1978.

Barry, R., Study of climatic effects on fast ice extent and its seasonal decay along the Beaufort-Chukchi coasts, in *Environmental Assessment of the Alaskan Continental Shelf, vol.2 : Physical Science Studies, final report*, pp. 272-375, 1979.

Barry, R. G., Energy budget studies in relation to fast-ice breakup processes in Davis Strait : A climatological overview, University of Colorado, Institute of Arctic and Alpine Research, Boulder, CO, 1978.

Barry, R. G., R. E. Moritz, and J. C. Rogers, The fast ice regimes of the Beaufort and Chukchi Sea coasts, Alaska, *Cold Regions Science and Technology*, 1, 129-152, 1979.

Barry, R. G., Schnell, R. C., and Miles, M. W. Study of leads in Arctic sea ice and their climatic effects : Final report (February 1988 - February 1990) to Cold Regions Research and Engineering Laboratory, U.S. Army, Hanover, N.H. 90. Boulder, CO, University of Colorado, Boulder.

Barry, Roger G. and Miles, Martin W. Lead patterns in Arctic sea ice from remote sensing data: characteristics, controls and atmospheric interactions. 2nd Conference on Polar Meteorology and Oceanography. 40-43. 88. Boston, MA, American Meteorological Society.

Barry, Roger G., Miles, Martin W., Cianflone, Richard C., Scharfen, Gregory R., and Schnell, Russell C. Characteristics of Arctic sea ice from remote-sensing data and their relationship to atmospheric processes. Proceedings of the Symposium on Ice Dynamics. 9-15. 89. Cambridge, International Glaciological Society. Annals of Glaciology; no.12.

Barry, Roger Graham, Moritz, Richard Edward, and Rogers, Jeffery C. Studies of Climate and Fast Ice Interaction during the Decay Season along the Beaufort Sea Coast. Science in Alaska : Proceedings of the 27th Alaska Science Conference. v.2, pp. 213-228. 76.

Barton, R., Croasdale, K. R., Hnatiuk, J., and Smith, J. G. Ice island count, south Beaufort Sea, 1972. 72. Calgary, Alta., Distributed by APOA (APOA Project no. 53. COGLA code 9442-94-J01-00-NXX-AI(72). 2 microfiche.).

Bauman, M., Fast ice fractures at Harrison Bay, *Prudhoe Bay Journal*, 1, 1983.

Bilello, M. A., Ice thickness observations, North American Arctic and Subarctic, 1960-61, 1961-62, CRREL, Hanover, NH, 1964.

Bilello, M. A., Ice thickness observations in the North American Arctic and Subarctic, parts 2-3, CRREL, Hanover, NH, 1966.

Bilello, M. A. Maximum thickness and subsequent decay of lake, river and fast sea ice in Canada and Alaska. 80.

Bilello, M. A. and R. E. Bates, Ice thickness observations: North American Arctic and Subarctic, Parts 1-4, CRREL, Hanover, NH, 1961-1969.

Bilello, M. A. and R. E. Bates, Ice thickness observations: North American Arctic and Subarctic, 1966-67, 1967-68, CRREL, Hanover, NH, 1971.

Bilello, M. A. and R. E. Bates, Ice thickness observations : North American Arctic and Subarctic, 1967-68, 1968-69, CRREL, Hanover, NH, 1972.

Bilello, M. A. and R. E. Bates, Ice thickness observations: North American Arctic and Subarctic, 1968-69, 1969-70, CRREL, Hanover, NH, 1972.

Bilello, M. A. and R. E. Bates, Ice thickness observations, North American Arctic and Subarctic 1970-71, 1971-72, CRREL, Hanover, NH, 1975.

Bilello, M. A. and R. E. Bates, Ice thickness observations : North American Arctic and Subarctic, 1972-73 and 1973-74, CRREL, Hanover, NH, 1991.

Bilello, M. A. and V. J. Lunardini, Ice thickness observations: North American Arctic and Subarctic, 1974-75, 1975-76, CRREL, Hanover, NH, 1996.

Bilello, Michael A. Decay Patterns of Fast Sea Ice in Canada and Alaska. Pritchard, R. S. Sea Ice Processes and Models. 313-326. 80. Seattle, WA, University of Washington Press.

Billfalk, L. Formation of shore cracks in ice covers due to changes in the water level. IAHR International Symposium on Ice : Proceedings, Vol.2. 650-662. 82. Québec, Canada, Université Laval.

Borgert, Neil. Ice conditions along the Alaskan coast during breakup. Proceedings of the 3rd International Conference on Port and Ocean Engineering under Arctic Conditions. 1, 555. 76.

Breslau, L. R., James, J. E., Trammell, M. D., and Behlke, C. E. The underwater shape of a grounded ice island off Prudhoe Bay, Alaska. Proceedings of the 1st International Conference on Port and Ocean Engineering under Arctic Conditions. 1, 119-139. 71. Trondheim, Norway, Technical University of Norway.

Brown, R. D. and P. Cote, Interannual variability of landfast ice thickness in the Canadian High Arctic, 1950-89, *Arctic*, 45, 273-284, 1992.

Bryan, M. L. and M. G. Marcus, Physical characteristics of near-shore ice ridges, *Arctic*, 25, 182-192, 1972.

Buehner, M., K. R. Thompson, and I. Peterson, Inverse method for tracking ice motion in the marginal ice zone using sequential satellite images, *Journal of Atmospheric and Oceanic*

Technology, 14, 1455-1466, 1997.

Bump, J. K. and J. R. Lovvorn, Effects of lead structure in Bering Sea pack ice on the flight costs of wintering spectacled eiders, *J. Mar. Sys.*, 50, 113-139, 2004.

Campbell, W. J., Ice lead and polynya dynamics, *Professional paper (United States Geological Survey)*, no.929, 340-342, 1976.

Campbell, W. J., Gloersen, P., Zwally, H. J., Ramseier, R. O., and Elachi, C. Simultaneous passive and active microwave observations of near-shore Beaufort Sea ice. Proceedings of the 9th Offshore Technology Conference. 1, 287-294. 77.

Cavalieri, D. J. and R. G. Onstott, Arctic coastal polynya observations with ERS-1 SAR and DMSP SSM/I, *ESA SP*, 359, 77-78, 1992.

Cavalieri, Donald J. and Onstott, Robert G. Arctic coastal polynya observations with ERS-1 SAR and DMSP SSM/I. Proceedings of the First ERS-1 Symposium; Space at the Service of our Environment. 295-299. 93. Paris, European Space Agency.

Chu, P. C. and W. D. Hibler, III, An air-ice-ocean coupled model for the formation of leads or polynyas, in *MIZEX: A program for mesoscale air-ice-ocean interaction experiments in Arctic marginal ice zones*, pp. 79-88, CRREL, Hanover, NH, 1986.

Colony, R., Dynamics of near shore ice-Task 5, in *Environmental Assessment of the Alaskan Continental Shelf. Quarterly Reports of Principal Investigators, Oct-Dec 1978, v.2*, pp. 273-276, 1979.

Colony, R., A Markov model for nearshore ice trajectories, in *Outer Continental Shelf Environment Assessment Program (OCSEAP). Final Reports of Principal Investigators, 1985 : v.72*, pp. 1-55, 1990.

Comfort, G. and D. Lapp, Alaskan Beaufort Sea nearshore ice conditions, Arctic Canada Limited, Kanata, Ontario, 1978.

Cooper, P. F., Movement and deformation of the landfast ice of the southern Beaufort Sea, Beaufort Sea Project, Victoria, B.C., 1975.

Cooper, P. F., Landfast ice in the southeastern part of the Beaufort Sea, in *The coast and shelf of the Beaufort Sea ...*, edited by J. C. Reed and J. E. Sater, pp. 235-242, Arctic Institute of North America, Arlington, VA, 1974.

Cornett, S. and B. Danielewicz, Grounded ridge frequency and the stability of landfast ice in the Beaufort Sea, Dome Petroleum Ltd., Calgary, Alberta, 1982.

Cornett, S. and B. Danielewicz, Winter ice conditions near the Mukluk location in Harrison Bay, Dome Petroleum Ltd., 1983.

Cox, Gordon F. N. and Dehn, William S. Summer ice conditions in the Prudhoe Bay area, 1953-1975. POAC 81; the Sixth International Conference on Port and Ocean Engineering under Arctic Conditions. 2, 799-808. 81.

Croasdale, K. R. Movement of Arctic landfast ice: its measurement and influence on offshore drilling. 2nd International Conference on Port and Ocean Engineering under Arctic Conditions: Proceedings. 617-636. 74.

Croasdale, K. R. and L. G. Spedding, Landfast ice movement -- Mackenzie Delta 1972, APOA, Calgary, Alberta, 1972.

Crout, R. L. and F. M. Fetterer, Arctic lead statistics and motion vectors, *Eos*, 73, 290, 1992.

Crout, R. L. and F. M. Fetterer, Arctic lead statistics at several spatial scales, *Eos*, 73, 149, 1992.

Cunningham, Glenn F., Kwok, Ronald, and Banfield, Jeff. Ice lead orientation characteristics in the winter Beaufort Sea. IGARSS '94; International Geoscience and Remote Sensing Symposium. Surface and Atmospheric Remote Sensing: Technologies, Data Analysis and Interpretation. 1747-1749. 94. Piscataway, NJ, Institute of Electrical and Electronic Engineers.

D.F. Dickins Engineering, Ice survey flight notes, Inuvik to Point Hope, Alaska, March 21 to 23, 1979, D.F. Dickins Engineering (Sponsored by Canadian Marine Drilling Ltd.), Yellowknife, N.W.T., 1979.

De Abreu, R. A. and LeDrew, E. F. Multitemporal analysis of fast sea ice albedo using AVHRR data. IGARSS'96 : International Geoscience and Remote Sensing Symposium. Remote Sensing for a Sustainable Future. 1, 639-641. 96. New York, Institute of Electrical and Electronics Engineers.

Dethleff, D., Sea ice and sediment export from the Laptev Sea flaw lead during 1991/92 winter season, *Berichte Zur Polarforschung (Russian-German Cooperation: Laptev Sea System. Edited by H. Kassens et al.)*, 78-93, 1995.

Dethleff, D., P. Loewe, and E. Kleine, Laptev Sea flaw lead: detailed investigation on ice formation and export during 1991/1992 winter season, *Cold Regions Science and Technology*, 27, 225-243, 1998.

Dethleff, D., Dynamics of the Laptev Sea flaw lead, *Berichte Zur Polarforschung = Reports on Polar Research* , 144, 49-54, 1994.

Dey, B., Variations of August ice cover in the Beaufort Sea, *Bulletin of the American Meteorological Society*, 61, 214-217, 1980.

Dey, B., Monitoring winter sea ice dynamics in the Canadian Arctic with NOAA-TIR images, *Journal of Geophysical Research*, 86, p.3232-3235, 1981.

Dey, B. and U. Feldman, Observations of winter polynyas and fractures using NOAA AVHRR TIR images and Nimbus-7 SMMR sea ice concentration charts, *Remote Sensing of Environment*, 30, 141-149, 1989.

Dey, B., H. Moore, and A. F. Gregory, Monitoring and mapping sea-ice breakup and freezeup of Arctic Canada from satellite imagery, *Arctic and Alpine Research*, 11, 229-242, 1979.

Divine, D., R. Korsnes, and A. Makshtas, Variability and climate sensitivity of fast ice extent in the north-eastern Kara Sea, *Polar Res.*, 22, 27-34, 2003.

Divine, D., R. Korsnes, A. P. Makshtas, and F. Godtliebsen, Atmospheric-driven state transfer of shore-fast ice in the northeastern Kara Sea, *J. Geophys. Res.*, 110, doi: 09010.01029/JC002706, 2005.

Divine, D. V., R. Korsnes, and A. P. Makshtas, Temporal and spatial variation of shore-fast ice in the Kara Sea, *Cont. Shelf Res.*, 24, 1717-1736, 2004.

Dokken, Sverre Thune. Characterization of coastal polynyas in SAR images from the Arctic Ocean. IGARSS 2000; Proceedings; IEEE 2000 International Geoscience and Remote Sensing Symposium. 1334-1336. 2000. Piscataway, NJ, IEEE.

Dokken, Sverre Thune, Winsor, Peter, Askne, Jan, and Bjork, Goran. Temporal variability of polynyas from combined ERS and SSM/I investigations. IGARSS '99 Proceedings: Remote Sensing of the System Earth -- A Challenge for the 21st century. 317-319. 99. Piscataway, NJ, IEEE.

Dumas, J., E. Carmack, and H. Melling, Climate change impacts on the Beaufort shelf landfast ice, *Cold Reg. Sci. Tech.* , 42, 41-51, 2005.

Dyment, L. N., Application of cluster analysis to identify areas with homogeneous ice breaks in the Arctic basin = Primeneniye klasternogo analiza dlya vydeleniya rayonov s odnorodnymi sistemami razryvov v ledyanom pokrove Arkticheskogo basseyna, *Russian Meteorology and Hydrology*, 12, 37-43, 2000.

Eicken, H., I. Dmitrenko, K. Tyshko, A. Darovskikh, W. Dierking, U. Blahak, J. Groves, and H. Kassens, Zonation of the Laptev Sea landfast ice cover and its importance in a frozen estuary, *Global Planet. Change*, 48, 55-83, 2005.

Erlingsson, Bjorn and Kotlyakov, V. M. Sea ice deformations in the proximity of coasts. Arctic research: advances and prospects; proceedings of the Conference of Arctic and Northern Countries on Coordination of Research in the Arctic. 129-137. 90. Moscow, Nauka.

Esso Resources Canada, Beaufort Sea freeze-up and break-up patterns., Esso Resources Canada, [S.l.], 1981.

Fett, R. W., K. L. Davidson, and J. E. Overland, Opening and closing of the "Husky 1" lead complex, in *Polar oceans and their role in shaping the global environment*, edited by O. M. Johannessen, R. D. Muench, and J. Ed. Overland, pp. 455-473, 1994.

Fett, R. W., R. E. Englebretson, and S. D. Burk, Techniques for analyzing lead condition in visible, infrared and microwave satellite imagery, *Journal of Geophysical Research*, 102, 13657-13671, 1997.

Fett, R. W., Major cloud plumes in the Arctic and their relation to fronts and ice movement, *Monthly Weather Review*, 120, 925-945, 1992.

Fett, R. W., S. D. Burk, W. R. Thompson, and T. L. Kozo, Environmental Phenomena of the Beaufort Sea Observed During the Leads Experiment, *Bulletin of the American Meteorological Society*, 75, 2131-2145, 1994.

Fett, R. W., R. E. Englebretson, T. L. Kozo, W. T. Thompson, S. D. Burk, and J. R. Clark, Detection of newly-opened leads in coastal fast ice in the Alaskan Beaufort Sea, *Eos*, 75, 381, 1994.

Fetterer, F. and J. Hawkins, Data set of Arctic AVHRR imagery for the study of leads, *Annals of Glaciology*, 17, 398-404, 1993.

Fetterer, F. M. and Cambridge, V. Lead area and orientation derived from satellite imagery of the Lincoln Sea with a Hough transform algorithm. 2nd WMO Workshop on Operational Remote Sensing of Sea Ice: Abstracts. 15. 91. Environment Canada.

Fetterer, F. M. and J. D. Hawkins, AVHRR data set for the Arctic leads, U.S. Navy. Naval Oceanographic and Atmospheric Research Laboratory., 1991.

Fetterer, F. M. and Holyer, R. J. Hough transform technique for extracting lead features from sea ice imagery. Proceedings, U.S. Naval Ocean Research and Development Activity. 89?

Fetterer, F. M. and Holyer, R. J. Hough transform technique for extracting lead features from sea ice imagery. International Geoscience and Remote Sensing Symposium, Proceedings, v.2. 1125-1128. 89. IEEE Geoscience and Remote Sensing Society.

Fetterer, F. M., A. E. Pressman, and R. L. Crout, Sea ice lead statistics from satellite imagery of the Lincoln Sea during the ICESHELF acoustic exercise, spring 1990, U.S. Naval Oceanographic and Atmospheric Research Laboratory., 1990.

Fily, M. and D. A. Rothrock, Opening and Closing of Sea Ice Leads: Digital Measurements from Synthetic Aperture Radar, *Journal of Geophysical Research*, 95, 789-796, 1990.

Fily, M., Rothrock, D. A., and Guyenne, T. D. Measuring lead area changes in sea ice imagery. IGARSS'88 ; International Geoscience and Remote Sensing Symposium: moving towards the 21st century. 799-800. 88. Noordwijk, ESTEC, ESA Publications Division. ESA SP.

Flato, G. M. and R. D. Brown, Variability and climate sensitivity of landfast Arctic sea ice, *Journal of Geophysical Research*, 101, 25767-25777, 1996.

Fontneau, Carl S. An oceanographic and climatological atlas of the Chukchi Sea. 90. U.S. Coast Guard.

Frolov, S. V. and Klyachkin, S. V. The influence of the orientation of leads relative to the general course of an icebreaker upon the speed and efficiency of ice navigation. Proceedings of the 15th International Conference on Port and Ocean Engineering under Arctic Conditions, v.2. 561-567. 99?

Gineris, D. J. and F. M. Fetterer, Hough transform algorithm for sea ice lead analysis: an evaluation, U.S. Naval Research Laboratory, 1993.

Golovin, P. N., Convective mass transport in the underice layer of winter fractures in the Arctic basin, *Oceanology*, 35, 778-786, 1996.

Gorbunov, IU. A., I. D. Karelin, and S. M. Losev, Nature of winter ruptures in sea ice covers =

Priroda narushenii sploshnosti morskogo ledianogo pokrova v zimnee vremia, *Materialy gliatsiologicheskikh issledovanii*, 55, 131-134, 1986.

Groves, J. E. and W. J. Stringer, The use of AVHRR thermal infrared imagery to determine sea ice thickness within the Chukchi polynya, *Arctic*, 44, 130-139, 1991.

Hanley, T. O., A field study of rough shore-fast sea ice, *Journal of Glaciology*, 30, 230-234, 1984.

Hibler, W. D. III, Ackley, S. F., Crowder, W. K., McKim, H. L., and Anderson, D. M. Analysis of shear zone ice deformation in the Beaufort Sea using satellite imagery. Symposium on Beaufort Sea Coast and Shelf Research. 285-296. 74. Arlington, VA, Arctic Institute of North America.

Hibler, W. D. III and E. M. Schulson, On modeling sea-ice fracture and flow in numerical investigations of climate, *Annals of Glaciology*, 25, 26-32, 1997.

Hibler, William D. Model simulation of near shore ice drift, deformation and thickness. Muggeridge, D. B. POAC 77 : Proceedings of the Fourth International Conference on Port and Ocean Engineering Under Arctic Conditions, v.1. 33-45. 78. Saint John's, Newfoundland, University of Newfoundland.

Hirose, T. and P. W. Vachon, Demonstration of ERS Tandem Mission SAR interferometry for mapping land fast ice evolution, *Canadian Journal of Remote Sensing*, 24, 89-92, 1998.

Hnatiuk, J., Sea ice beyond the landfast zone, in *Technical memorandum (National Research Council of Canada. Associate Committee on Geotechnical Research) ; no. 121*, pp. 17-18, National Research Council Canada, Ottawa, 1977.

Holland, D. M., An impact of subgrid-scale ice -- ocean dynamics on sea-ice cover, *Journal of Climate*, 14, 1585-1601, 2001.

Holt, B. and S. A. Digby, Processes and imagery of first-year fast sea ice during the melt season, *Journal of Geophysical Research*, 90, 5045-5062, 1985.

Holt, B. and S. Martin, The effect of a storm on the 1992 summer sea ice cover of the Beaufort, Chukchi, and East Siberian Seas, *Journal of Geophysical Research* , 106, 1017-1032, 2001.

Hopkins, M. A., On the mesoscale interaction of lead ice and floes, *Journal of Geophysical Research*, 101, 18315-18326, 1996.

Inall, M. E., Arctic leads, in *Technical report (Scott Polar Research Institute. Sea Ice Group) ; no. 91-1*, pp. 1-31, 1991.

Jacobs, J. D., R. G. Barry, and R. L. Weaver, Fast ice characteristics, with special reference to the eastern Canadian Arctic, *Polar Record*, 17, 521-536, 1975.

Kane, D. L., Carlson, R. F., and Seifert, R. D. Alaskan Arctic coast ice and snow dynamics as viewed by the NOAA satellites. The Third International Symposium on Ice Problems. 567-577. 75. International Association of Hydraulic Research.

Kantha, L. H., Numerical model of Arctic leads, *Journal of Geophysical Research*, 100, 4653-4672, 1995.

Key, J., J. A. Maslanik, R. S. Stone, and A. S. McLaren, Lead detection and mapping with reference to relationships between scale, sensor characteristics, surface conditions and atmospheric properties : Annual report, April 15, 1990 - April 14, 1991, University of Colorado, Cooperative Institute for Research in Environmental Sciences, Boulder, CO, 1991.

Key, J., Schweiger, A. J., and Maslanik, J. A. Mapping sea ice leads with a coupled numeric/symbolic system. ACSM-ASPRS Annual Convention : Technical Papers, v.4. 228-237. 90. Bethesda, American Congress on Surveying and Mapping.

Key, J. R., Lead width distributions observed in Landsat imagery and their relationship to model distributions, *Eos*, 71, 99-100, 1990.

Key, J. R., J. A. Maslanik, and E. Ellefsen, The effects of sensor field-of-view on the geometrical characteristics of sea ice leads and implications for large-area heat flux estimates, *Remote Sensing of Environment*, 48, 347-357, 1994.

Key, J. R., R. Stone, J. A. Maslanik, and E. Ellefsen, The detectability of sea-ice leads in satellite data as a function of atmospheric conditions and measurement scale, *Annals of Glaciology*, 17, 227-232, 1993.

Key, J. R. and S. Peckham, Probable errors in width distributions of sea ice leads measured along a transect, *Journal of Geophysical Research*, 96, 18417-18423, 1991.

Key, Jeffrey R., Stone, Robert, and Maslanik, James A. Lead retrieval using visible and thermal AVHRR imagery: testing theoretical atmospheric and geometric effects with LEADEX data. IGARSS'94; International Geoscience and Remote Sensing Symposium. Surface and Atmospheric Remote Sensing: Technologies, Data Analysis and Interpretation. 1012-1014. 94. Piscataway, NJ, Institute of Electrical and Electronic Engineers.

Khandekar, M. L., On the development of a model for fast ice movement, Canada. Atmospheric Environment Service., 1979.

Kloster, K. ERS-1 SAR ice analysis in NE-Barents Sea in March 1992. 92. Nansen Environmental and Remote Sensing Center. Technical report (Nansen Environmental and Remote Sensing Center).

Korsnes, R., Regime shifts in mesoscale deformations of sea ice during the winter, *Journal of Geophysical Research. C. Oceans*, 103, 8167-8176, 1998.

Kovacs, A. and W. F. Weeks, Dynamics of near-shore ice, in *OCSEAP: Environmental Assessment of the Alaskan Continental Shelf. Annual Reports of Principal Investigators for the Year Ending March 1981, vol.VII: Hazards*, pp. 125-135, 1981?

Kovshov, V. A. and Yu. N. Sinyurin, Breaks in sea ice cover = Razryvnyye narusheniya morskogo ledyanogo pokrova, *Meteorologiya i Gidrologiya*, 7, 99-106, 1990.

Kozo, T. L. and R. W. Fett, Wind-forced lead genesis in the Alaskan Beaufort Sea's coastal ice zone (CIZ), *Eos*, 74, 176-177, 1993.

Kozo, T. L., W. T. Thompson, S. D. Burk, J. R. Clark, and R. W. Fett, Lead creation in fast ice produced by a mesoscale Arctic storm, *Eos*, 75, 381-382, 1994.

Kozo, T. L., R. W. Fett, L. D. Farmer, and D. S. Sodhi, Clues to causes of deformation features in coastal sea ice, *Eos*, 73, 385, 388-389, 1992.

Kozo. Thomas L., Torgerson, Lenora J., and Saeki, Hiroshi. The Role of Alternating Cyclones and Anticyclones in Triggering Sea Ice Fracture in the Canadian Arctic Basin. Proceedings: 9th International Symposium on Ice . 1. 88. International Association for Hydraulic Research, Committee on Ice Problems.

Kwok, R., Sea ice concentration estimates from satellite passive microwave radiometry and opening from SAR ice motion, *Geophysical Research Letters*, 29, 4p., 2002.

Kwok, Ronald and Cunningham, Glenn F. Use of time series SAR data to resolve ice type ambiguities in newly opened leads. IGARSS'94; International Geoscience and Remote Sensing Symposium. Surface and Atmospheric Remote Sensing: Technologies, Data Analysis and Interpretation. 1024-1026. 94. Piscataway, NJ, Institute of Electrical and Electronic Engineers.

Li, F., Kelley, J., and Uematsu, U. Spring ice conditions from SAR images near the Alaska coast of the Chukchi Sea. 92. Fairbanks, Alaska, Polar Ice Coring Office.

Lindsay, R. W. and D. A. Rothrock, Arctic sea ice leads from advanced very high resolution radiometer images, *Journal of Geophysical Research*, 100, 4533-4544, 1995.

Lissauer, I. M. and Baird, D. A. Aerial photographic surveys analyzed to deduce oil spill movement during the decay and breakup of fast ice, Prudhoe Bay, Alaska. 82. U.S. Coast Guard.

Lowings, M. and E. Banke, Ice edge break-up in Lancaster Sound, Dome Petroleum, Calgary, Alberta, 1982.

Lussenburg, J. L. Regional ice conditions in the southern Canadian Beaufort Sea, winter 1989-1990 : final report. 91. Calgary, Alta., Micep Consulting Inc.

Lyden, J. D. and R. A. Shuchman, A digital technique to estimate polynya characteristics from synthetic aperture radar sea-ice data, *Journal of Glaciology*, 33, 243-245, 1987.

Mahoney, A., H. Eicken, L. Shapiro, and A. Graves, Defining and locating the seaward landfast ice edge in northern Alaska, 18th International Conference on Port and Ocean Engineering under Arctic Conditions. POAC '05, Potsdam, N.Y. June 26-30, 2005

Marko, J. R. Satellite observations of the Beaufort Sea ice. 75. Victoria, B.C., Beaufort Sea Project. Beaufort Sea technical report.

Marko, J. R. and R. E. Thomson, Spatially periodic lead patterns in the Canada Basin sea ice: a possible relationship to planetary waves, *Geophysical Research Letters*, 2, 431-434, 1975.

Marko, J. R. and R. E. Thomson, Rectilinear leads and internal motions in the ice pack of the western Arctic Ocean, *Journal of Geophysical Research*, 82, 979-987, 1977.

Markus, T. and B. A. Burns, A method to estimate subpixel-scale coastal polynyas with satellite passive microwave data, *Journal of Geophysical Research*, 100, 4473-4487, 1995.

Martin, S., R. Drucker, R. Kwok, and B. Holt, Estimation of the thin ice thickness and heat flux for the Chukchi Sea Alaskan coast polynya from Special Sensor Microwave/Image data, *J. Geophys. Res.*, 109, doi: 10.1029/2004JC002428, 2004.

Martin, S., R. Drucker, R. Kwok, and B. Holt, Improvements in the estimates of ice thickness and production in the Chukchi Sea polynyas derived from AMSR-E, *Geophys. Res. Lett.*, 32, doi: 05510.01029/02004GL022013, 2004.

Martin, S. and R. Drucker, The effect of possible Taylor columns on the summer ice retreat in the Chukchi Sea, *Journal of Geophysical Research*, 102, 10473-10482, 1997.

Massom, R. A. and J. C. Comiso, The Classification of Arctic sea ice types and the determination of surface temperature using Advanced Very High Resolution Radiometer data, *Journal of Geophysical Research*, 99, 5201-5218, 1994.

Matthews, J. B. and W. J. Stringer, Spring breakup and flushing of an Arctic lagoon estuary, *J. Geophys. Res.*, 89, 2073-2079, 1984.

McHenry, M. and B. Danielewicz, A short summary of ice and wave conditions of Harrison Bay, Alaska, Dome Petroleum Ltd., Calgary, Alta., 1982.

McIntire, T. J. and J. J. Simpson, Arctic sea ice, cloud, water, and lead classification using neural networks and 1.6-muum data, *IEEE Transactions on Geoscience and Remote Sensing*, 40, 1956-1972, 2002.

McNutt, S. Lyn, Labelle-Hamer, Nettie, and Overland, James E. Combining SAR and AVHRR to understand sea ice dynamics in the seasonal and perennial ice zones of the Beaufort and Chukchi Seas. IGARSS 2001: proceedings: IEEE 2001 International Geoscience and Remote Sensing Symposium: Scanning the present and resolving the future. 177-180. 2001. Piscataway, NJ, IEEE.

Melentyev, V. V., Pettersson, L. H., Sandven, S., Kloster, K., and Dalen, O. Use of satellite radar mapping of ice features to describe the fall freezing conditions: a case study from the Ob estuary. Tuhkuri, J. and Riska, K. eds. POAC'99, Proceedings of the 15th International Conference on Port and Ocean Engineering Under Arctic Conditions, v.1. 1, 249-255. 99. Helsinki, Helsinki University of Technology.

Melling H., Detection of features in first-year pack ice by synthetic aperture radar (SAR), *International Journal of Remote Sensing*, 19 , 1223-1249, 1998.

Metzner, R. and L. H. Shapiro, Ice conditions on Alaska's Beaufort Sea coast: extending the observations, *The Northern Engineer*, 11, 22-27, 1979.

Miles, M. W. and Barry, R. G. Large-scale characteristics of fractures in multi-year Arctic pack ice. POAC 89: The 10th International Conference on Port and Ocean Engineering Under

Arctic Conditions, v.1. 103-112. 89. Research report TULEA.

Miles, M. W. and R. G. Barry, A 5-year satellite climatology of winter sea ice leads in the western Arctic , *Journal of Geophysical Research. C. Oceans*, 103, 21723-21734, 1998.

Miles, M. W., R. G. Barry, and E. L. Andreas, Lidar remote sensing analysis of leads in Arctic sea ice, *Eos*, 69, 1278, 1988.

Miles, M. W., A climatology of leads in Arctic sea ice in winter, derived from satellite imagery, thesis, Ph.D. dissertation, University of Colorado, Boulder, CO, 1993.

Miles, Martin William. A climatology of leads in Arctic sea ice in winter, derived from satellite imagery [abstract]. Dissertation Abstracts International. Section B: Physical Sciences and Engineering 54(10), 5070-B. 94.

Milne, A. R., The transition from moving to fast ice in western Viscount Melville Sound, *Arctic*, 23, 45-46, 1970.

Mironov, Ye. U., Spichkin, V. A., and Sergeyeva, I. A. Dynamics of landfast ice development on the shelf of the Barents and Kara Seas = Teplovyye, dinamicheskiye i morfograficheskiye usloviya razvitiya pripaya na shel'fe Barentseva i Karskogo morya. ICETECH '2000, Sixth International Conference on Ships and Marine Structures in Cold Regions. 500-507. 2000. St. Petersburg, Russia, Krylov Shipbuilding Research Institute.

Morison, J. H., M. G. McPhee, T. B. Curtin, and C. A. Paulson, The oceanography of winter leads, *Journal of Geophysical Research*, 97, 11199-11218, 1992.

Morris, K., S. Li, and M. Jeffries, Meso- and microscale sea-ice motion in the East Siberian Sea as determined from ERS-1 SAR data, *Journal of Glaciology* , 45, 370-383, 1999.

Newbury, T. K., Under landfast ice, *Arctic*, 36, 328-340, 1983.

Onstott, R. G. Study of the temporal nature of Arctic leads during spring using ERS-1 SAR. 3rd ERS Symposium on Space at the Service of Our Environment : Proceedings, v.2. 937-941. 97. Noordwijk, European Space Agency.

Onstott, R. G., Wackerman, C. C., Shuchman, R. A., and Fett, R. W. Use of satellite remote sensing to monitor lead dynamics. IGARSS'95; International Geoscience and Remote Sensing Symposium: Quantitative remote sensing for science and applications, v.2. 848-850. 95. New York, Institute of Electrical and Electronics Engineers.

Osterkamp, T. E. and Seifert, R. D. Fast ice on the northern coast of Alaska. 75. U.S. Environmental Protection Agency. Ecological research studies.

Ou, H. W., A time-dependent model of a coastal polynya, *Journal of Physical Oceanography*, 18, 584-590, 1988.

Overland, James E., Walter, Bernard A., and Davidson, Kenneth L. Sea ice deformation in the Beaufort Sea. Third Conference Polar Meteorology and Oceanography. 64-67. 92. Boston, MA, American Meteorological Society.

Parker, M. N. Breakup patterns of the landfast ice regime: southern Beaufort Sea, 1974-1986. 87. Scientific Services, A.E.S. Western Region.

Pease, C. H., The size of wind-driven coastal polynyas, *Journal of Geophysical Research*, 92, 7049-7059, 1987.

Pinkel, R., M. Merrifield, and H. Ramm, Probing the interior of Arctic leads: investigations using high-frequency sound, *Journal of Geophysical Research*, 100, 4693-4705, 1995.

Piwowar, J. M., Wessel, G. R. I., and LeDrew, E. F. Image time series analysis of Arctic sea ice. IGARSS'96, International Geoscience and Remote Sensing Symposium: Remote sensing for a sustainable future, v.1. 645-647. 96. New York, Institute of Electrical and Electronics Engineers.

Pritchard, R. S., Dynamics of near shore ice, *OCSEAP Annual Reports of Principal Investigators for Year Ending March 1978: vol.XI, Hazards*, 39-49, 1978.

Pritchard, R. S., Beaufort Sea ice motions, in *The Alaskan Beaufort Sea: Ecosystems and Environments*, edited by P. W. Barnes, D. M. Schell, and E. Reimnitz, pp. 95-113, Academic Press, Orlando, FL, 1984.

Pritchard, Robert S. Sea ice leads and characteristics. IAHR 92; 11th International Symposium on Ice. Proceedings. 1176-1187. 93. Edmonton, Alberta, University of Alberta, Department of Civil Engineering.

Pritchard, R. S. and D. R. Thomas, Chukchi Sea ice motions, 1981-1982, *Outer Continental Shelf Environment Assessment Program (OCSEAP) : Final Reports of Principal Investigators, 1985* , 72, 239-255, 1990.

Ramseier, R. O., W. J. Campbell, W. F. Weeks, L. Drapier-Arsenault, and K. L. Wilson, Ice dynamics in the Canadian archipelago and adjacent Arctic basin as determined by ERTS-1 observations, in *Canada's Continental Margins and Offshore Petroleum Exploration*, pp. 853-877, Canadian Society of Petroleum Geologists, Calgary, Alberta, 1975.

Rearic, D. M., P. W. Barnes, and E. Reimnitz, Arctic shoals: their effect on the intensity of ice-gouge processes, *Eos*, 68, 1317, 1987.

Reimnitz, E. and Kempema, E. W. Pack Ice Interaction with Stamukhi Shoal, Beaufort Sea, Alaska. Barnes, P. W., Schell, D. M., and Reimnitz, E. The Alaskan Beaufort Sea; ecosystems and environments. 159-183. 84. Orlando, Academic Press.

Reimnitz, E., L. J. Toimil, and P. W. Barnes, Arctic Continental Shelf Morphology Related to Sea Ice Zonation, Beaufort Sea, Alaska, *Marine Geology*, 28, 179-210, 1978.

Rogers, J. C., Sackinger, W. M., and Nelson, R. D. Arctic coastal sea ice dynamics. Proceedings of the 6th Offshore Technology Conference, v.2. 133-145. 74. Dallas, Texas.

Roots, E. F., Shore fast sea ice, in *Technical memorandum/ National Research Council of Canada, Associate Committee on Geotechnical Research ; no.101* , pp. 8-10,24, 1971.

Sackinger, W. M. and Rogers, J. C. Dynamics of breakup in shorefast ice. Symposium on Beaufort Sea Coast and Shelf Research: Proceedings. 367-376. 74. Arlington, Va., Arctic Institute of North America.

Schlatter, T., Shore ice, *Weatherwise*, 50, 36-37, 1997.

Schneider, W. and G. Budeus, Estimation of the surface heat budget and the thickness of thin sea-ice in Arctic polynyas with Landsat 5 TM, *International Journal of Remote Sensing*, 20, 3149-3164, 1999.

Schnell, R. C., R. G. Barry, M. W. Miles, E. L. Andreas, L. F. Radke, C. A. Brock, M. P. McCormick, and J. L. Moore, Lidar detection of leads in Arctic sea ice, *Nature*, 339, 530-532, 1989.

Schulson, E. M. and W. D. Hibler, III, The Fracture of ice on scales large and small: Arctic leads and wing cracks, *Journal of Glaciology*, 37, 319-322, 1991.

Schulson, E. M. and W. D. Hibler, III, The fracture of ice on scales large and small: Arctic leads and wing cracks, *Journal of Glaciology*, 73, 294, 1992.

Schwab, D. L., Beaufort Sea ice movement from Landsat imagery analysis, Gulf Oil Canada, Calgary, Alta., 1978.

Searcy, C., K. Dean, and W. Stringer, A river-coastal sea ice interaction model: Mackenzie River Delta, *Journal of Geophysical Research*, 101, 8885-8894, 1996.

Seifert, R. D., The structure of shorefast ice off the North Slope of Alaska, thesis, M.Sc. thesis, University of Alaska, College, Alaska, 1973.

Shapiro, L., Barnes, P. W., and Reimnitz, E. Processes and mechanisms responsible for the repetitive occurrence of the pack ice boundary shear zone. Arctic Energy Technologies Workshop. Proceedings. 79-90. 85.

A preliminary study of the formation of landfast ice at Barrow, Alaska, winter 1973-74. Shapiro, L. H. Geophysical Institute Report no. UAG R-235. 75. Fairbanks, AK, University of Alaska.

Shapiro, L. H. A preliminary study of ridging in landfast ice at Barrow, Alaska, using radar data. 3rd International Conference on Port and Ocean Engineering under Arctic Conditions (POAC). 1, 417-425. 76. University of Alaska.

Shapiro, L. H., Distributed stresses in landfast ice, *OCSEAP Principal Investigators' annual reports for the Year Ending March 1978, vol.10: Transport*, 752-760, 1978.

Shapiro, L. H., Mechanical properties of sea ice deformation in the near shore zone, in *OCSEAP Final Reports, v.72*, pp. 357-584, U.S. Dept. of Commerce, NOAA, 1987.

Shapiro, L. H., R. C. Metzner, A. Hanson, and J. B. Johnson, Fast Ice Sheet Deformation during Ice-Push and Shore Ice Ride-Up, in *The Alaskan Beaufort Sea: Ecosystems and Environments*, edited by P. W. Barnes, D. M. Schell, and E. Reimnitz, pp. 137-157, Academic Press, Orlando, FL., 1984.

Short, A. D. and W. J. Wiseman, Jr., Coastal breakup in the Alaskan Arctic, *Bulletin of the Geological Society of America*, 86, 199-202, 1975.

Skokov, R. M., Determining horizontal shifts of stable fast ice = Issledovanie gorizontal'nykh podvizhek ustoichivogo pripaia, *Trudy (Arkticheskii i antarkticheskii nauchno-issledovatel'skii institut)*, 376, 134-140, 1981.

Skokov, R. M., Forecasting the breakup of fast ice = K prognozu vzloma pripaia, *Gidrometeorologicheskii nauchno-issledovatel'skii tsentr SSSR. Trudy*, 270, 52-57, 1985.

Smith, S. D., R. D. Muench, and C. H. Pease, Polynyas and leads: an overview of physical processes and environment, *Journal of Geophysical Research*, 95, 9461-9479, 1990.

Smith, S. D., Review of oceanography and meteorology of Arctic leads and polynyas, University of Washington, Applied Physics Laboratory, Seattle, WA, 1988.

Smith, S. D., Review of the oceanography and micrometeorology of Arctic leads and polynyas, *Eos*, 69, 1269, 1988.

Smith, S. D., Review of the oceanography and micrometeorology of Arctic leads and polynyas, *CRREL Monograph*, 90-1, 123-126, 1990.

Spedding, L. G. Break up pattern of the landfast ice in the Mackenzie Delta region for the spring of 1975. Ottawa, Ontario, Energy, Mines and Resources Canada, Canada Oil and Gas Lands Administration. Report (Imperial Oil Limited).

Spedding, L. G., Ice reconnaissance flights from Herschel Island and Tuktoyaktuk, November 14, 1971, Distributed by APOA, Calgary, 1972.

Spedding, L. G., Landfast ice movement - Mackenzie Delta 1972-73, Distributed by APOA, Calgary, Alberta, 1973.

Spedding, L. G., The extent and growth pattern of landfast ice in the southern Beaufort Sea - Winter 1972-73, Distributed by APOA, Calgary, Alberta, 1974.

Spedding, L. G., Landfast ice movement - Mackenzie Delta 1973-74, Distributed by APOA, Calgary, Alberta, 1975.

Spedding, L. G., Landfast ice movement - Mackenzie Delta 1974/75, Distributed by APOA, Calgary, Alberta, 1975.

Spedding, L. G., Landfast ice movement - Mackenzie Delta 1975/76, Distributed by APOA, Calgary, Alberta, 1977.

Spedding, L. G. Break up pattern of the landfast ice in the Mackenzie Delta region for the spring of 1975. 78. Calgary, Alberta, Imperial Oil Ltd., Production Research Division.

Spedding, L. G. Landfast and shear zone ice conditions in the southern Beaufort Sea - winter 1977/78. 79. Calgary, Alberta, Esso Resources Canada Ltd. Beaufort E.I.S. reference work, no. RWI09.

Spedding, L. G. Landfast ice motion observed in the MacKenzie Delta region in the southern Beaufort Sea in the 1972/1973 winter. Proceedings of the 5th International Conference on Port and Ocean Engineering Under Arctic Conditions, v.1. 23-37. 79. Trondheim, Norway, University.

Spedding, L. G., Landfast and shear zone ice conditions in the southern Beaufort Sea - winter 1977/78, Esso Resources Canada Ltd., 1980.

Spedding, L. G., Artificial islands and ice : further information on seasonal variabilities of break-up and climatic conditions, Esso Resources Canada Ltd., 1983.

Spedding, L. G. A large landfast ice movement. The Seventh International Conference on Port and Ocean Engineering under Arctic Conditions, v.3. 203-213. 83. Espoo, Finland, Technical Research Centre of Finland.

Spedding, L. G. and B. W. Danielewicz, Artificial islands and their effect on regional landfast ice conditions in the Beaufort Sea, Esso Resources Canada ; Dome Petroleum Ltd., 1983.

Squire, V. A., How waves break up inshore fast ice, *Polar Record*, 22, 281-285, 1984.

Squire, V. A., On the critical angle for ocean waves entering shore fast ice, *Cold Regions Science and Technology*, 10, 59-68, 1984.

Squire, V. A., The breakup of shore fast sea ice, *Cold Regions Science and Technology*, 21, 211-218, 1993.

Stander, E., R. M. W. Frederking, and J. P. Nadreau, The effects of tidal jacking on ice displacement and strain in the nearshore environment, Memorial University of Newfoundland, Centre for Cold Ocean Resources Engineering, St John's, Newfoundland, 1987.

Steffen, Konrad, Heinrichs, J., Maslanik, James A., and Key, Jeffrey R. Sea ice feature and type identification in merged ERS-1 SAR and Landsat thematic mapper imagery. Proceedings of the First ERS-1 Symposium; Space at the Service of our Environment. 361-365. 93. Paris, European Space Agency. ESA SP.

Stern, H. L., Rothrock, D. A., and Kwok, R. Sea ice lead dynamics from ERS-1 SAR. Proceedings of the 2nd ERS-1 Symposium : Space at the Service of Our Environment, v.1. 269-270. 94. Paris, European Space Agency.

Stone, R. S. and J. R. Key, The detectability of Arctic leads using thermal imagery under varying atmospheric conditions, *Journal of Geophysical Research*, 98, 12469-12482, 1993.

Stringer, W., Shorefast ice in vicinity of Harrison Bay, *Northern Engineer*, 5, 36, 1973-1974.

Stringer, W., Morphology of Beaufort, Chukchi and Bering Seas near shore ice conditions by means of satellite and aerial remote sensing, in *Environmental assessment of the Alaskan continental shelf. Principal investigators' annual reports for the year ending March 1978. vol.X: Transport*, pp. 1-220, Outer Continental Shelf Environmental Assessment Program, Boulder, Colorado, 1978.

Stringer, W. J., Morphology of the Beaufort Sea shorefast ice, in *The Coast and Shelf of the Beaufort Sea*, edited by J. C. Reed and J. E. Sater, pp. 165-172, Arctic Institute of North America, Arlington, VA, 1974.

Stringer, W. J. Morphology and hazards related to nearshore ice in coastal areas. Proceedings of POAC 79 : the Fifth International Conference on Port and Ocean Engineering under Arctic Conditions, v.1. 1-22. 79. Trondheim, Norway, Norwegian Institute of Technology.

Stringer, W. J., Nearshore ice characteristics in the eastern Bering Sea, Geophysical Institute, University of Alaska, Fairbanks, AK, 1980.

Stringer, W. J., Physical hazards and pollutant transport mechanisms in the Bering Sea nearshore area : Special report to the Outer Continental Shelf Environmental Assessment Program, University of Alaska, Fairbanks, AK, 1980.

Stringer, W. J., Characteristics of nearshore ice in southwestern Alaska, *Journal of Environmental Sciences*, 25, 23-29, 1982.

Stringer, W. J. Sea ice morphology and characteristics : marginal ice zone bibliography. 85. Glaciological data. Report.

Stringer, W. J. and S. A. Barrett, Landsat survey of near-shore ice conditions along the Arctic coast of Alaska : final report, University of Alaska, Fairbanks, AK, 1978.

Stringer, W. J. and Barrett, S. A. LANDSAT survey of near-shore ice conditions along the Arctic coast of Alaska. 78. U.S. National Aeronautics and Space Administration. NASA contractor report.

Stringer, W. J., S. A. Barrett, and L. K. Schreurs, Nearshore ice conditions and hazards in the Beaufort, Chukchi and Bering Seas, Geophysical Institute, University of Alaska, Fairbanks, AK, 1980.

Stringer, W. J. and Groves, J. E. A study of possible meteorological influences on polynya size. Alaska OCS Region 1987 Arctic Information Transfer Meeting, conference proceedings. 141-144. 88. Anchorage, Alaska, Alaska OCS Region. OCS Study.

Stringer, W. J. and J. E. Groves, Location and areal extent of polynyas in the Bering and Chukchi Seas, *Arctic*, 44, 164-171, 1991.

Stringer, W. J., J. E. Groves, R. D. Henzler, and C. Olmsted, Distribution of floe sizes in the eastern Beaufort Sea shear zone, University of Alaska, Geophysical Institute, Fairbanks, Alaska, 1982.

Stringer, W. J., J. E. Groves, R. D. Henzler, L. K. Schreurs, and J. Zender-Romick, Location of the shear zone in the eastern Beaufort Sea, Geophysical Institute. University of Alaska Fairbanks, Fairbanks, AK, 1982.

Stringer, W. J. and Sackinger, W. M. LANDSAT survey of near-shore ice conditions along the Arctic coast of Alaska : quarterly progress report. U.S. National Aeronautics and Space Administration. NASA contractor report.

Stringer, W. J., J. Zender-Romick, and J. E. Groves, Width and persistence of the Chukchi polynya, Geophysical Institute, University of Alaska, Fairbanks, AK, 1982.

Stringer, W. J., Nearshore ice characteristics in the eastern Bering Sea, in *The eastern Bering Sea shelf : oceanography and resources, v.1*, edited by D. W. Hood and J. A. Calder, pp. 167-187, University of Washington Press, Seattle, WA, 1981.

Stringer, W. J., Morphology and hazards related to nearshore ice in coastal areas, *Coastal Engineering*, 5, 229-245, 1981.

Stringer, William J. and Sackinger, William M. Ice hazards to offshore oil operations in Arctic Alaskan waters. Proceedings of the 31st Annual Petroleum Mechanical Engineering Conference. 76.

Sukhorukov, K. K. and Smirnov, V. N. In situ investigations of the shore-ice-grounded hummock interaction. Proceedings of the 12th IAHR Symposium on Ice, v.1. 442-446. 94.

Thomas, D. R., Harrison Bay sea ice conditions relating to oil spills, in *Environmental assessment of the Alaskan continental shelf, v.6: Transport. Principal Investigators' annual reports for the year ending March 1981*, pp. 275-309, Outer Continental Shelf Environmental Assessment Program., Boulder, CO, 1981.

Thomson, R. B., Breakup patterns of landfast ice : southern Beaufort Sea, 1975-1982, Atmospheric Environment Service, Ottawa?, 1983.

Tremblay, L. B. and L. A. Mysak, On the origin and evolution of sea-ice anomalies in the Beaufort-Chukchi Sea, *Climate Dynamics*, 14, 451-460, 1998.

Tschudi, M. A., Curry, J. A., and Maslanik, J. A. Airborne observations of leads in the Beaufort Sea. IGARSS'98; International Geoscience and Remote Sensing Symposium: Sensing and managing the environment. 986-988. 98. New York, Institute of Electrical and Electronics Engineers .

Tschudi, M. A., J. A. Curry, and J. A. Maslanik, Characterization of springtime leads in the Beaufort/Chukchi Seas from airborne and satellite observations during FIRE/SHEBA, *Journal of Geophysical Research*, 107, SHE9.1-SHE9.14, 2002.

Tucker, W. B. CRREL investigations relevant to offshore petroleum production in ice covered waters. Proceedings of the International Symposium on Remote Sensing of Environment: Remote Sensing for Exploration Geology, v.1. 207-215. 83.

Tucker, W. B., Weeks, W. F., Kovacs, A., and Gow, A. J. Nearshore ice motion near Prudhoe Bay, Alaska. Proceedings of the Symposium on Sea Ice Processes and Models, v.2. 23-31. 77?

Van Dyne, M. and Tsatsoulis, C. Extraction and analysis of sea ice leads from SAR images. IGARSS'93; International Geoscience and Remote Sensing Symposium: Better understanding of earth environment, v.2. 629-631. 93. New York, Institute of Electrical and Electronics Engineers.

Van Dyne, M. M., C. Tsatsoulis, and F. Fetterer, Analyzing lead information from SAR images, *IEEE Transactions on Geoscience and Remote Sensing*, 36, 647-660, 1998.

Vesecky, J. F., Smith, M. P., and Samadani, R. Remote sensing of pressure ridge and lead characteristics using SAR images of sea ice. IGARSS'90 ; International Geoscience and Remote Sensing Symposium: Remote sensing science for the nineties. 1871-1874. 90. New York, Institute of Electrical and Electronics Engineers.

Vesecky, J. F., M. P. Smith, and R. Samadani, Extraction of lead and ridge characteristics from SAR images of sea ice, *IEEE Transactions on Geoscience and Remote Sensing*, 28, 740-744, 1990.

Wackerman, C. C., Shuchman, R. A., Onstott, R. G., and Fett, R. W. Monitoring lead dynamics with ERS-1 synthetic aperture radar imagery. Johannessen, J. A. and Guymer, T. H. Oceanic Remote Sensing and Sea Ice Monitoring. 106-113. 94. Bellingham, WA, SPIE.

Walter, B. A. and J. E. Overland, The response of lead patterns in the Beaufort Sea to storm-scale wind forcing, *Annals of Glaciology*, 17, 219-226, 1993.

Weaver, R. L., Barry, R. G., and Jacobs, J. D. Fast ice studies in Davis Strait. 3rd International Conference on Port and Ocean Engineering Under Arctic Conditions, v.1. 455-466. 76. Fairbanks, Alaska, University of Alaska.

Weeks, W. F., A. Kovacs, S. J. Mock, W. B. Tucker, W. D. Hibler, III, and A. J. Gow, Studies of the movement of coastal sea ice near Prudhoe Bay, Alaska, U.S.A. *Journal of Glaciology* , 19, 533-546, 1977.

Weeks, W. F., Tucker, W. B., Frank, M., and Fungcharoen, S. Characterization of the surface roughness and floe geometry of the sea ice over the continental shelves of the Beaufort and Chukchi Seas. Proceedings of the Symposium on Sea Ice Processes and Models, v.2. 32-41. 77?

Weingartner, T. J. Circulation on the north central Chukchi Sea shelf. 98. Fairbanks, Alaska, University of Alaska, Coastal Marine Institute . OCS study.

Weller, G. The role of sea ice in the Arctic coastal environment. Science in Alaska 1976: proceedings of the Twenty-seventh Alaska Science Conference, v.1. 133-149. 78. Fairbanks, Alaska, Alaska Division, American Association for the Advancement of Science.

Winebrenner, D. P. and Sylvester, J. Inversion of wideband microwave reflectivity to estimate the thickness of Arctic lead-like sea ice. IGARSS'96; International Geoscience and Remote Sensing Symposium: Remote sensing for a sustainable future, v.2. 1205-1207. 96. New York, Institute of Electrical and Electronics Engineers.

Wiseman, W. J., Jr., Suhayda, J. N., Hsu, S.-A., and Walters, C. D., Jr. Characteristics of nearshore oceanographic environment of Arctic Alaska. Symposium on Beaufort Sea Coast and Shelf Research. 49-64. 74. Arlington, VA, Arctic Institute of North America .

Appendix C.   List of catalogs and digital media

Catalogs

AVHRR imagery reviewed for this study: Disk 2

RadarSat SAR imagery reviewed for this study: Disk 2

Digital Media

Variability of landfast ice widths and water depths at the SLIE for all 8 annual cycles (222 SLIEs) for all 200 coastal locations: Disk 1

Geodatabases of (i) SLIEs for all 8 annual cycles and (ii) leads for all 11 annual cycles: Disk 1

GeoTiffs, grids and shapefiles of (i) SLIEs for 5 annual (1996-2001) cycles and (ii) leads for all 11 annual cycles: Disk 1

GeoTiffs, grids and shapefiles of SLIEs for 4 annual (2001-2004) cycles: Disk 2

Summary statistics of lead data for all 11 annual cycles: Disk 1

Monthly averages of the SLIE in ArcGIS format: Disk 1

Metadata templates for ArcGIS deliverables: Disk 2

Monthly lead recurrence probability maps: Disk 2

Bibliography of sea ice leads and landfast ice: Disk 2

SF298 Report Documentation Page: Disk 2

OCS Study MMS 2005-068, PDF and Word version: Disk 1

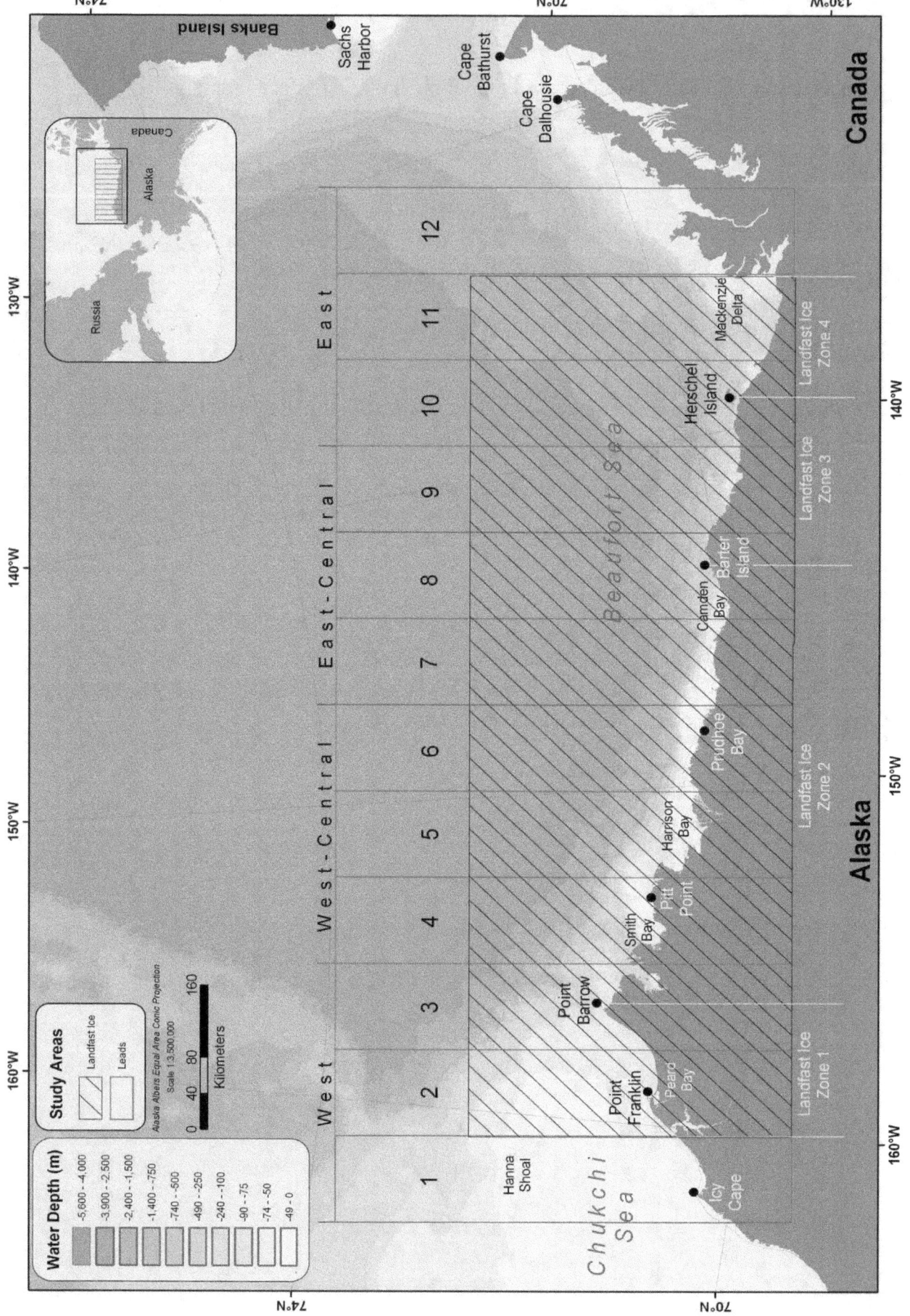